THE DEVIL'S BUTCHER SHOP

REPORTER: What was it like in there?

INMATE: Man, what can I tell you?
It was like the Devil had his
own butcher shop, and you could
get any cut you wanted.

New Mexico is the anomaly of the Republic.
It is a century older in European civilization than the rest, and several centuries
older still in a happier semi-civilization
of its own. It had its little walled cities
of stone before Columbus had grandparents-
to-be; and it has them yet. The most incredible pioneering the world has ever seen
overran it with the zeal of a prairie fire
three hundred and fifty years ago; and the
embers of that unparalleled blaze of explo-
ration are not quite dead today. The most
superhuman marches, the most awful priva-
tions, the most devoted heroism, the most
unsleeping vigilance wrested this bare,
brown land to the world; and having wrested
it, went to sleep. The winning was the wake-
fullest in history—the afternap eternal.
It has never been wakened—one does not
know that it ever can.

Charles Lummis,
The Land of Poco Tiempo

To open the blind eyes, to bring out the
prisoners from the prison, and them that
sit in darkness out of the prison house.

Isaiah 42:7

FOR DAVID AND ZOË

STEPCHILDREN EXTRAORDINARY,
WHO TAUGHT ME ABOUT LOVE,
WHO SHARED THE SKY AND MOUNTAINS,
AND WHO, CHARACTERISTICALLY,
WOULD WANT THIS BOOK AS WELL
FOR OTHER DAUGHTERS AND SONS.

THE DEVIL'S BUTCHER SHOP

TAKEOVER

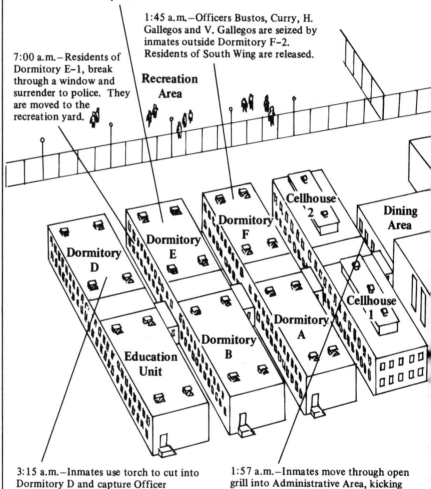

1:40 a.m.—Inmates seize Capt. Roybal, Lt. Anaya and Officers Schmitt and R. Martinez in Dormitory E-2.

1:45 a.m.—Officers Bustos, Curry, H. Gallegos and V. Gallegos are seized by inmates outside Dormitory F-2. Residents of South Wing are released.

7:00 a.m.—Residents of Dormitory E-1, break through a window and surrender to police. They are moved to the recreation yard.

Recreation Area

Dormitory D

Dormitory E

Dormitory F

Cellhouse 2

Dining Area

Cellhouse 1

Education Unit

Dormitory B

Dormitory A

3:15 a.m.—Inmates use torch to cut into Dormitory D and capture Officer Hernandez.

1:57 a.m.—Inmates move through open grill into Administrative Area, kicking Officer Bustos down the corridor.

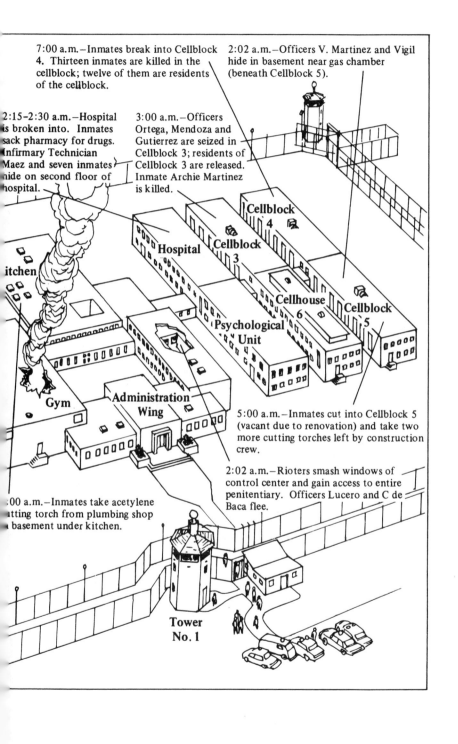

7:00 a.m.—Inmates break into Cellblock 4. Thirteen inmates are killed in the cellblock; twelve of them are residents of the cellblock.

2:02 a.m.—Officers V. Martinez and Vigil hide in basement near gas chamber (beneath Cellblock 5).

2:15–2:30 a.m.—Hospital is broken into. Inmates sack pharmacy for drugs. Infirmary Technician Maez and seven inmates hide on second floor of hospital.

3:00 a.m.—Officers Ortega, Mendoza and Gutierrez are seized in Cellblock 3; residents of Cellblock 3 are released. Inmate Archie Martinez is killed.

Cellblock 4

Hospital

Cellblock 3

Kitchen

Cellhouse 6

Cellblock 5

Psychological Unit

Gym

Administration Wing

5:00 a.m.—Inmates cut into Cellblock 5 (vacant due to renovation) and take two more cutting torches left by construction crew.

2:02 a.m.—Rioters smash windows of control center and gain access to entire penitentiary. Officers Lucero and C de Baca flee.

:00 a.m.—Inmates take acetylene cutting torch from plumbing shop in basement under kitchen.

Tower No. 1

ROGER MORRIS

THE
Devil's
BUTCHER SHOP

THE NEW MEXICO
PRISON UPRISING

University of New Mexico Press
Albuquerque

Brief passages of this book have appeared in
substantially different form in *Playboy*, the
Santa Fe Reporter, and the *Santa Fe New Mexican*, and
acknowledgment is gratefully given those publications.

Excerpt from "Penal Madness" by Ray Bremser. © by
Ray Bremser. Reprinted by permission of the author.

"The Little Man Who Wasn't There" by
Hughes Mearns © by Mrs. Petra Cabot.
Reprinted by permission of Mrs. Petra Cabot.

Diagram of New Mexico State Penitentiary by John Trevor.
© *Albuquerque Journal*. Reprinted by permission of
John Trevor, *Albuquerque Journal*.

Morris, Roger.
  The devil's butcher shop: the New Mexico prison uprising/Roger Morris.
      p. cm.
  Reprint. Originally published: New York: F. Watts, 1983.
  Bibliography: p.
  Includes index.
  ISBN 0-8263-1062-1 (pbk.)
  1. New Mexico State Penitentiary. 2. Prison riots—New Mexico-Santa Fe. I. Title.
[HV9475.N62N45 1988]
365'.641—dc19   88-4005
                                                                        CIP

19   18   17   16   15   14   12   13   14   15   16   17

ISBN-13: 978-0-8263-1062-0

CONTENTS

PREFACE

In the cold early hours after midnight on Saturday, February 2, 1980, convicts seized the New Mexico State Penitentiary at Santa Fe, taking twelve guards hostage. When the institution was surrendered thirty-six hours later, rampaging inmates had murdered and mutilated almost beyond recognition at least thirty-three men, tortured eight of the hostage guards, and raped, wounded, and terrorized scores of other prisoners in the most savage penal riot in American history. Gutted by fire and by flooding, blood-soaked sewage, the penitentiary stood in the Sunday mountain twilight a dank and acrid charnel house, the butchery so complete that anthropologists would later sift through the muck for occasional shards of bone as if searching some prehistoric burial ground.

This is the story of that event, and of its origins and aftermath.

The tracing of so much hate began in love. I first came to New Mexico in the early 1970s, driving to Santa Fe without remarking the haunted prison on its outskirts. What inspired me then, and what drew me back to a new life there, was the utter magnificence of the land, and an equal beauty of feeling among its native Spanish, whose dignity and depth are one of the least understood and most admirable gifts America has been given in conquest of a continent.

I am writing in part, then, of that place and people. The book takes its special backdrop in the hard, clean air and crystalline blue skies, the purple mountains and lunar valleys where a desultory Spanish colonialism gave way to the caste rule of an American backwater and where, as on the high desert itself, the surface tranquillity hid a seething, pitiless, often lethal harshness. For the proud Spanish remnant here, its children disappearing into an alien and empty television culture, its authentic community dispersed and shunted ever northward, politely gerrymandered into a last congressional redoubt, the penitentiary riot amid its larger history is in a sense one of the final battles. For both Hispanic and Anglo, for Indian or black, for guards, inmates, and citizens alike in New Mexico, the state prison and the politics and policy that produced it constitute in many ways a betrayal of public trust as witless and mean-spirited as any recently inflicted by rulers upon the ruled in this country.

Yet make no mistake about this: the deeper meaning of the New Mexican riot is national. In the end, there is nothing *local* about prisons. The shocking misrule behind this butchery is altogether multiracial, bipartisan, and commonplace in the United States. That it happened on this relatively exotic frontier on a bleak February weekend in 1980 makes only the texture of the story regional, not the political and social essence—or the omen. For most of America's blighted penal system, drifting toward Armageddon like some decrepit ungovernable empire, the blood frenzy at Santa Fe is scarcely an aberration or relic of the past. It is a terrifying glimpse of our future nationwide.

This book belongs to so many people whom mere acknowledgment can never adequately repay. Not least are the scores of brave men and women of New Mexico corrections on both sides of the bars, they and their families, captives all. During hundreds of hours of interviews they shared their experiences, however painful, and asked me in return simply to protect their privacy and to make an honest effort to tell it as it was—and is. I hope I have done both.

Then there are debts I can only distinguish alphabetically: Jeanette Antunez for her remarkable insight and gallantry of spirit; Dwight Duran of the National Prison Project of the American Civil Liberties Union for his singular wisdom and friendship and for an example of heroism that gives this terrible history its redemption; Lisette Ellis for giving me her shrewd overview of criminal justice policy gained as a nationally-recognized prison architect; Jerilou Hammett for her thoughtful bilingual perspective on the larger cultural tensions; my colleagues of the 1981 Inter-Media Investigative Group—Toni Drew, Kingsley Hammett, David Hendry, Karen McDaniel, Peter Morris, Mary Lynn Roper, Niki Sebastian, Diana Stouffer, and Charlie Zdravesky— for their indispensable contributions to this record; Sylvia and Conrad Keller for their exceptional valor in speaking out when they stood alone; John and Johnna Bustamante Lopez for their guidance at important turns and for the model of their dedication; Lloyd McClendon of the Ohio Department of Corrections for spending a drizzly day with me in Columbus, brightened by his profound feeling and intelligence about criminal justice as well as his own moving story; Richard McCord, copublisher and editor of the *Santa Fe Reporter*, for the courageous journalism that inspired much of my work on the prison from that first February 1980 phone call from an unknown writer who'd found something in Washington; *Playboy* editor, Jim Morgan, who gave me the first chance to write about the riot itself and whose superb editing and staff, especially Mary Zion, contributed so much along the way; Lee Page for sharing the expertise of his brilliant public service as a consultant on prison standards in several states; Dick Winterbottom for giving me his public defender's unique knowledge and perspective on the takeover; Susan Yakutis for her sparkling intellect and sensibility in fathoming the madness; and the attorneys and investigators of both the riot defense and the prosecution, who have asked not to be named but who gave similarly valuable help.

Without my gifted young editor, Elizabeth Hock, who believed in this book devotedly through many intervening projects, the larger story could never have been told. Liz is owed a debt of honor by so many people she will never know, and I gratefully acknowledge it here.

Finally, there is my collaborator in all this, and my conscience and authority on humanity's enduring good amid the atavism and butchery, my wife Kathy. She gave herself and her home over to the hectic journalistic prelude to this book, researched, interviewed, functioned as an astute chief of intelligence, edited the manuscript, and passionately argued me out of several satisfying distortions. Whatever is right and thoughtful here comes of Kat and all the others. The mistakes are stubbornly mine.

And for yet another book, I'm fortunate to have had the generous cooperation of both the New Mexico State Library and the Fogelson Library Center of the Christian Brothers' College of Santa Fe.

Roger Morris
Santa Fe, 1983

SOURCES

Attribution for quoted remarks and salient parts of the narrative is given in the Notes at the end of the book. Every condition of weather, circumstance, and state of mind, all feelings, thoughts private and public, and all actions have documentary support.

Like anyone who looks seriously at this uprising or at prison revolts in general, I have been indebted from the outset to the two-part *Report of the Attorney General* produced under legislative mandate in June and September 1980 by then New Mexico AG, now U.S. Senator, Jeff Bingaman and his staff. Though the report obviously had its official limits (and my own differences with it are plain in this account), the two volumes in many respects remain a starting point for authentic research.

Beyond published sources, the narrative derives from an assembled archive of official documents, including post-riot investigative files, eyewitness statements and interrogations recorded by the State Police, reports of the penitentiary intelligence office, and various other records from the prison, state corrections department headquarters, and other agencies. This collection, along with extensive primary documents from inmate and official monitors in the *Duran* case and the primary files from various journalistic investigations of the New Mexico prison system in 1980 and 1981, will fill several cabinets at the New Mexico State Library in Santa Fe, making its way, as it should, from bureaucratic shadows to public sunlight, for future scholars (and—who can tell?—maybe even a future guard or governor) to sample the tenor of this history firsthand.

I have drawn as well on over two hundred interviews, many with eyewitnesses of all uniforms, many interviewed several times to check and sharpen details. When recollections have clashed with the documents, I have tended to side with the written record unless the interview evidence was clearly preponderant and from several independent sources. Not that official documents in this story were not by definition suspect; fractured or self-serving memory was often simply more so.

Among those journalists writing about the riot, I have admired and drawn gratefully from the work of Jack Cox, Tom Day, Peter Katel, Robert Mayer, Ernie Mills, Steve Penrose, Craig Pyes, and John Robertson. Mayer's article in *Rocky Mountain Magazine* and Katel's account in *Corrections Magazine*, both cited in the Notes, were especially valuable.

Finally, for reasons that should be clear in the narrative, I have not been able for purposes of scholarship to trust the authenticity of much of the evidence presented by post-riot prosecutions, and so have not generally convicted men in print for myriad crimes committed in the riot, even when they have ended up "guilty" in the tangled web of plea bargains, judicial politics, and the handful of actual jury deliberations. From Torquemada to Vyshinsky, we have learned that trials can make dubious history, and what happened in the judicial aftermath in Santa Fe was no exception. It was scarcely a reckoning on the disaster, but rather part of it. "Who's on trial here?" a lawyer once asked sarcastically in a typical and usually successful effort to cut off evidence embarrassing to the state. The answer, he should have known, was all of us.

FORESHADOW

Do you know how many
unnumbering days
I have waited
and waited, immobile?
Insane with the brawn
of oppression, the bane
of a thousand and radical hardons,
lusty with dreams.

Ray Bremser,
"Penal Madness"

i

t is a fashionable, lovely place, this site of massacre.

"So fresh the strike of breath in that air, so clear the endowment of sight in that light," writes an admiring author, that every day in Santa Fe seems "a new beginning." At 7,000 feet, the desert plateau wears a crisp, unearthly brilliance. By day the sky is everywhere, a vastness of startling blue. Near, yet unoppressive, the sun unfurls sharp, dark shadows and bathes the cool, dry ground in a gentle warmth. The landscape is almost never unlit. Even in the desert darkness, its craters clearly visible to the naked eye, the moon casts its own phosphorescent light and inky silhouettes, seeming somehow to hover longer in the eastern rise, savoring an unaccustomed splendor. And in the infinity beyond, seen only black and empty from lesser altitudes, countless stars suddenly fill the sky as if they have just blazed into existence.

It is a vista in which men have long felt wonder—and frailty.

The Spaniards come at the end of the sixteenth century for their own new beginning, plodding with their priests and sheep along the Rio Grande valley from El Paso del Norte and the border of Old Mexico three hundred miles to the south, switching back and forth up the rocky escarpment they will reverently call La Bajada, the great descent, gaining the high plateau in hope of silver bars lying in the arroyos. Instead they find drought and hunger and poor, dun-colored pueblos soon defiant at the intrusion.

Even in their disappointment, Santa Fe having become one more lonely, dusty presidio at the extremity of a moribund empire, the Spanish are in thrall to the setting. Across the broad valley of scrub and piñon to the west rises the Jemez range, a craggy volcanic face ever changing in the angular light. Yet it is the mountain chain to the north and east, where the plateau washes up on a last great spur of the North American Rockies, that dominates the scene. The colonists nestle their mud-brick Royal City of Holy Faith and Saint Francis hard among the foothills and thin *acequias* that slope from that majestic basin. Over the peaks draw fiery, haunting sunsets, a swift drain of color, crimson to gray, horizon to ground, as if the mountains were flushed and then suddenly stricken and dying of some massive internal wound. In awe, the pious Spanish come to call the mountains Sangre de Cristo, the blood of Christ.

For a time after the American seizure in 1848, Santa Fe remains an obscure outpost, trail town booty of the Mexican War. By the twentieth century, though, it has captured its new conquerors as well. Artists make the pilgrimage to its singular clarity of light and boundless horizon. Immigrants with college degrees abandon pay and prestige elsewhere and wait on tables or lay adobe bricks just to live in the sunsets. In the Latin vestige there seems a haven for both creative and social freedom, what writer Paul Horgan calls a "long tradition of sanctuary," a beguiling blend of gentle village manner and Bohemian sophistication that from the 1920s affords individuality, even eccentricity, a search for values. "This curious city," Oliver La Farge says of it affectionately, "attracting and holding people of sensitivity." La Farge and others are utterly charmed by the painters in their sculpted adobe houses along the Camino del Monte Sol, the sleepy native barrio and the mood it supplies of Mediterranean exile right here in the Great American Desert, the hale old Spanish and Anglo politicians who pass out dollar bills for votes within sight of the polls, the raw, seductive local chic of Santa Fe belles at Fiesta riding their horses raucously into the bar at the La Fonda Hotel as late as the Eisenhower fifties.

Still, not everyone is held by the spell, nor is every pilgrim so sensitive. Like all shrines, it is a site, too, of shattered dreams, of the old illusion that a place somehow provides more than people bring to it. Some artists languish, becoming merchants, drunks, or mere oddities. Fresh starts often peter out, like the old Spanish mines south of town. Part of the city's avant-garde smacks of failure and fraud. Along with the heavenly and cultivated charms come successively larger waves of tourists, monied migrants, young strays, affluent dropouts, blue-jeaned refugees from the rest of American life, "an open conspiracy of hedonism," as Horgan once deplored their sometimes self-conscious alienation and decadence. For many of these émigrés, as for the Japanese Americans herded into a wartime compound along the Alameda, the city is a kind of internment camp, replete with camp costume of long skirts, turquoise, and designer cowboy hats.

Now, in 1980, Santa Fe is more than ever a settlement of art and artifice, its inspiring sensibility increasingly crowded by the vulgar. Condominiums eat into the hills. Real estate predators pick over the remains of the old plaza. *Esquire* magazine is about to pronounce it anew "the place to be."

Meanwhile, largely unseen and unadvertised by *Esquire* or the Chamber of Commerce, quite another Santa Fe lives alongside the resort. In quiet blocks behind the landmarks and expensive galleries is a small, ingrown state capital, in which the poor and a struggling, provincial middle class, much of it Hispanic and of traditional values, coexist uneasily (as they always have) with the expatriate youth and wealth with its paler skin. What La Farge twenty years earlier called nimbly "the race question" is still no historical abstraction in that Santa Fe. And there, widespread official corruption and a blighted educational system are no longer picturesque. It is a place of cruder arts where flushed corporate lobbyists congregate and New Mexico's coveted resources are exploited at vast private gain, where public treasuries are rifled and services are stunted, where a generally co-opted or indolent press masks the multiple abuses of local power, and where the fashionable and artistic seldom descend.

Eleven miles outside this capital, on the rolling, windswept plain the settlers crossed from the crest of La Bajada, stands a state penitentiary, a monument to the squalor and ruin of the public interest beside the exquisite vogue and quaint backwardness. This prison is not—never has been— a "place to be." But it is about to mark the City of Holy Faith with the newest distinction of its legend. Until now, the pen has been part of the unseen, unfashionable Santa Fe. Like the sunset hemorrhaging over the mountains, however, blood will make it visible—at least for a while.

for months the kites are everywhere. Notes scrawled, rumors, meetings on murmured agendas, premonitions felt in noisy, clamorous action or in the silent eyes of caged men, it is all the furtive telegraph by which a prison talks to itself. As usual, the kites flow outward. The keepers in the New Mexico pen and beyond are among the first to know. But the messages move in both directions, reverberating deep into the corridors and cell blocks in the sights and sounds of official provocation and persistent, contemptuous negligence, until it will seem to many that the state officials are not merely ignoring the beast taking shape before them, but actually inviting it in.

In April 1979 a guard named Bob Runyon proposes to his superiors an organized intelligence system to replace the pen's haphazard reliance on informants and random, usually unchanneled staff reports. A former air force intelligence operative with a degree in criminology, Runyon sees his proposal ignored for several weeks and then, like so many other conscientious guards before him, resigns in apprehension and disgust. "Lacking this system," he has written in a prophetic letter to Deputy Secretary of Corrections and former Warden Felix Rodriguez, "I anticipate serious incidents in the near future of corruption, the introduction of contraband, escapes, riots, hostage-taking and ruthless killings of inmates." The letter is dated July 6, 1979.

A month later, two seemingly unconnected events give Runyon's letter added portent. In the long, cool days of the late New Mexico summer, the prison administration begins an overdue renovation of the riot-control grilles that close off the south wing dormitories from the main corridor of the institution. The remodeling is to allow the prison control center to shut the grilles electronically, swiftly sealing off the dormitories by the remote command of a few buttons. At any point, the work can be completed in "several days," concludes a later inquiry, but the administration feels "no sense of urgency or priority," and the new electronic controls will still not be installed by February 1980. Now, though the grilles are usually closed manually, renovation leaves the old routine operation by key "cumbersome," according to prison officials' subsequent reports. From August, the riot-control doors are simply not used.

As the grilles stand open, the U.S. Justice Department's Community Relations Service has begun a crucial mediation between New Mexico corrections officials and penitentiary inmates represented by attorneys of the American Civil Liberties Union. The mediation stems from a landmark con⸱itutional suit brought by convicts against the state in 1977 to improve prison conditions, *Duran* v. *King*, captioned for Dwight Duran, the convict who led the plaintiffs, and Bruce King, the state's current Democratic governor. After presiding indifferently over the first stages of the case, local Federal Judge Santiago Campos suggests mediation, and the two sides agree. With the state dragging its feet, the mediation takes more than a year to get started. But this August there is genuine optimism among embittered inmates as the talks begin. The Justice Department mediators have resolved similarly volatile disputes among California unions, at Kent State, at Wounded Knee, and in school desegregation battles from Boston to Dallas. "It looks like we have a chance of changing things with the feds around," one prisoner writes his mother on Labor Day. As the first chill autumn nights descend over the Cerrillos plain, as the leaves blanch to pale yellow in the sparse trees near the administrators' houses and the guards' trailer courts on the pen grounds, the negotiations drag on fitfully through September. Then, abruptly, in early October Deputy Secretary Rodriguez takes charge of the state's case, and the federal mediators are told to leave, their good offices "no longer utilized" as a Justice Department official describes it to a reporter four months later, after events have made the breakdown pregnant with tragedy. When Rodriguez next negotiates with inmates, there will be no Washington intermediaries, and the issues will be more stark.

In early November prison officials begin yet another renovation, this one of the locking system in cell block 5, a maximum-security unit at the north end of the building housing some of the pen's most violent men. The need for repair in cell block 5 is not unusual. Though little more than a quarter-century old, the penitentiary has been shoddily built and poorly maintained, the product of original and continuing graft of one sort or another. Guards will remember especially the locks. They seem perpetually faulty. Now, because the prison is decaying, the dangerous men from 5 must be transferred. It is prescribed corrections practice in such cases to put the displaced inmates in other maximum-security cells or, failing that, at least to disperse and separate them among lower-security units, lest they band together in their temporary housing. But because the New Mexico prison is also overcrowded, more than 1,100 men in an institution designed to hold safely and humanely no more than 850, the remaining high-security cell blocks are already beyond capacity. Almost all the men from 5 will be moved into dormitories, the least secure units of a prison. Yet, at that, they will not be dispersed. Most of them this November are sent together down the long central corridor to dormitory E-2, on the second floor of the south wing. There, as renovation of their cell block proceeds at the usual leisurely pace, the new hard-core men from 5, a coalition of Chicanos and whites, soon begin to expel the dormitory's few blacks and establish their rule. They will still be in E-2, beyond the open, too "cumbersome" grilles, as the winter wears on.

On Thanksgiving, many of the pen's inmates are served spoiled turkey, what one later describes as "smelling, green, rotten." Hundreds suffer from diarrhea after eating only the other parts of the meal. Guards and prison food administrators ridicule their angry protests. Then, a few days later, as several convicts were to remember vividly, there is the strange repetition of a recent incident. At about five-thirty in the evening, the pen is suddenly plunged into darkness while the mess hall is still crowded with prisoners. When the lights come on minutes later, the men, though murmuring and occasionally catcalling, are still sitting or standing passively where the blackout found them. But a special contingent of guards, fully equipped with helmets, shotguns, riot clubs, and teargas launchers, has quickly materialized in the corridor and at the entrance of the mess. The armed group is made up largely of what inmates call the "goon squad," officers allegedly involved in frequent gang beatings of prisoners. Some of them are not assigned to the regular swing shift staffing the penitentiary at that hour, and they have apparently been ready for the blackout. Since nothing develops in the darkness, however, helmeted officers pause awkwardly before the quiet men in the relit hall and then leave as the meal goes on. It has all happened like this once before in the last few months, several inmates remark afterward: a sudden blackout and the instant appearance of a battle-ready riot squad, although at other incidents such as fights or stabbings it can take several minutes for a single guard to arrive on the scene. Later, there will be no record of a power failure at the Penitentiary of New Mexico during those weeks.

With the collective transfer of the cell block 5 men to E-2, the rancid turkey, and the blackout, November brings as well two specific warnings, both given to ranking officials, both ignored. Around November 30, the New Mexico pen's director of psychological services, Marc Orner, goes to senior prison officials in visible alarm. Orner is a controversial figure. Distrusted by some inmates, protected by others, he wields the awesome, arbitrary power of release or repression with his psychological evaluations, and represents a part of the convoluted world of the prison snitch system, the cultivated treachery that will soon issue in such annihilating rage. "I get good information whenever there is going to be heavy shit," Orner later tells State Police agents in recorded testimony. Now, in the last days of November, four inmates come to Orner one by one to tell him there is going to be "trouble"—an escape and a takeover of the institution with hostages, perhaps Orner and some of his own staff, including women. A black, two whites, and a Chicano, the prisoners are not usually informers. But they have seen the kites as never before, and the black man believes he is on a hit list of those to be executed in the revolt.

There will be an escape, then a riot, Orner tells administrators. "A follow-up breakout?" State Police subsequently ask the psychologist about his warnings. "No, not a follow-up breakout," he answers emphatically, "but a follow-up riot...supposed to be a riot in the gym." The escape would be "only the beginning," Orner goes on. "They are trying to start a riot...there was going to be a riot....I heard just that a riot was going to happen." The insistent repetition in Orner's later testimony about what he knew and warned will be itself as significant as his initial report. For he will testify to the State Police on his unheeded intelligence on January 7, 1980, *after* half of his warning has already proved rather dramatically accurate, but still *before* the predicted follow-up. His information will be ignored even then, however, much as it was ignored weeks earlier.

He has hardly been alone in having advance warning of the "trouble," Orner recalls to the State Police in his later statement. "There was a bunch of people who knew about it." Among them are several guards who tell their superiors of the specific date of the planned major escape within a day or two. Orner will later recount two meetings with corrections officials that November. At one there are repeated reports of an impending disturbance, and Rodriguez orders that two of the inmates named most frequently be locked away in maximum security. But at a second session, when Orner brings a precise list of conspirators, he is ridiculed. He has come with his report of escape and riot to Deputy Warden Robert Montoya and Superintendent of Correctional Security Manuel Koroneos. As Orner hands over his list of names, Montoya pointedly lifts a paper off his desk and says, according to Orner's statement, "That is okay. I've got twelve names." But Montoya and Koroneos will not act on the intelligence. "I'm not going to be in this fucking place with twenty officers on a weekend," Orner remembers telling them nervously, "and they laughed...they thought it was funny." Then later, when this foreknowledge is the object of an outside investigation, Orner and others on the prison staff are told they are "all one family" and must "be careful what we say." What did that mean? Orner is asked, and he answers simply, "Keep your mouth shut." Then, later, "There is a group of people [in the prison administration] who keep all the fucking information," Orner concludes in his January testimony.

While the deputy warden and his security chief are laughing at Orner, yet another augury comes from the other side of the bars. Soon to be paroled, Dwight Duran, the leading plaintiff in the prison reform suit, joins another inmate, Ralph Gonzales, in writing an extraordinary letter to his nominal opponent in the case, the state's governor, Bruce King. Unless there is immediate action to better conditions, Duran and Gonzales warn King, the Penitentiary of New Mexico faces catastrophe. Since he filed his brief in 1977, Duran's life has been a symbol of moderation, legal redress, and negotiation in the raw-edged, blackly cynical cell houses of Santa Fe. But in the closing weeks of 1979 he senses that time is running out, and perhaps gone. To the failure of reform, he tells the governor, there will be "terrible consequences," and the situation will be soon "out of control." Marked "privileged legal correspondence," the Duran-Gonzales letter disappears into the maw of penitentiary mail and state bureaucracy. Months afterward, the governor's staff cannot recall ever receiving it. In any case, though this letter speaks with grave new urgency and authority, Bruce King has been hearing similar warnings for years during his two terms as chief executive. They have all had similar effect.

By December, winter has begun to toy with the prison on the barren Cerrillos Plain. Days are alternately mild and biting, the nights steadily frigid. A thin snow falls, disappears, oozes back to a frozen crust on the worn, empty ground around the cell blocks and dormitories. In the cold the prison closes in on itself, crouches, windows fogged by breath where men can reach them, sound ricocheting sharper and farther through the wings. But this winter, outside or in, the signs of what is coming continue to gather, and to be ignored.

On Friday, December 7, there is an obscure but historic gathering in Santa Fe. Ostensibly, it is a routine meeting of the parties to discuss the course of the prison reform suit now that the Justice Department mediators have been dismissed. For the inmates come Dwight Duran and fellow plaintiffs and inmates Lonnie Duran and Sharon Towers, along with two ACLU attorneys. Representing the state are Ralph Muxlow, for some years the corrections department lawyer on the attorney general's staff, Deputy Secretary Rodriguez and Rodriguez's chief aide, Joanne Brown. But amid the perfunctory legal jockeying, Duran and the other convicts deliver to the state officials a somber, unmistakable warning, just as they have tried to warn the governor. "The prison's going to blow," a witness remembers Duran saying. He and the others then describe the mounting tension of the past weeks. But no one contradicts their view, asks for more information, offers a tangible response. As the convicts and their lawyers part later in the courthouse hallway, someone jokes bitterly about the date; it is Pearl Harbor Day.

Two days after Duran's warning and plea, the event takes place, on schedule, which Orner and several other penitentiary staff have forecast for more than a week and which fulfills the first of the kites' prophecies. Eleven men escape from the New Mexico pen with apparent ease. Moments past five o'clock that afternoon, following the evening meal, ten inmates gather in cell house 2. Six are from another block, but are undetected by the lone guard supervising the area. Five of them are convicted murderers. While an eleventh convict occupies a swing-shift guard captain in a conversation at the entry to the cell house, the ten break a cell window and use a stolen saw to hack through bars already partially cut. Within an hour, all ten get out the hole and— using knotted sheets, stocking caps, and clothing—pull down protective concertina wire and climb to the roof of the central corridor. Across the roof they drop a dozen feet to the ground. They make their way toward the fence along a cell block wall just out of sight of the front tower.

In the gray early nightfall a tower guard eventually sees a portion of sheet left hanging and asks a foot patrol officer to investigate. But while the guard is finding the sheet, the escapees cross unseen a 50-yard lighted expanse of the penitentiary's front lawn and lie by the fence, once more just beyond the tower's field of vision. Incredibly, the foot patrol reports having seen the sheet but routinely resumes his rounds. The escaping men wait for the siren. None sounds. For twenty minutes an inmate grinds on the inner perimeter fence with a pair of pliers stolen from a contractor at a prison work site, and then, through a jagged 2-by-3-foot hole, the men are gone.

Almost ninety minutes later, the eleventh man ends his conversation with the guard captain, walks back into the cell house to leave by the same route, scales the roof, drops to the front yard, and then walks almost casually along the fence for what a later report calls "several minutes" before he finally finds the hole and disappears. It will be more than an hour after the escape before the State Police are notified, nearly three hours until roadblocks are set up.

"A lot of dumb luck," one fleeing con explains the break-out later. With little evident planning for the outside, all but one of the fugitives are captured over the ensuing days and weeks. But the mass escape is more than happenstance. Not only are reports from Orner and others ignored, but a subsequent attorney general's inquiry reveals as well that three of the plotters have been witnessed and *reported* planning the event, while another off-duty guard has received a tip and called the pen to alert officials to the escape two hours before it begins. Still, senior officers said to receive these reports, among them Koroneos and the guard who advises Orner to "keep my mouth shut," cannot remember the information. No one asks more. Only after the escape is it discovered that "much of the fence line" cannot be seen from the front tower, while it and other towers are commonly left with broken equipment and even without binoculars. But administrators responsible for tower security and provisioning go unquestioned.

As the attorney general prepares in mid-January to release his inquiry into the escape, newspaper accounts report that prison officials had prior warning of the breakout. Despairing guards immediately circulate to the governor and the news media an anonymous letter saying the reports are true, that the pen is dominated by "a large click [sic]," and that "measures have to be taken or other incidents will definate [sic] occur." The letter is ignored.

The attorney general's escape report concludes that there is "factionalism, poor communication and apathy" at the pen, and under current conditions officials are "playing Russian roulette with the lives of inmates, staff and the public." California corrections consultants called into the inquiry observe that "this [the escape] or something similar should have happened long before this and will no doubt be repeated if the staffing and training problem is not addressed, and quickly." But despite such stark language, the report remains unaccountably vague on specific responsibility for the intelligence lapses, and any other question of management beyond added staffing. In its wake, two young tower guards are fired, while Charles Becknell, a black corrections secretary who has sought vainly to curb Rodriguez's power, resigns as the public scapegoat for the shocking escape. But Governor King will not ask the legislature for the higher guard salaries and added prison staff the report has so urgently recommended.

Not everyone suffers from the debacle. Senior prison officials are implicitly exonerated. Rodriguez becomes acting secretary of corrections, the heir apparent to the position. And the attorney general's chief investigator of the escape, the author of the published inquiry, it turns out, is a former corrections department staff lawyer under Rodriguez. Not long after the report, he is appointed by Governor King to fill a vacant district judgeship.

A manageable embarrassment on the outside, the effect of the escape is electric inside the prison. It wreaks havoc with the always fragile facade of security by which a penitentiary staves off anarchy. The keepers have blundered, but with impunity. The scapegoats are too junior or too distant to matter. For better or for worse, the system will go on. A few days after the escape, one convict later tells a television interviewer, several prisoners watch as a guard, obviously drunk, weaves through his work in charge of the control center. The holes methodically chewed in the window of cell house 2 and the perimeter fence have returned to the convicts their most valued and volatile possession—control. At the same time, the escape also fastens the inmate population into a rapid spiral of overcrowding. Transfers to more lenient satellite institutions have been cut off in October after a stabbing at the work camp in the mountains south of Albuquerque. Now, movement out of the maximum-security hell in Santa Fe is frozen indefinitely. The census climbs from 957 to 1,157 in less than three months, squeezing men together, pressing their faces into the stench of dirty feet in packed cells, robbing them of the last shreds of prison privacy, and of transfer's last incentive for decent behavior. Without the mass escape in December, the folly and cover-up and the mood it leaves in the cell blocks and dormitories, at once bravado and despair, the New Mexico pen riot is far more difficult to imagine.

As Christmas approaches, there are numerous kites bruiting that hostages will be taken during the holidays. Earlier in the month there has been talk of a seizure during a special radio broadcast from the pen by the inmates' favorite disc jockey, Mr. Hot Lix of the University of New Mexico's public station KUNM, who plays 1950s oldies every Saturday night to accompanying dedications between the prisoners and their loved ones. Taking Hot Lix hostage will give the cons a dramatic captive as well as an instant broadcast facility through which to air their grievances. But someone warns the administration, and the special concert is canceled, though no other precautions are taken.

Another plan has it that a picked group of convicts will capture civilian and guard staff, order the rest of the inmates evacuated, and hold up in the institution during a televised siege the holiday week, dramatizing their grievances to the nation. "We're going to have a goddamned riot," an inmate clerk and staff officers hear Deputy Warden Montoya abruptly announce to a classification meeting in mid-December. The subordinate men around the room are stunned and say nothing. Montoya, apparently satisfied with his effect and in any case vouchsafing no details, resumes the regular agenda. On December 20, five inmate assistants are called together by one of their fellow clerks in the psychological unit and warned not to interfere if female members of the psychologist's staff are taken hostage. Some of the clerks say they will resist any assault on the women. At the same meeting, according to later testimony to the State Police, the clerks are told that "one of the primary goals" of an uprising is "to open cell block four and kill all the snitches and, besides, any snitches that were out in population." December 20: it is one of the first references to planned executions of the informers, a first allusion to cell block 4, the protective custody wing at the far northwest corner of the building. A riot always has been—will be—far more than a political act to expose mistreatment and wring concessions. For many, it is the long-dreamed-of chance for "payback," an orgy of retribution. Murder will be no random by-product of the chaos but a cherished purpose, and officials know it. The threat to the informers will be duly reported, and dismissed, before Christmas.

At year's end two essential sequels will be played out. Around December 23, by their later account to state investigators, two worried guards send Koroneos a memorandum on the danger of the renovation contractor's tools being left each night unsecured in cell block 5. A hacksaw from there already has been used in the escape. Among the equipment are powerful blowtorches and even tanks of reserve fuel for them. Afterward, Koroneos will claim he never saw the memo, and apparently never thought of the tools. Finally, just before New Year's Eve, another guard notices that the small blue night-lights in dormitory E-2 are evidently burned out, leaving the unit and its new occupants from cell block 5 in a thick nighttime darkness almost impenetrable to corrections officers on rounds. The guard reports the bulbs out, but they will go unreplaced. The year 1980 dawns in a pale blue day, the snow already heavy in the Sangre de Cristos. Santa Fe has had its posh New Year's Eve parties behind adobe walls lit by the charming traditional fires of *farolitos* and *luminarias*. Behind other walls at the penitentiary, the open grilles, the political and legal neglect, the administrative negligence, the blowtorches, the burned-out lights, and the men—all are already in place for what one con will call "the biggest party ever held."

In January one inmate chronicler of events would remember "plenty of secret meetings" between the pen's racial gangs, plotting their uneasy coalition in an uprising. The psychological unit clerks are now notified the target date is January 8. They repeat their readiness to defend the female employees, while later passing on the report to a staff psychologist, who passes it in turn to prison security. At the same time, inmates quietly begin to request transfers from E-2 and other dormitories, a textbook omen of imminent prison violence. In early January, according to later State Police interrogations, inmates are widely discussing how to get added weapons into the institution from the prison-industries building nearby on the reservation. These plans, too, are reported. Preparations and the official indifference to them are becoming almost too blatant. Convicts, one wrote later, "began to wonder if The Man was daring them to start something."

On January 11, the day Becknell resigns as corrections secretary, Orner sends a memo to Security Chief Koroneos. A distillation of numerous early reports in the psychological unit, Orner's memo warns that men in E-2 may have homemade guns and may plan to take hostages. The later attorney general's report on the riot will call this memorandum "the first indication of a possible hostage seizure," though it merely repeats a portion of the intelligence that officials have had from various sources with numbing frequency for several weeks. In response to Orner's written report, guards perfunctorily shake down dormitory E-2 but, as usual, find nothing, although in the vents and pipe chase there is, as usual, a small arsenal of blades and bludgeons as well as a crude miniature distillery made of garbage bags and cardboard boxes.

On January 15 Jerry Griffin, the pen warden since 1979 and a former Rodriguez aide, yet a figure almost invisible in his powerlessness, attempts to change the prison's organization chart, allowing underlings to report more directly to the warden rather than through Montoya and the dense layer of other second-echelon administrators. Griffin has been shocked by the escape, and knows only a small fraction of the daily accumulating intelligence on a riot. But his redrawing of paper lines will have no impact on the pen's flesh-and-blood power, now in the grip of a handful of officials and a few inmates. At any rate, it will come too late.

Far more important is an unannounced event the same day: the installation of a large bay window between the control center and the main corridor. Three main panels and two smaller side panes projecting slightly into the hallway, the new glass follows a 1979 architect's recommendation to replace several smaller windows in the bay and thus afford a freer view of the corridor where inmates often pass or gather. The $1\frac{3}{16}$-inch glass is bulletproof and slightly tinted to provide a partially reflective, one-way effect. It is also breakable.

Deputy Secretary Rodriguez ceremoniously tests security glass with a sledge hammer two weeks before installation and finds it unbreakable. But the glass he tests is not the same kind installed in the bay window of the control center. When officials do decide to test the same glass about to be installed in the control room of a new medium-security prison south of Albuquerque, three inmates with hammers bash a gaping hole in it in less than thirty seconds. With several guards instantly alarmed and complaining to superiors about the glass at Santa Fe from the day it is put in, one of Griffin's deputies sends a memorandum to the architect on January 17, asking that a section of the new glass be framed for testing. Griffin also discusses briefly with aides the prospect of placing some sort of steel reinforcement behind the glass. But there are no more discussions and no further tests. On the day the glass is installed, prisoners joke openly about it. One convict watches as the work is completed and then walks back down the corridor to his unit. Passing a guard in the hall, he brazenly thanks the officer, in the words of a later inquiry, "for giving the institution away."

A day after the deputy's memo about testing the glass is sent to the architect, a Santa Fe County grand jury sharply criticizes prison officials for nepotism in hiring and promoting guards. But such grand jury reports are by now almost routine, never acted upon by the state or district attorney, and the finding is soon filed away with the many others like it. Meanwhile, there are more requests for transfer out of E-2. By January 18, too, the ruling convicts in E-2 begin to smuggle in from the kitchen fresh supplies of raisins and yeast for a new blending of home brew.

On January 23, Montoya reports to Griffin intelligence of a possible takeover and seizure of hostages in cell block 3, the maximum-security cell block caging the pen's most violent men. Again, a shakedown finds nothing, though at this moment the cell block is bristling with "shanks," the ingenious, lethal homemade prison knives. Now Koroneos does recommend that some protective-custody inmates housed in cell block 3, most of them labeled snitches, be transferred for their safety. But nine days later, the cell block will still have inmates ostensibly in "protection," and they will be the first to scream and to die.

Aware of the palpable tension if not the intelligence, Griffin now asks his officers in the last week of January to review the prison's riot-control plan. The plan had been issued in 1977, the device of an earlier, more orthodox warden from out of state, and it is little more than a collection of conventional handbook nostrums and procedures, with no adaptation to the inmate and non-inmate society of the pen or to the prison's geography. Typical of administrative mentality, it reassuringly attributes any disturbance variously to "agitators," "reckless and unstable" prisoners, "racial strife," or "a general revolt against authority," and only vaguely and toward the bottom of the list to "conditions." It does, however, list plainly the "signs of unrest," including "undue tension," inmates avoiding usual contact with prison staff, "a flood of requests for quarter [sic] changes," all of which are evident in the weeks before the Santa Fe mayhem. The plan also sets forth clearly the "order of responsibility" in dealing with a riot. Officers are to protect "general public safety," hostages, and other staff personnel first, and only then to consider the "welfare" of the inmates (along with the preservation of state property). Most of this will be academic in any case. Copies of the plan are nowhere to be found these last days of January 1980, although they are supposed to be available for study in the shift captain's office. Later, though regulations stipulate that "each employee is required to attest by his signature that he is familiar with this plan," only two guards will remember seeing it at all prior to the riot. "You say there's a new riot plan," one guard had said to a reporter years before when the plan was issued. "Well, we haven't been told about it. The only plan we've heard about is when the national guard comes in and we leave."

At least the prison's officers cannot find the plan. Marked "confidential" and "never to be left where inmates would have access to it," copies of both the "Riot Control Plan" and "Escape [prevention] Plan" circulate among the inmates and are later casually mailed out of the penitentiary marked "legal papers." The institution's most sensitive security documents thus exit the prison under privilege, while Dwight Duran's warning letter about the riot, sent to Governor King under the same imprint, apparently never gets through.

As the forlorn order goes out to review the riot-control plan, inmates now begin to warn openly friendly staff members. "When I come and tell you not to come to work the next day, don't come to work," one prisoner tells a woman employee. The precise warning never comes, however, and she does not report the incident until after the riot. Another convict warns a female guard and teacher that "something's coming down soon." This time the incident is reported, and the prisoner, unpopular with the administration, is conspicuously called in to be questioned about the warning. A few days later, an unrecognizable clump of charred bone and flesh, the young convict will have paid with his life, in part for this gesture. Afterward, officials will claim that they ordered guards during this last week to "keep on your toes," and that prisoners under suspicion of planning a takeover were "locked down" in maximum-security segregation. But there are no special orders or briefings. And when housing records are reconstructed after the riot, they show that only three inmates have recently been moved to cell block 3, none for being suspected of plotting a riot. Meanwhile, at least two convicts who have been reported as instigators, one named in the January 11 Orner memorandum, remain in dormitory E-2. Neither the caseworkers who must deal with them nor the guards who must watch them at night are given Orner's memo or are even told that the men are suspects in a long-predicted uprising. "They knew and they kept telling us, 'It's going to come down,'" guard lieutenant Marshall Lujan tells reporters afterward about comments by the pen administration, but there is "nothing specific" about the warnings.

It is Thursday, January 31. The pen's new intelligence chief, Larry Flood, has called an "intelligence-sharing meeting." After more than twenty years as an army MP and two as a New Mexico prison guard and counselor, Flood has been acting intelligence officer for only two weeks. But it has been long enough for him to grow nervous about the evidence gathering on his desk. He convenes the meeting to appraise the information and alert his superiors. To the session come

Rodriguez, Griffin, Montoya, and Koroneos, other administrators, State Police intelligence officers and agents, members of the attorney general's staff, and Eugene Long, one of Koroneos's predecessors as security superintendent, a longtime Rodriguez subordinate, and now a corrections department adviser. Rodriguez chairs. In perfunctory, manly tones, they discuss the prospect of a hostage seizure, another escape, smuggled weapons, racial unrest. Koroneos tells them a "white supremacy group" may be planning a disturbance in E-2, but not until next spring. One pen official says an inmate has told him that "E-2 is getting hot." Still another remarks that the men seem to be "acting differently in several ways." Flood adds that the mood of the prison population strikes him as "quite ugly."

Perhaps too accustomed to harsh omens, Rodriguez and his men, the men of power at the table, hear all this—and do almost nothing. No special precautions or procedures are ordered, no routine security practices or spot checks enforced, no alerts or even briefings given the captains and guards who will be left in the pen when the meeting is over and the men of power have gone home beyond the fence. What matters here at this meeting is not the intelligence memos, or Flood's short time in the job, or the slight, fatal discrepancies in the warnings. What matters is power, and *el jefe*, the chief and *patrón* of the system, Felix Rodriguez, and those he commands. Together with pliant and captive politicians, a willfully ignorant public, and a shallow press, they have shaped the history that has come down to this moment. It will be largely their creation, their domain, that will soon erupt in the most savage bloodletting in prison annals. Yet their relative sangfroid on the eve is not so surprising. For more than a quarter-century they have survived grand juries, governors, corrections secretaries, attorneys general, reformers, and other disturbances. They have defied, ignored, delayed, succeeded. They will approach this climactic event with much the same assurance.

As their cars leave the prison parking lot in the scarlet Thursday dusk, however, few will sense that in the long run it is indeed the end of an era. Afterward, their harshest critics will fantasize that the responsible officials somehow, in some twisted logic, wanted it all to happen: a nicely confined little rumble, perhaps to prompt the legislature then sitting languidly in Santa Fe, perhaps to make heroes of those at the top and cement or even advance their positions. But the angry speculation of conspiracy does not matter. Though what is about to unfold grows ineluctably from the character and regime of the New Mexico State Penitentiary, no one can plan or control the full horror.

There are prisons, into which whoever
looks will, at first sight of the people
confined, be convinced that there is some
great error in the management of them.

John Howard,
The State of Prisons (1777)

they danced the quadrille with requisite dignity and "tripped merrily the jolly waltz," as a correspondent described the scene. "The ladies with their rich, bright colored toilets, the gentlemen in full dress, with a profusion of flowers everywhere visible, presented an ever changing variety of kaleidoscopic views as the gay revelers promenaded about the hall." On the cool evening of August 6, 1885, a hundred carriages had crowded the dusty Cerrillos Road south of Santa Fe to bring the guests to a gala "house warming" of New Mexico's first public building, the newly completed territorial penitentiary.

Concerned at the $30,000 a year it would cost to house convicts in outside institutions, the New Mexico Territory built its first prison in 1884–85, "a centre building and one cellhouse wing" in what the local *New Mexican* would call a "magnificent structure."* "If it were properly and wisely handled," said the paper, apparently in hopes of gaining profit-making hard labor and ensuring minimum future attention or expenditure on such disagreeable matters, "it would very soon become self-sustaining." And local legend will have it that Santa Fe chose the prison over the state university, which went to upstart Albuquerque, because the jail seemed likely to be better patronized and to produce more jobs and revenue. Three decades earlier they had tried to put a penitentiary near the site of the federal courthouse in the old city, but residents had blocked the project, and funds had mysteriously disappeared. The new location was more than

*By 1980 that $30,000 would cover little more than the cost of incarcerating two inmates for a year in a state pen.

three miles from the plaza and capitol, at the end of what would be Pen Road, comfortably out of town, it was thought. In any case, the opening was an event to be celebrated. Up a broad stairway on the second floor of the central building, more than twenty white-aproned waiters "rushed to and fro," as the newspaper account described them, arranging four long tables where the visitors were to "feast" later in the evening. From a platform at one end of the spacious "grand chapel hall" on the floor above, the Thirteenth U.S. Infantry band, not long returned from futile forays against the Chiracahua Apaches, played to a floor and gallery filled with the territory's more elegant citizenry. It was not until after ten that the dancing stopped and the civic-minded revelers returned home in their carriages, rarely to look back. Eleven days later, the territory's first public building began to receive more permanent guests.

Outwardly, the prison was at first a mute Victorian fortress, slowly enveloped by the growing town and almost a part of it. A brick plant was added in 1893, and older homes in the area still stand among their adobe neighbors in stolid penitentiary brick. Convict laborers were commonly seen in Santa Fe manicuring state lawns or constructing public buildings. A portent of things to come, early and desperately needed additions to the pen were delayed because the bricks and gang labor were being used elsewhere to pad the state budget. Later, neighborhood children, seizing one of the few smooth sidewalks in town, bicycled around the prison's dark red homemade walls. But a few feet away from the children, on the other side, was what one former inmate called "an endless nightmare" of overcrowding, primitive sanitation and brutality. Before the turn of the century, a swelling inmate population had overflowed from the old cell house into temporary yard buildings. By 1916 there was an average daily census of 427 in space intended for 300. Nor would the prison and its brick plant be as self-sustaining as the *New Mexican* had hoped, and the legislature traditionally starved and ignored the institution anyway. "They are the poorest paid lot in the service of the state," said a warden of his guards in 1912 at the moment New Mexico entered the Union. And as in that year of statehood, forty years later prisoners would still be periodically beaten and brutalized by their fearful, low-paid keepers; would still be using chamber pots and open latrines; would still suffer regular bouts of dysentery.

A food riot broke out at the end of 1948, followed by another six months later, and yet another in November 1950 in which several guards were hurt. Inmates killed an officer in a thwarted escape in June 1952, and the attempt triggered a violent general strike and the resignation of the warden. Six months later several inmates nearly escaped again after taking guns from a supposedly impenetrable vault, and within a few weeks of that near disaster, pitched gang fights led to numerous stabbings and to the murder of one prisoner. On June 15, 1953, in the fourth major violent incident in less than a year, convicts seized the decrepit prison hospital and took twenty-one guard and staff hostages. They were quelled only when a 30-30 carbine was smuggled to one of the captives, a deputy warden, who promptly shot and killed two of the riot leaders in a drama no fiction could have improved. After this bloody sequel, local editorialists no longer thought the old territorial pen so "magnificent." "A New Pen—Now!" headlined the capital paper that June. "Monday's riot could not have happened in a modern penitentiary. In all but archaic prisons like ours, trouble in one section can be isolated and snuffed out quickly before it spreads," the *New Mexican* pronounced in the summer of 1953 with a certain lack of foresight. The next observation, however, was to be more prophetic, "As long as the hideous physical conditions at the penitentiary exist, as long as men are required to live in degradation, we will have violence at the penitentiary." A consultant called in at the same time, a San Quentin warden and the first of a line of outside "experts" contracted over ensuing years from the bigger, supposedly better California penal system, drew similar and even more relevant conclusions. Violent acts were the "symptoms and not causes of bad conditions," he told the state government. "In the last analysis, the prison conditions are the responsibility of the legislature which expresses the will of the people. You have an opportunity to develop a constructive program through legislative support and continuing evaluation of the penitentiary program and personnel."

The state responded to all this by erecting a brand new pen by 1956 and by razing (with the presumably grateful help of convict labor) the old territorial relic to the last dark, embarrassing brick—though not before wide-eyed Santa Fe schoolchildren, a little like the carriage crowd seventy years before, were trooped through both institutions to witness the obvious progress at hand.

Once again, the new prison was placed suitably out of town, to the south, on an exposed, treeless plain but in a larger setting of stark beauty. Near the old quarry where Willa Cather's immortal Archbishop Lamy took the stones to chisel his incongruous, nostalgic French provincial cathedral in Santa Fe, the pen commands on two sides the majestic Jemez and Sangre de Cristo; to the south, sunken below La Bajada, the soft Ortiz Mountains round gently toward Albuquerque and, far beyond, the Mexican border.

With a grudging appropriation of $8 million, the statehouse's favored architects shoddily built the new penitentiary on the "telephone pole" model. Ten two-story dormitories, cell houses, and maximum-security cell blocks formed the north and south wings, all connected by a single central corridor that ran wing to wing for nearly two city blocks, threading through a middle administrative area housing the prison offices, mess halls for inmates and guards, kitchen, gymnasium, chapels, and control center. With each wing and the intersecting units running off it sealed by riot-control grilles, the single-corridor design was intended to conserve staff, ease security, and, most of all, confine disturbances to their point of origin—"isolated and snuffed out," as the *New Mexican* had imagined the solution. All in all, boasted Governor John Simms in an echo of other openings before and since, the prison commissioned on April 20, 1956, was surely "among the most advanced correctional institutions in the world."

Before the institution was completed or occupied, however, there were ugly rumors about the land it stood on, tales of shady swaps that were later fueled when a lucrative racetrack sprouted across the Albuquerque Highway opposite the pen. Back in town, the former site of the old brick dungeon seemed even more intriguing. A new shopping center would go up nearby to handsome profits, and an adjacent structure would be built and leased to the U.S. Postal Service by a public-spirited landlord named Senator Joseph Montoya (no relation to the Deputy Warden), a prospering local politician who would achieve some notoriety on the Watergate Committee. Some years later, as an elderly former warden lay on his deathbed and was visited by a grandson who had become a prison reformer suspicious of widespread corruption in the system, the dying man whispered cryptically, "Look for the land; look for the land." The real estate transfers were never officially investigated, however, and outwardly the maze of leases and purchases of valuable state and private property seemed in order, with no obvious local fraud or official beneficiaries, though the archives would show at least one interesting connection between the disposal of the old pen ground and the politics surrounding the riot in the 1980s. The state assistant attorney general who officially sanctioned some of the pen site transactions in the fifties was the same man who later as a federal judge would preside over the major reform suit challenging the whole long-entrenched political and bureaucratic corrections establishment in New Mexico: Santiago Campos.

Far worse than the real estate lore it left behind, however, was what the new penitentiary of the mid-fifties promptly took with it from the old—the squalid, racist sociology of the state's penal system. The custody of its felons, like other menial jobs, New Mexico tended to leave to a poor, meagerly educated underclass of native Hispanics. Low-paying, hazardous, unskilled— at least as it was commonly practiced—prison work only reflected larger New Mexican society beyond the walls. There, the dwindling Spanish majority, a people of proud cultural parochialism and a revered ancestry in this land before the Pilgrims landed at Plymouth Rock, had lived since the Yankee conquest in social and economic subordination to the pretense of their own small transplanted gentry and to the Anglo minority whose men and money ruled the state. Over the next quarter-century, as on the other razor's edges of race in American life, there would be a genuine softening of such inequality. If most of New Mexico's Hispanic men of the forties and fifties were gardeners, gas station attendants, poor farmers, unskilled laborers, and penitentiary guards, their sons and even daughters were by the sixties and seventies moving in increasing numbers into white-collar jobs, many in the state government clerkdom, and from there into Albuquerque or Santa Fe subdivisions as a fledgling middle class. Despite that apparent mobility and affluence, however, despite the relative residential integration that had long blurred ethnic lines in northern New Mexico in particular, there remained a hateful, insidious division between Spanish and Anglo. In a sense it was one of the most subtle and obdurate cultural problems in the United States and a bleak portent for the rest of the country of the limits of de jure equality—in this case two peoples not even separate and equal, but largely together in schools, workplace, and neighborhoods yet persistently unequal.

To begin with, it was a uniquely colonial setting. Unlike

other social frontiers where immigrant minorities came upon, struggled into, and slowly transformed the prevailing Anglo-Saxon culture, the Americans had encountered and promptly subjugated in New Mexico a people who had governed, held grants of land vast and yeoman, and practiced their own dominant European culture for more than two hundred years before the U.S. Cavalry arrived on its civilizing mission. In part, this clash of presumptions produced simple and predictable mutual bigotry, cast in tribal stereotypes. Immigrant Anglos comforted themselves with slurs about shiftless, devious "natives," "Mexicans," and, later "wetbacks," all parodied in their singsong English dialect, while the Spanish, riven between early arrivals and late Mexicanos, between the nobility or the pollution of Indian blood, depending on one's genealogy, looked on with a superior culture's moral and social contempt for the rootless, mercenary, dishonorable gringo who had scant respect for either history or himself. Both the Spanish and the Anglos deplored the prospect of intermarriage, which delivered "inferiors" into the family. Both elbowed into corners of the marketplace where, at least in government jobs or the patronage-riddled school system, native Hispanics came after World War II to have the dubious privilege of exercising a thinly veiled reverse discrimination.

But the encounter was also more complex, the progress of the Spanish more precarious. With the state government payroll as New Mexico's principal welfare institution, with palpable power as well as a respectable dole in the government jobs, Hispanics tended to become, like most other entrenched welfare recipients, jealous and resentful of other claimants. Yet precisely as the state and its bureaucracy grew after the fifties to play that major welfare role, more and more Anglos were arriving, better equipped by an acquisitive culture as well as education for the bureaucratic and business order that was supplanting the languid old regime. Pride notwithstanding, it was soon an uneven contest for a people of gentle family-centered culture and comparatively modest ambitions. Ironically, in their newly realized status there would be no real escape for many Hispanics from the old insecurity and inequality. Quietly bitter, the already fractured Spanish community retreated into the time-honored responses of nepotism, accusations of bigotry, and an often rancorous self-pity. Clinging stoically if not always effectively to their cultural separatism, they only deepened in their pride and suspicion the educational deficit that lay at the heart of the tragedy. State schools relentlessly hired and promoted from within, and became relentlessly mediocre. At the same time, by the very force of its tradition, in the grip of a primitive Catholicism, the Spanish population proved barren ground even for homegrown rescues. When Reyes Tijerina and his militant if unsophisticated Alíanza de Mercedes burst forth from the dark villages of the north in the sixties to tear at the raw old lesion of land titles and theft, much of the white society was suitably terrified, promptly throwing Tijerina in jail for murder and later into a federal insane asylum for his politics. The New Mexico Hispanic constituency, however, remained mostly quiescent. The brief abortive revolt touched deep chords, but its crude strategy and pointless violence sustained nothing.

Politically, the core of the Spanish community seemed to prefer the more venerable and proven patronage of traditional Anglo politicians like Bruce King, men who had grown up with established colonial castes or coalitions, who for their own power in the Democratic party machine had fashioned their own alliances with the native majority. And on the strength of such patronage and alliances, yet another social schism opened, this one defined by class. Adopting the Protestant ethic if not the religious heresy, some "successful" Hispanics in this postwar era climbed up through education and status in commerce or politics and became part of the state's knit-suit, good old boy establishment, seldom glancing back at the deeper, enduring problems of poverty and discrimination, though also rarely more than token members or servants of the ruling white caste.

For their part, not surprisingly, the native Anglos were prone to accept these arrangements as part of the local charm, while more recent arrivals, particularly those in competition for jobs, reacted with alternating puzzlement and guilt at the hostility they discovered so close to the surface. For a moment in the seventies it was still possible to ignore what was really happening. During New Mexico's resort boom there were more jobs, higher land values, more prosperous development than ever before. Money salved the Anglo's racial guilt, and even obscured among Hispanics the atrophy of values and space, and the implacable imposition of an alien face and timetable on the land. Yet all the while, the profound subterranean anger and fear between ruler and ruled in this strange desert colony coursed just beneath the state's fervent, full-color public mythology of bicultural harmony, secreted in playground fights, jailhouse or police brutality, wherever the hate and hurt, like body bruises, could be hidden from passing view. Though schoolchildren were spared the historical truth, General Stephen Kearny's troops had pranced into Santa Fe more than a century before to the wailing of women and angry dark eyes behind latticed windows. The wailing had died away while the angry dark eyes remained. But that uglier reality was still behind closed doors. Otherwise, everyone seemed to agree, it would only detract from the tourist trade.

The effect of all this on the penitentiary was decisive. In the politics of the state's poverty and discreet racism, the payroll of the institution promptly became in the postwar years a fount of bureaucratic nepotism, fostering the inevitable clan of administrators and guards tied—by family, by unspoken complicities, and often by a shared incompetence—to jobs that none could afford to lose, or at least lose the option to resume. To the eve of the riot, the chronically understaffed guard ranks were a state sinecure where impatient young men might leave for a seasonal construction job and promptly return when the weather snapped cold. Moreover, as a major employer among the extended families of the region's Hispanic society (albeit not quite as the Santa Fe city fathers had hoped in originally contemplating the mercantile potential of a pen), the prison came to provide votes, patronage, and campaign contributions for those politicians who saw and harnessed its potential in the counties around Santa Fe.

At the most rudimentary level—the daily encounter between keepers and captives—the system took an awful toll. Ignorant, unschooled guards and administrators meant caprice, brutality, and, not least, exploitation of staff and inmates alike by the more cunning prisoners. Added to the common oppressions of prison life, the entrenched nepotism made change or relief seem all the more hopeless. Through the corridors and cell blocks throbbed the ethnic suspicion and loathing between the predominantly Spanish guard corps and the one-third to one-half of the inmates who were Anglo and the handful who were black or Indian. Yet the worst abuse and brutalization were by every reckoning reserved for Spanish prisoners. Not only were they more severely mistreated physically, but, by the perverse colonial logic brought inside the pen from the society outside, they were also often presumed by Hispanic officials to be less educable, trainable, and salvageable than their Anglo cellmates. Sophisticated observers would see the typical Santa Fe pen guard acting out the tragic social role of oppressed as oppressor, playing an assigned part in an institution and legal system that were historically artificial in his culture. But whatever the cause, the result was savagely simple. The fear and fury of the Spanish turnkey from his trailer or barrio house fell most heavily on the "homeboys," the Hispanic inmates who were a living reflection at once of the guard's social vulnerability and yet also of his vestige of control and manhood.

At the next level, within the prison staff, the system was no less pervasive or self-reinforcing. Nepotism thwarted the very dependence on security that was the only governance of the pen its untrained overseers understood. It was hardly a penitentiary where educated new guards were welcomed or promoted, where embarrassing intelligence was reported or given credence, where old friends, relatives, or fellow members of the staff clique were reprimanded for minor matters such as unclosed grilles or similar lapses. Though federal funds were available by 1974 to help guards get college or even advanced degrees, the administration offered neither incentive nor work schedules for extra schooling. And again, until the very moment of the riot and even afterward, briefings at the change of guard shifts might frequently be given in the local colloquial Spanish, leaving to their own devices those who did not understand the language.

Finally the circle closed with politicians who had little reason to clean out a willfully ignored state patronage system that was a virtual commissary of votes, money, and manifold other advantages. Once the prison was consigned to its ethnic and political function, to look too closely at its management or efficiency as a penal institution was to upset the basic balance of power and rewards. Then, too, there was still less incentive for reform or even occasional tampering when the long-tenured prison officials had come to know so much about the politicians; to know which inmates they wanted favored or paroled and why; to know who was profiting so consistently on the outside from the big contracts; to know who benefited from the fat, dubious vouchers and where their political support then went. All these politics enshrouded the New Mexico pen. And as if that were not enough, there was as well the customary budgetary indifference and stinginess toward corrections; the regional bigotry and political primitivism of powerful delegates from New Mexico's southeastern quarter, aptly called "little Texas"; and the usual shallowness of oversight by a part-time, pay-by-the-mile legislature. When the riot was over and the bodies were pieced back together, official autopsies of cause would strain to find how New Mexico was different, while tactfully ignoring the larger political malfeasance that made it typical.

The history was vivid in the lives of men who made it.

Felix Rodriguez—thickened in middle age but still an impressively tall man with the square, dark, heavy-browed countenance of his lineage—to many the hovering gargoyle of the system, came to February 1980 atop more than a quarter-century in the New Mexico penal system. Born in 1929 to one of the older families, he was feared and respected in the streets of the east side of Santa Fe where, at well more than six feet, he towered over most of his Spanish peers. Later his sheer size explained part of his power and distinction in a prison where guard corps and inmates were so largely native Hispanics of smaller stature. He dropped out of Saint Michael's, the local Catholic high school, in the eleventh grade. After nearly two years in the army ending as staff sergeant and an eight-month hiatus following discharge, he went to work at the old territorial pen in October 1953 at $250 a month. From that moment he had found his vocation, and he rose as a kind of guard prodigy. In five months he was a lieutenant, in less than three years a captain at nearly twice his starting pay.

When the new prison opened in 1956, the new Captain Rodriguez would be, by his own description, "in charge of installation of all security and key control procedures, locking devices, et cetera." By 1957 he was certified as having passed his high school equivalency exam or GED, and only months later he began more than a decade's tenure as associate warden, second in command and with "overall control of all phases of [the] operation," as he later described his position. Once acting warden himself for a period in 1967, he was now paid almost six times his first salary. When J. E. Baker, a popular, relatively progressive warden of only brief term, was pressured out by the legislature—some suspected with his deputy's encouragement—Rodriguez became warden in his own right in February 1970, almost a decade to the day before the riot. By now he listed on his résumé twenty-three quarter-hours and three semester hours of college credits, all apparently earned while working at the pen. After five years as warden, he was promoted to director of adult institutions; he went on to become deputy secretary of the corrections department in 1978. For a quarter-century before the catastrophe, through a succession of wardens and state corrections secretaries, no other official would be so continuously in authority or so responsible day by day at the New Mexico State Penitentiary.

His career soon became part of the rich, melancholy folklore of the pen. A generation of inmates would portray him as a stern yet generally fair man who left the enforcement to his underlings, who was deeply affected long afterward by the killing of a guard at the old brick prison, and who confided in one convict his anxieties about his own children after seeing so much homosexuality in the prison society that was his universe. Just as colorfully, a generation of colleagues and subordinates would describe him as the imposing *patrón* of the ingrown prison staff, with the gifts and instincts of the shrewdest con, dispensing rewards and penalties, reaping the perquisites of his great, unchallenged power in this small, closed domain. At one point introduced by a friendly professor at old Saint Michael's College to politicians like Bruce King who were looking for contacts among state officials, over the years he nurtured the relationship by doing them favors whenever he could. A simple yet complex man, he was never at home in the outside world. When he had risen to the level of senior officialdom and so had to appear at public hearings, he was clearly uneasy and reportedly took the coaching of Joanne Brown, a stout, ambitious young California lawyer who became by the end of the seventies his ranking aide. Still later, he would be visibly wounded, somehow almost puzzled, like a great forest animal caught in a clearing, when post-riot journalism and politicians were suddenly critical of his public record. But inside the walls, in the province he knew so well for so long, he was unquestionably in control—*el jefe*, the chief.

There he ran the institution with a staff of similar background. In a guard corps where a turnover rate of 80 percent had become common by 1980, most of the ranks were new, inexperienced young officers whose starting salary was barely $700 a month on the eve of the riot and of whom fewer than a third received even minimal training. The rest, hardly better schooled, were those who had stayed and risen, almost entirely Rodriguez's men. They included the security chief, Koroneos, one-time roofer and truck driver, a high school dropout with no previous corrections experience who applied to the pen in 1962, explaining on the state personnel form as his reason: "I want [a] steady job." He was duly promoted to lieutenant, cited for his vigilance in watching the visitors' room, and eventually made superintendent of correctional security. Before Koroneos had come Eugene Long, another local high school dropout who tried taxidermy, drove heavy equipment, and worked briefly in an army disciplinary barracks before joining the old brick prison as a guard the same year Rodriguez was hired. Later, with a GED and 104 college credits claimed from part-time study, Long rose through captain, assistant warden, and superintendent of the women's prison as well as chief of pen security. Adelaido Martinez—another one-time security chief and associate warden, another participant along with Koroneos and Long at the January 31, 1980, intelligence meeting—similarly went to work at the new pen as a guard in 1956 after three years at a local mission high school, rising steadily to lieutenant, captain, and onward.

Snaking in and around such records and power were the ties of clan and cronyism. At the time of the riot, Rodriguez's brother-in-law, once a prison security officer, was head of prison industries. Long was married to Rodriguez's cousin, who once taught cosmetology classes at the pen. One captain had a brother on the prison infirmary staff; another supervised two sons as junior guards. Martinez's nephew worked in prison administration, while the penitentiary staff included two pairs of husband-and-wife guards, a father and two sons who were corrections officers, three more officials in various offices who were all from the same family. Beyond Santa Fe, a former parole officer was rewarded with the deputy warden's chair at a satellite prison; a former security captain became a warden elsewhere in the state; a former guard was a security chief of a prison farm; Griffin had gone from Rodriguez's outer office to a facility in the south where he was superintendent. The tentacles of faction reached throughout the state, following inmates and staff wherever New Mexico put men or women in captivity. And so it went. From sensitive positions in security or administration to temporary secretarial or maintenance jobs, the institution presented a revolving door for relatives and retainers at all levels, a ready payroll for the *primos*,

the "cousins" who crowded an inbred society that felt itself en-
titled by both default and tacit bargain to such pockets of patronage. There were a few younger, better-educated men, though
they, too, were unmistakably part of the system. Robert Montoya,
the deputy warden in 1980, was hardly thirty when he was named
to the job in 1975 with a bachelor's degree in psychology from
Northern Arizona University and five years as a juvenile corrections officer. In the end Montoya's management of the pen under
(and in spite of) several wardens would be indistinguishable from
the rule of the others. The ill-fated riot warden, Jerry Griffin,
held a college degree from New Mexico Highlands and had served
eleven years in the state system. He had been singled out early,
however, as Rodriguez's personal assistant when the latter was
warden, and the patronage of Griffin's subsequent promotions,
was plain. By the mid-seventies other officers, outside the clique
and bitterly frustrated, had come to characterize such men with
the story of a favored guard who flunked an ostensible merit
examination with the worst grade recorded, yet was promoted
anyway. They would call him "Lieutenant Forty-One," for his
score on a scale of one hundred.

Rodriguez and his men presided over a pen buffeted periodically by the changing styles and theories of a train of wardens
and cabinet secretaries, now with a scattering of rehabilitation
programs and relative autonomy, now under the fist of some stern
new drive to reestablish "discipline." But whatever the veneer of
the regime, the institution bore indelibly the marks of its permanent government for the quarter-century before the riot. One
way or another, as a later official inquiry would document, it
was a prison ruled by a craven, unstable coalition between a few
of the dominant felons of maximum security and an administration
that could govern no other way. Whether given rein with flourishing drug traffic and other corruption, or simply in the con-
vulsive violence and turmoil that erupted when out-of-state wardens
tried in vain with an indifferent staff to take back control, it was
this alliance of keepers and kept that filled the vacuum of management and political oversight. Similarly, the penitentiary was
long notorious for lax security and capricious authority. Pervasive
nepotism not only fostered incompetence, but it also spawned,
as in a 1971 creation of several new captaincies to satisfy clique
claimants, a chaos in inmate discipline in which each newly
empowered commander ruled the cell blocks and houses his own

way. Eight-hour shifts became satrapies with different spoils for different officers of the old guard. Finally, and perhaps most characteristic, the Santa Fe pen was a community constituted in treason. In its inherent weakness, the administration became incessantly dependent on inmate informers for the most rudimentary intelligence and security. And, in turn, it passed along its preoccupation with treachery, like some lethal contagion, into the vulnerable bloodstream of convict society.

Most of those sentenced to Santa Fe were ravaged by the system. Even by dubious official statistics, one in four would be charged with another crime soon after release. Many who watched both paroles and prosecutions in the state, from prison reformers to law enforcement officials, believed the real rate of long-term recidivism to be nearer 80 percent, with the prison turning out hardened repeat offenders in roughly the same proportion it turned over its guards. Adding to this its own official corruption, it was thus calculable that the Penitentiary of New Mexico by the end of the seventies was propagating anew altogether more crimes than those for which its bulging population had been sentenced to begin with.

The few who beat the odds did so hardly because of the sytem's ostensible rehabilitation, but in spite of it. One of the most remarkable was a young Oklahoman named Lloyd Miller. Veteran of a reformatory and a state prison while still in his teens, he had visited Santa Fe not long after the new pen was built, and in a strange premonitory moment drove out the Cerrillos Highway to look at the fresh gray rows of cell blocks. A few years later he was back for more than curiosity, sent to death row at twenty-six for the murder of a store clerk. After twenty-four months facing the gas chamber, Miller won a new trial on a technicality, and in 1966 was resentenced to life imprisonment.

A bitter, belligerent loner, he took a first step forward when Rodriguez was trying to start soft furniture production in prison industries (for what would become a lucrative business in repairing and supplying state government agencies), and records showed Miller had worked in a foster mother's upholstery shop. Miller taught another convict to run the furniture operation, and a year later, in 1968, he enrolled in an IBM-sponsored keypunch class and was soon training a few other inmates in a burgeoning prison computer shop. By 1970 he was supervising more than a hundred men, writing his own training manuals, and turning out for various state agencies computer work of such high quality that it saved taxpayers nearly half a million dollars a year. Over the next four years, Miller taught in the prison high school, was both administrator and student in a prison college program offered by the local Christian Brothers College of Santa Fe, where he took honors degrees in business and education, and was hired on a work release arrangement to work as a full staff member in the college admissions office. By the spring of 1974 he had won a job as a planner for the Governor's Council on Criminal Justice Planning. He was then paroled in July, and a year later became a key administrative assistant to the secretary of corrections. At the end of the seventies, less than fifteen years after he was sentenced to death in Santa Fe, he had changed his name to Lloyd McClendon and left New Mexico to become deputy director of prison industries in Ohio, managing a multimillion-dollar business as a senior and much-honored government official.

Yet however inspiring, however stunning its rebuke to the presumptions of the death penalty or to the popular image of irredeemable felons, McClendon's triumph was to be the exception that proved the rule in Santa Fe. "If society had known here's Lloyd's plan, he'd never gotten out," said a man who watched it intimately. "Here's an animal getting up. And they don't like it. Don't ever forget that. Don't ever let anyone forget that." Behind McClendon's success were the enduring harsh realities of the New Mexico pen. The keypunch and educational projects flourished largely through the devotion of McClendon and a handful of similarly bright, ambitious, dauntless young cons, and few of the programs survived the departure that was the reward of the men who made them work. By the end of 1973, the once astounding keypunch operation was abruptly abolished when its staff sponsor resigned. As federal funds ran out a year later for Project Newgate, the program that helped a hundred inmates every year progress from high school into the college curriculum, the pen did not even request state funds but simply disbanded the instruction. By 1976 the school release McClendon and others used so effectively to build careers was almost unknown. And over the next four years inmates received altogether little more than half as many college degrees as earlier convicts had won in 1974 alone.

The fleeting achievement was enshrouded, too, in the prison's pervasive racism and corruption. Most of the success stories belonged to Anglos, a fact that deepened the bitterness of equally able Spanish prisoners who accurately saw their Hispanic prison masters more often granting entry to programs and educational privileges to whites because, by the logic of this local reverse racism, they were thought more likely to complete the job or the course, and so less prone to embarrass the administration. In the same way, the studious Anglos, and an occasional well-educated Latin, were enlisted to prepare school papers or even take tests for penitentiary officials accumulating their own educational credits and the bureaucratic promotions they promised. For a remarkable moment in the late sixties and early seventies, captives and captors went to school side by side at Santa Fe, "grew up together," as McClendon would later describe it. But it would be the inmates who got the education and then left, taking with them the real impetus of the rehabilitation. The officials remained.

As Lloyd McClendon was becoming an aide at corrections headquarters in Santa Fe, Dwight Duran was returning to the pen in 1976 for his third sentence, and his equally moving experience would symbolize the plunge the prison now took toward catastrophe. With thick black hair, a rugged Spaniard of a man, Duran wore beneath his handsomeness the scars of a castoff's life. His grandfather had been New Mexico's last territorial warden. His mother was born on the grounds of the old brick penitentiary. His lineage crisscrossed some of the state's most venerable citizens, both Anglo and Spanish, including a senator and a prominent publisher. Yet in the splintered destiny of so many Hispanic families, two uncles had also done time in the state prison, and Duran had been a public ward for much of his life since infancy. After foster homes and a harsh boarding school in New Mexico, there was juvenile prison in California, more jail in Tijuana, Mexico, and the three terms in the Santa Fe pen, one for assault, ending in 1967, and the last nine years later, at thirty-six, for forging a $35 check.

What Duran found in his third term, however, was to change his life—and ultimately the history of New Mexico. During his absence the deterioration of conditions and the men in them had been relentless, McClendon and short-lived rehabilitation programs apart. Duran now saw those effects in sharpened contrast against his earlier years at Santa Fe, and the scene shocked even a man who had spent much of his life in the worst prisons of two countries.

By the mid-seventies the New Mexico penitentiary was a physical as well as psychological horror. Rats and roaches infested the building. Poor ventilation made it stifling by summer. Inadequate heating left the cell blocks sickly chill in winter. Drinking and waste-water systems were cross-connected, spewing sewage into sinks. Food practices were primitive and unsanitary with rodent feces openly visible in the kitchen and often in the food. Intestinal diseases were pandemic. Inmates used what passed for mashed potatoes to paste posters to walls, where the potatoes congealed and hardened. With exposed and frayed wiring everywhere, successive fire marshals' reports warned of potential holocaust. On seeing the pen for the first time, a visiting warden thought it "a national disgrace" and "the filthiest institution I'd ever seen." There was no full-time doctor for more than a year in 1979–1980, and neither a resident dentist nor psychiatrist for a population now far over capacity. A chaotic classification system threw petty forgers and first-time nonviolent offenders in with habitual murderers, rapists, and armed robbers. Inmates were packed into cells until many slept on mattresses on the floors, feet pressed against bars, heads touching the toilets. Gang rape was so common that prisoners regularly made book—as if it were the daily races at nearby Santa Fe Downs—on who the "punk" would be, when it would happen, and how many would sodomize him.

Minor uprisings in 1971, 1973, and 1976 had been cruelly repressed. Guard brutality was commonplace. Convicts would remember the screams of the victims of rape and of the engraved batons of the official goon squad as part of the endless cacophony of penitentiary life, day and night. Men watched as the victims were carried back to dormitories or cell houses in blankets, slung limp and bleeding in these "Santa Fe stretchers."

One personal yet typical experience with the savagery of the regime moved Duran to act. Not long after he returned, another con, a boyhood friend from New Mexico, had begun to suffer the torture of heroin withdrawal. But when the addict went to the prison hospital for help, he was quickly thrown naked into the hole, the isolation cell in the basement of the maximum-security cell block. There he stayed for more than a month, untreated, slowly going mad in his agony, at the end smearing his own excreta on himself or the cell walls while guards laughed or administered periodic beatings, which included kicking him repeatedly in the scrotum. When he staggered from the strip cell at the end of his ordeal, he would never be the same. Duran and others cared for him as best they could for the next year and finally went to authorities in desperation to ask that he be hospitalized. Simply for making the request they, too, were threatened with the hole. Examined at a Santa Fe hospital, the young con was found to have an advanced malignant tumor on his testicles. He was quickly released to the forensic section of the state mental hospital. Two weeks later he was dead.

The year Duran returned there were several escapes, and two inmates were murdered by fellow prisoners. Added to the customary barbarity of life at Santa Fe were the new men, the new prisoners who created the new prisons of the decade. Reflecting the civil rights revolution in the outside world, the convicts of the seventies were no longer members of servile minorities without a voice, no longer simply doing their time. Throughout the nation, penal institutions obviously remained a place of the poor. Nine times as many blacks were imprisoned as whites; indigents received harsher sentences than those from middle-income levels who committed the same crime. A 1978 Justice Department report found that 45 percent of all male inmates in the United States earned an annual income before detention of less than $3,000, and the median income of all prisoners prior to arrest was hardly a third of that of the general population. Yet there was a palpable change in mood and behavior among that vast underclass, a growing defiance and rebellion, what prison argot would call the "payback."

In Santa Fe and elsewhere, the payback often issued in sudden rage and violence, much of it inflicted on the easier target of other inmates, and in a seething that was finally to erupt with historic ferocity in February 1980. For Duran and a handful like him in other prisons, however, it took shape as a new determination to use the same legal system that had allowed their torment. Still working toward a college degree in social work and with no formal legal education, Duran painstakingly began research in the New Mexico prison library early in 1977. He was joined by fellow plaintiffs Sharon Towers and Lonnie Duran as well as other cons, among them Harmon Ellis, who had helped draft the historic *Battle* v. *Anderson* prison-reform brief in Oklahoma, and whose escapes, including the December 1979 mass breakout, would make him a pen folk hero. For weeks they poured over cases in Oklahoma and Alabama, hunting for precedents page by page through densely forested federal records. Still more time went into learning the empty but obligatory arcana of form and jargon that cloak the legal guild. By November 1977 Duran was ready with a lengthy brief, meticulously printed by hand and single-spaced on long, white legal paper. Filed in federal court on behalf of the two Durans, Towers, and "all those similarly situated," the petition systematically catalogued the most inhumane conditions at the New Mexico penitentiary, cited the judicial strictures against such abuses, and charged the state with basic constitutional violations in cruel and unusual punishment. Into Duran's carefully handwritten letters was inked an outline for the most sweeping reform ever proposed for any single prison in American history.

When the Duran suit breached the walls of the Santa Fe pen at the end of 1977, it was soon taken up by the American Civil Liberties Union as a landmark case in the ACLU's nationwide effort to defend prisoners' rights. Neither national advocacy nor Duran's patient idealism in the prison law library, however, reckoned with the political wilderness into which the petition promptly fell in New Mexico.

Outside the penitentiary the landscape of justice was nearly as desolate as within. As Duran and his colleagues mailed off their desperate pages, the Land of Enchantment, as its license plates proclaimed, was still in the grip of its tradition, where State Police were reported to have ignored a booming narcotics trade and several drug-related murders,* where patrolmen had been seen fencing stolen television sets out of their squad cars and then had risen to the top of their service, where ballots had been burned, where votes had been bought and sold, and where the very bench itself was awash in alcoholism, nepotism, decisions bartered for sexual favors, blatant interference with prosecutions, and other assorted malfeasance. To no quarter was there fair appeal. The same year Duran documented the outrages at Santa Fe, the powerful Democratic chairman of the Legislative

*One local investigative report on unsolved murders and other questionable police practices provoked a multimillion-dollar libel suit from the state police chief, but the suit went largely unpursued and the chief finally dropped it in exchange for the offending newspaper simply running a story about his retirement.

Finance Committee pronounced it "unreasonable" to consider a pay raise for prison guards, whose salary level was then thirty-ninth out of the fifty states.

"You know what the political process is in Santa Fe," pen psychologist Orner would tell the State Police agents in his post-escape interview in January 1980. "If you could find a legislator after five o'clock, except for the last two weeks, they don't want to be disturbed."

"Go to the Bullring," offers a policeman, referring to a bar near the capitol.

"Go to the Bullring or go to their room," continues Orner. "They are either fucking or sucking or drinking. I mean that's a fact."

"That is right," another agent replies. "I understand."

Initially it would be *Duran* v. *Apodaca*. The suit came to the statehouse of Jerry Apodaca, a former teacher and shoe sales-man from Las Cruces who was narrowly elected the first New Mexican governor of Spanish surname in the modern era. Apo-daca was soon gone, however, and the crucial response to the petition would fall to his successor.

At fifty-four, Democrat Bruce King won a second term in the governor's mansion in 1978 by less than four thousand votes. A large, paunchy man, educated only at a rural New Mexico high school before World War II, King with his snakeskin cowboy boots and his tenor twang was to many a comic caricature of the good old boy politicians who had long misgoverned the state. He was launched on his family's fortune from one of the region's largest feedlot operations, became a Santa Fe County commis-sioner about the same time Rodriguez joined the prison guard corps, entered the legislature in 1959 with large vote margins around Santa Fe, was made the powerful speaker of the state House from 1963 to 1969, served for a year as state Democratic party chairman, won the governorship first in 1970, and then sat out the ensuing Apodaca term of 1975–79 because the state constitution barred consecutive terms. Through it all his politics were a curious mixture of decency and fecklessness, supportive of education or other public needs, yet largely inert in the face of environmental abuses, bureaucratic corruption, and fiscal ine-quities, wherever issues brushed the hoary special interests of his constituency. His administrative motto was said to be "If it ain't broke, don't fix it," and he seemed often myopic when it came to the breakage of institutions and ethics. In the end his regime would die in a pall of corruption and paralysis.

In any case the politician and the penitentiary *patrón* had known each other for years. Rodriguez was warden throughout King's first term. They had weathered together a prison disturbance harshly put down in 1971, and the near-exposure of a pervasive state parole scandal in 1973–74. However kindly Bruce King the grandfather, however cheerful the politician pumping hands and singing his greetings about the state House, it was not surprising that the indebted governor would continue in 1979–80 to preside uncritically over the state's corrections disgrace—and ignore the prophetic Duran petition.

Beyond legislators and governors, one more figure might have made a difference. The U.S. district judge who inherited Duran's suit and the constitutional shame of the New Mexico penitentiary was one of the state's own, Santiago Campos. Named by President Jimmy Carter to the court in the summer of 1978, at fifty-two Campos was the first Hispanic to sit on the federal bench. He was known warmly to his Democratic party friends as Jimmy, a small man with the dignified mien and wavy graying hair of a movie-script magistrate. But Campos came to his historic judgeship from a past that made his reaction to the prison problem all too predictable. Though he had been a hardworking postwar student who finished first in his 1953 University of New Mexico law school class, at a moment when racial discrimination was still deeply felt there as elsewhere in the state, there was little in Campos's record as either lawyer or local judge to suggest the sensibility or political independence the moment demanded.

After a brief period of lone law practice, he had joined a state Democratic regime as an assistant attorney general in the mid-fifties (where he approved the sale of some of the old pen land) and then entered a flush Santa Fe law firm with major corporate and mining clients. There followed seven years in a smaller partnership that dissolved; Campos later listed his practice as "personal injury claims cases more than any other type." Campos was nominated and elected as a Democrat without opposition to fill the vacant seat of a state district judge in 1970. He was reelected, after again running unopposed, to a full term on the local bench in 1972. Along the way he was one of the attorneys embroiled in the Colonias de Santa Fe, a development of scenic lands from one of the northern New Mexico pueblos that ended in fiery scandal when unknown protesters burned the developers' sales office on the site and the original contract was broken.

Otherwise, as a lawyer Campos had by his own accounting tried almost no cases in a federal court, and scarcely 5 percent of his practice was in criminal matters. Although as a state judge he was respected by lawyers for his knowledge of procedure, when asked on a questionnaire in competition for the federal appointment to show any and all writing of distinction as either a lawyer or judge over a quarter-century in the law, Campos simply wrote "none." For that matter, law students would later find few Campos opinions in the record even as a federal judge. Some believed that his studied reticence to leave judicial tracks was part of his deliberately cautious politics in jockeying to be the first Hispanic elevated to a higher bench, even perhaps to the U.S. Supreme Court. Of the same political party, alliances, and traditions challenged so directly by the Duran suit, Campos would apparently see scant urgency in 1978 or afterward in recognizing or remedying conditions at the state pen. He would endorse minor consent orders negotiated by the two sides, but never apply the meaningful injunctive relief that might have made the life-and-death difference. And his inertia was to continue long after the prison lay in smoking, bloody debris.

Such were the men and institutions standing by as the New Mexico pen neared its day of cannibalism. Though *Pravda* and other organs of the anti-American press would later claim otherwise, there was nothing inevitable about the New Mexico prison riot. Different representatives, a different governor, a different judge might have taken any number of steps that could have staved off the riot even in January—a trip to the pen that might have enhanced security, a gesture on the Duran suit that might have held out some hope to the convicts, a warning to the administrators that might have provoked them to greater vigilance or conciliation, almost any action that could have promised some new attention and eased the convicts past the combustible moment of hopelessness and rage and official negligence that occured in February 1980. But there was to be no reprieve. "Inadequate people were surrounded by inadequate people," said a former prison counselor of the years and months before the riot. "The officials became indistinguishable from the inmates, and the riot, in a way, was simply a continuation of administration." But even after the event, when blame was unavoidably fixed on the guards and administrators nearest the scandal, there was only a faint sense, and much willing ignorance, of how much the calamity belonged to others still more responsible before the public trust—to the legislature, to King, to the Anglo establishment, to Campos, and ultimately to an indifferent press and citizenry.

At the end of a gray, cold Friday, February 1, 1980, Lloyd McClendon would be gone to his future out of state, and Dwight Duran would be in Albuquerque looking for odd jobs after being paroled a few weeks before. Meanwhile, in Santa Fe the legislature slowly gathered for its annual session; King sat heavily in his statehouse office behind an engraved desk plate gaudily announcing his name; Campos headed home to his comfortable house in the hills above the capital. Despite McClendon and Duran and their prophecy, the men of power would leave it—as they had left it for so long, as white policy had left it—to the overseers.

TAKEOVER

At the womb they call Center!
Chief—Deputy squats—or captain
fatly abides in the mother-tongue
chair at the lip—at the sperm
that is gathered lieutenantly into the vat
where the keys to the kingdom
prevail!
where the morbid machine

                    INTERCOM

has its source
In the wide teethless mouths of the little
alternative lords!

                    Ray Bremser,
              "Penal Madness"

friday, February 1, 1980. The day dawns after seven with high, soiled clouds dimming the sun. The wind whips the treeless plateau less harshly than usual, dying through the day and night until, the next morning, smoke from smoldering cell blocks and corpses will curl almost motionless over the desert. But daybreak is still cold, harsher than the 20 degrees recorded on thermometers at the guards' trailer court just to the west on the prison grounds.

Inside the pen the morning heat is triggered. It pushes unevenly over the familiar official contours as the prison stirs to the day. There are the hard textures of concrete and tile and pockmarked porcelain, poorly painted flaking steel, and tattooed skin. Ordinary sounds here—lone footsteps, doors shut, sudden voices down a corridor—are hollow and crashing. And those who lived in it would never forget the odor, even when they had left it far behind. Not quite fecal, speaking more of rust and ruin and cheap disinfectant and a mixture of private and public staleness, the hidden sour scent of a thousand confined men. On this February morning, over four hundred of those men have nothing to do—no educational program or work or even porters' rounds—except to mark again their sounds and smells. "Man, when I get out of here there may be some things I'll have the guts to do," one inmate has written in a poem to his parents, "but one thing I promise: your boy Tom don't tease no monkies [*sic*] in the zoo again."

In the first moments of light, the secretary to the prison intelligence officer calls in sick. She fears some kind of "disturbance," she will explain subsequently to an official inquiry, although she has no "specific knowledge." Now the secretary simply tells the pen that she is staying home. Later in the morning, a prisoner pointedly drops out of a college program. Before noon he explains to a staff officer that he is afraid that hostages will be taken sometime that day in the school dorm. A guard notices an unusually large group of convicts gathered in the central corridor just after lunch, whispering and agitated. But the officer apparently does not report it until days afterward. "They knew," a guard will say bitterly about the administration a few days later. "They knew," he will insist, whatever is reported or unreported in these last hours.

In the psychological unit that Friday afternoon, the well-connected inmate clerks hear that something will finally happen Monday, February 4, around the morning work call. But as one of the clerks closes his part of the unit and walks home early to his south wing dormitory, he feels the mood of the penitentiary change, feels it go "raw," as he later testifies. "My gut-level feeling told me that something was not right," he will remember. The clerk goes back to the psychological section until the day's visitors leave, ten local women who are there meeting with the unit's acting class.

In the prison's incoming and classification unit, Friday is usually a light day. They do not often process new convicts at the weekend. But this Friday there are still three or four inmate files to be worked and entered in the official count when the pen computer access routinely shuts down at 4:00 P.M. The files are left, a staff worker will remember later, in the desk drawer of an associate warden, to be entered the next Monday morning. But then there will be no Monday morning for the office, and the files are never found. The new men are in the pen this Friday night, but they will never be counted among the 1,157 officially reconstructed from computer records as the population on February 1, 1980. Afterward, without knowing about the files in the drawer, an inmate clerk in administration remembers the late commitments and realizes that for the weekend the only accurate census of prisoners would be on a wax board in the control center on which guards recorded and adjusted the count in grease pencil. The inmate clerk and a guard from the day shift that Friday remember the grease-board talley vaguely as "eleven hundred sixty-something." It is the beginning of chaos in inmate accountability that will reach eighteen months beyond this weekend, spinning a sequel of blunder and evasion and of still unanswered questions about how many men would actually die in the horror of the next thirty-six hours.

At 5:30 P.M. the sun is down. A clearing desert sky annihilates the frail heat of the day. The temperature sinks swiftly into the teens. A plump fluorescent moon appears over the Sangre de Cristo, and inmates with windows in its glow will recall superstitiously the "ghost white" light and the lunar astrology of violence. A full moon, some believe, compels killing, and this night only proves it. By midevening, however, what is far more compelling for the moment is the pungent, unmistakable aroma wafting through the south wing and into the central administrative area. By 8:00, later testimony will document, at least half the pen "absolutely reeks" of the home brew, crudely but efficiently fermented in the southwestern second-floor lateral of dormitory E-2. The nervous convict distillers in E-2 cannot quite believe the guards are ignoring the redolence, that they are not letting it hang there until the goon squad bursts in to mete out punishment. It is only the beginning of their fear and mounting disbelief.

The leaders of E-2 are "gladiators," the remaining heavies in population after the December escapees have been locked away in cell block 3. They have expelled the blacks from the dorm. By the pen society's natural selection on the basis of strength and bravado and gang cohesion, they have assumed their own control over the unit. The regime is a coalition of Spanish and Anglo and is not particularly despotic as convict governments go. They practice little extortion on their subjects. But this is clearly a "strong" dormitory, far more in charge of its own daily affairs than most sections of the penitentiary. Since their transfer from cell block 5 in the fall, the new men of E-2 have it "together," and they have it "good," as they will recount, from available homosexual favors and drugs to the petty deference to their authority.

The subsequent official explanation of the riot will ascribe it to a lack of inmate incentives for "order." No dormitory now benefits more from the prevailing order at the New Mexico penitentiary than E-2.

Among their perquisites is the home brew they are opening tonight. An 8-gallon store made in plastic garbage bags and a large cardboard box, it has been cooking away chemically in the pipe chase, the most obvious of hiding places. The box is then taken out and simply shoved to the side, between bunks, as guards come through for the evening count after 10:00 P.M. They're starting their drinking late in E-2. Some of the leaders, some who helped make the brew, get back from work assignments well after nightfall. Like dutiful suburban housewives waiting for their returning husbands for the first cocktail, E-2 holds off dipping until everyone is home from the office.

There is no general premonition abroad in the pen this night. A few men up and down the corridor feel something, like the taut sense felt earlier by the psychological unit clerk, and they lie awake. Yet many prisoners are in their bunks before midnight. Even in E-2 the drinking begins as one more party. Only fifteen of the dormitory's sixty-two inmates are the strong men. Scarcely jailhouse lawyers or convict polit- ical leaders like the Durans, they are what their lawyers will later aptly call them: the sansculottes, ruffians of the peni- tentiary revolt. Yet in the end there will be the riot's haunt- ing moral: that these prisoners' wild, reckless action and its hideous sequel will provoke more genuine reform than will the most eloquent pleading. Now, in the Friday night hours between 10:30 P.M. and 12:30 A.M., they drink heavily. As they drink they become surly and brash, and they boast and prod for some payback, some act of defiance. And as they agitate, they need no more numbers, no precise cause or plan. In Santa Fe's oppression, they are guerrillas in friendly terri- tory, fish in the proverbial sea of despair. Neither they nor the acquiescent majority in E-2 know what they will achieve, what they will bring down. But their imprisonment here describes a sheer hopelessness and boredom, a numbness, that moves them all to go along. "It wasn't over anything great and grandiose," one inmate swore afterward. By 11:30 they have almost decided to jump the graveyard-shift guards when they come through, with the usual slovenly security, in an hour or so to close down the dormitory dayroom, or common, with its television set. "They didn't secure any of those doors," one con told a television interviewer later. "They never secured those doors." At the same time, however, men who are later tried as "conspirators" are also by this hour dizzy if not drunk. If there is a grand conspiracy to kidnap a jail, as the state will claim, the scheming authors have senselessly dulled their minds for its execution. They will have talked about this night, this act, for two hours at the most. They are about to do it because, in the haze and alcohol-blurred extremity of the moment, any pen moment for decades, there seems no real reason not to.

At a quarter to twelve the morning guard watch gathers, with the usual murmurs and scuffing of shoes, for the routine briefing by Captain Joe B. Baca, a longtime guard and now shift commander of the evening crew. According to the later report of the attorney general's inquiry, Baca says nothing about a potential incident and apparently nothing about the odor of home brew in the south wing. The new shift taking over has been on graveyard for two months. There are twenty-seven employees all together. Nine are outside the pen in towers, on patrol, or on other duties. Two female officers watch the women's annex in an adjacent building within the compound but outside the penitentiary perimeter fence. And fifteen guards and one civilian medical technician are left inside the institution to oversee the 1,157 inmates then recorded there. They will be outnumbered nearly 80 to 1 in a prison configured to hold safely and humanely no more than 850.

The shift is almost a caricature of the history of pen staffing. Of these guards 60 percent have worked less than three years, some as little as four months—an illustration of the astronomical turnover rate. Only one officer has lasted more than three years yet less than twenty. The remainder are fixtures of two decades or more. Fewer than a third of the corps has even minimal training. In command is Captain Greg Roybal, fifty-two, a short, slack man with twenty-one years on the job. His deputy, the same age and physical condition, is Lieutenant José Anaya, who has worked as a guard for a quarter-century, with no written record in 1980 of any

formal training in corrections. Following Baca's shift briefing, Roybal makes the post assignments for his contingent.
Besides Lawrence Lucero in the control center, there are to
be seven guards for the south wing, five and the medical
technician for the north. Their average age is thirty-four, a
typical mingling of unschooled veterans and inexperienced
newer men. The recently hired men have been "lucky," one
guard later tells an official inquiry, to get more than a tour
of the pen as basic orientation. For all the men, old and new,
there are written post orders and policies supposedly governing procedures and basic security. But this night as so
many others, for example, no post order mentions the elementary precaution of closing the central corridor grilles
during evening and night shifts. Security Chief Koroneos has
not made an inspection of the grilles "for a long time," as
the attorney general gingerly puts it afterward. Besides, staff
men confide, some of the senior officers like to have the
grilles open in the corridor and on the south side, if only to
make it easier to sneak up on guards who are off sleeping
during the shift. The commanders tiptoe in, and there is said
to be great glee and a suitable ceremonial chewing out when
a dozing culprit is caught.

By midnight Roybal is satisfied that the evening count
is complete and thus routinely relieves Baca's watch. Twenty
minutes later Roybal and Anaya are in the inmates' mess to
check on the preparation of the next day's breakfast. At about
1:10 A.M. they begin to walk down the central corridor to the
south wing to do a customary check of the dormitories and
cell houses, and to help close down the dayrooms, where on
weekends prisoners are allowed to watch television until
1:30 A.M. Ahead of them are five other junior officers already
beginning to close down the nearest cell houses.

The two commanders begin their rounds by passing the
central corridor grille, and like the warden and his deputy,
like other ranking officials who have walked across the same
fateful boundary so often over the past months, they leave
the grille open. Still, there is one more chance here. Moments
after Roybal and Anaya pass the open grille, another officer
comes down the corridor. Herman Gallegos, nearly fifty, has
more than a quarter-century behind him as a guard, and
tonight he is joining the graveyard shift's close-down in ad-

dition to his duties as a work release officer. He is an easy man to get along with, fair with inmates and respected by them, and unlikely to provoke controversy with his employers. Gallegos cannot recall whether the central corridor grille was open or closed when he went by it that night, he will later testify, but he left it as he found it.

The first closings go without incident. Roybal and Anaya join guards Michael Schmitt and Ronnie Martinez to secure dormitory B-1 just across the hall and a story down from E-2. Schmitt is twenty-five, a burly officer of only a few years' experience. At eighteen Martinez has worked at the pen only since the previous autumn, and he is already solely responsible for the "care, custody and control" of more than two hundred inmates in three southside dormitories, including E-2. After locking B-1, Anaya turns left toward the end of the south wing to help another guard secure dormitory D-1. The other group of four guards is up the corridor shutting dorms A-1 and A-2. It is almost 1:30 A.M. Roybal, Schmitt, and Martinez climb the stairs across the hall and prepare to close down E-2.

As he takes the steps toward E-2, Martinez has with him the keys to that dorm as well as to B-1 and B-2, the other units under his supervision. Schmitt carries the keys to E-1. Since the other group of guards working up the corridor is similarly spread out to cover several dorms and cell houses, the keys to all the south units are now in the wing at the same moment. So are Roybal and Anaya. Again, though neither Santa Fe's post orders nor written policy expressly prohibits it, standard prison security dictates that the shift supervisor and his deputy should never be together on one side of the pen or in one unit, leaving the rest of the institution without supervision.

At the door of E-2 the guards pause, once more routinely. Schmitt, following procedure, gives young Martinez the keys to E-1. Two, sometimes four, officers, including both shift supervisors, usually close the day rooms. The guards gather at the door and give any other keys to the officer who will man the door. Within, through the dirty door window, the dormitory is shrouded in darkness. The small blue nightlights are still burned out, long ago reported but still unreplaced. Only the faint cast of lights from the lavatory outside the unit door and from the perimeter fence, through the dormitory's grimy barred windows, silhouettes the still forms in the room. Inside E-2 the tough men are scared, some lying in the blackness with heads still sickly reeling from the home brew, listening for the guards. One man sheepishly remembers long afterward that he almost defecates in his pants in the minutes before the officers climb the stairs. Another thinks he can hear hearts beating everywhere, a loudening drumbeat of the punks around him that will only alert the screws, he thinks with disgust, until he realizes it is his own pulse. But it is too late to stop. They have bragged and postured and spent too much. They are more afraid *not* to act. At least they will have the initiative. For all the warnings, snitching, and premonitions, there is no sign yet that their play is expected. When officers are in the dorm at night, especially near the dayroom at the far end, the guard at the door cannot distinguish them from inmates. He makes out only moving bodies.

The bunks of the dorm are, as always, doubled along the side, set perpendicular to the lateral wall. Two rows of single beds lie down the center of the dormitory flanking the double bunks, creating two narrow aisles on each side. In the crowded bunking, every space between the double beds is a nighttime hiding place from which a prisoner can jump someone in the aisle. The beds begin close enough to the dormitory entrance for inmates to strike the door in a short bound from where they lie. One officer who works the dorms regularly, who walks the 60-foot gauntlet past the double bunks to clear out and lock the dayroom at the end of the dormitory, will later tell an investigator that every time he reports for night duty he wonders whether he will leave the penitentiary alive. Tonight is the same. And the men are waiting unseen.

According to security procedures, the officer at the door is to let his fellow guards into the dorm and then, while they are closing the dayroom and checking the dorm, keep the door closed, shutting and securing it with an audible crack of the lock. Guards who go inside the units describe that sound at their back as one of the terrors of duty, a small metallic clap far louder than its actual report, a sudden resounding announcement to everyone that the keeper is now in the cage himself.

But more often in Santa Fe, the man at the door holds it open a few inches or else turns the key the other way to hold the snap lock and so closes the door without securing it, only giving the appearance of locking it. A few moments before, Roybal, Schmitt, and Martinez have come through a gate at the stairway to E-2, a gate that should be similarly secured. They have left it unlocked.

It is now almost 1:40 A.M. Martinez unlocks the door to E-2, opens it out toward him, and steps back to let Captain Roybal and Schmitt inside. The dormitory is quiet, the men apparently asleep and orderly—far too orderly, the convicts suddenly worry. But the guards do not seem to notice, and come on in. Schmitt walks quickly up the left aisle toward the dayroom, Roybal more slowly up the right. What Martinez does at this instant with the door will never be clear—whether he locks it, or leaves it ajar, or shuts it but leaves it unlatched. For only seconds later, Lieutenant Anaya comes up the stairs—like the other men, through the unused riot-control grille at the central corridor and through the unlocked gate at the stairway to E-2—to help in the closing. Anaya is at the door, and Martinez opens it again to let him in. But what happens to the door now will remain all too vivid in the memories of the men who lived the moment.

Anaya starts up an aisle. And for a fleeting time, incredibly, there is a last warning, as if the history about to unfold shrinks back one more time. In the quiet, dark, unusually subdued dormitory, an inmate near the door, one of the strong men, abruptly sits up in bed with a rustle, fully dressed, as if rushing his cue, which is exactly what he is doing. For a few seconds the officers and the anxious con look at one another in puzzlement, perhaps in the last glance of the old regime at Santa Fe. Then it is past. The con lies back down. The guards walk deeper into the room. Schmitt is just inside the dayroom, Roybal halfway along the right aisle, Anaya a few bunks down the same row.

Suddenly an inmate near the entrance hurls himself at the door, and a partner follows almost immediately. There is a thud as the door is hit and Martinez thrown back, a sudden scuffling as he pushes to hold the door. But the sound dies in the stairwell. At the crash Schmitt steps back into the left aisle. Roybal and Anaya turn toward the door. In a frozen moment, one of them is jumped by the first inmate—no one can remember precisely who—and at least some of the watching prisoners believe that if the guard simply throws off the attack, displays some sudden power, like a television hero, the uprising will be quashed.

But the con and the guard struggle an instant too long, the guard too weakly. A dozen men join the fight, springing from bunks onto the other two officers, pounding the door open and dragging Martinez inside. Out come the shanks, the ubiquitous homemade prison knives, and clubs and ax handles hoarded and secreted in preparation for violence. It is no match. Roybal and Anaya are small middle-aged men in poor shape to fight. Martinez is too young. Schmitt, though he has the youth and size to put up a struggle, is jumped by several men. The attackers are younger, quicker, stronger. Many are regular weight lifters in the pen gym.

This bloodiest, most anarchic of American prison riots now begins, not with a wild rush or screams but with an almost controlled pause and quiet. The inmates methodically strip, tie, and blindfold their four captive guards. Some of the cons in E-2 still do not believe it will work, still think that they can hold the officers for a while but that there will eventually be an attack, a "shit-stomping" by the other guards (as one of them later remembers his fears), and they will all go to the hole. But the adrenaline is flowing, burning away the haze of the home brew and their hesitation, and they soon act. At least one of them acts immediately, and by himself takes the insurgency further than anyone has imagined.

Within minutes after the seizure of the guards, a muscular young Hispanic con has put on Roybal's uniform shirt and a bandanna. Armed with a shank and reckless machismo, he tells the others he is going out alone, and then he plunges through the dorm door. He spills down the stairs, through the unlocked gate, and past the open riot grille into the dimly lit central corridor. He starts first across the hall to dormitory B, but then turns suddenly, whether at sound or instinct, to cross back diagonally to dormitory F, just north of E. He is clearly looking for the other guards he knows are closing down the rest of the wing. He runs through the open grille and stairwell gate in F, then up to the second floor. And there, in the small vestibule in front of the door to F-2, which they have just locked, he confronts four more officers. They are Herman Gallegos, the congenial veteran; Juan Bustos, in his mid-twenties with a year's experience; another Gallegos, Victor, only twenty-two and with little tenure on the job; and officer Elton Curry. At forty-nine, Curry has been a guard for three years; he is a large, physical man whom the prisoners call Big Foot.

It is another extraordinary scene. The men face each other in a moment of shock. Then the con brandishes his shank. Unarmed, Curry looks around desperately and reaches for a nearby trash can. He thrusts it forcibly at the inmate as the other three guards back up against the wall. For perhaps less than a minute, it is a close, even fight. Using the garbage pail as foil and lance, Curry wards off the shank and pushes the con to the stairwell, forcing him to bend back over the rail a story above the concrete floor below. Again the fate of the penitentiary, and of so many men, hovers in the seconds. Curry might have pushed the attacking con over the rail. The other guards might have gone back into F-2, called the control center, or even rushed past the fighting men to close the central corridor grille to the south wing. But they do not. The con holds on, slashes back at Curry. And by then other inmates from E-2 have ventured into the corridor, heard the fight, come to see the scene in front of F-2. Finding Curry grappling alone with their partner, the cons overpower him, wrenching away his protective trash can and stabbing and beating him viciously for putting up a fight. Then they also seize the other guards.

Out of this fateful joust, however, the inmates will have only three more hostages, not four, and the incident reveals the mixed character—now mad and chaotic, now strangely, almost casually calculated—the riot has assumed from the beginning. In the "confusion" of the attack by the railing, the attorney general's inquiry would later conclude, Herman Gallegos, the older, more benign guard, somehow slipped into F-2 and took refuge in its dayroom where he was "protected" by "sympathetic inmates." But several other accounts have the door to F-2 already locked when the lone con confronts the officers in front of it and then unlocked only by the inmates who moments later seize the guards and their keys. More likely, the prisoners simply let Gallegos go into the dormitory, a dispensation for his longtime decency. To *some* of their captives *some* of the rioters, even among the feral men of E-2, already high on their feat, will be "sympathetic," now and later. Though savage, the payback will not be blind. But amid so much atavism and treachery, the heroism and gentleness and loyalty will be largely overlooked. Such concepts do not easily fit into the preconceptions of the prosecutors and investigators who subsequently scavenge the history. After all, they only raise more questions—about the reasons for the violence, about the men who did it, about justice—than official inquiries are prepared to pose.

While a few inmates take the younger Gallegos and a bleeding Curry back to the E-2 dayroom where the other guards are being held, another group strips, binds, and blindfolds the remaining guard, Juan Bustos. After looping a belt around his neck, they drag him painfully down the stairs to the central corridor, his feet raking the hard sharp steps. As they reach the hallway, they pause with the blindfolded, terrified guard, pulling and kicking at him in their own fright and exhilaration as they contemplate how they will now use him. Inmates from E-2 and F-2 are now flowing into the hall, small clusters of them with captured keys beginning to unlock the adjacent dormitories, A and B and F-1. It is little more than ten minutes since Ronnie Martinez opened the door to E-2. Except for the running footsteps, the cries of Bustos as he is struck, muffled echoing shouts as liberators call out to their friends, the south wing is still curiously quiet. Outside, guards sense no eruption, only the occasional tapping on the tower windows of a faltering north wind.

At 1:57 A.M. the riot announces itself. The inmates have taken the officers' two-way radios as well as their keys. In the control center, guard Lawrence Lucero, an officer in his early twenties and with only three years experience, is startled from his graveyard-tour quiet as a strange voice, obviously an inmate's, suddenly crackles out of the sour night air of the pen from one of the two-way radios. "We've got the shift commander hostage," the voice tells the unknown receiver. "There had better be a meeting with the governor, the news media, and Rodriguez." It is a simple, stark notice and demand, spoken deliberately over the sound of running footsteps in the south wing, aimed at anyone and everyone down the long corridor to the rest of the prison. The message is strangely terse, mentioning nothing of the other hostages, the territory seized, the consequences if the demand goes unmet. But the first riot message is also unmistakably political. The guards have been jumped in E-2 in a drunken brashness, the entire south wing seized this Friday night in February almost on impulse. The future course of the uprising will frequently be aimless and wild, with shifting, uncertain leadership, and often politics will be an apparent afterthought. Yet this clipped ultimatum to Lucero will be testimony that the larger cause is always there. It is Roybal who counts with the clique, the inmate on the radio knows well. And it is King and Rodriguez who will decide the fate of any reform, and they will be held accountable—if at all— only by the media. Minutes into the takeover, the announcement captures the history and politics of the New Mexico penitentiary with a simplicity never improved upon in the tumult to follow.

The sound of the radio dies away, and Lucero is instantly shaken again by a jangling telephone. The call comes from a frightened Mike Hernandez, a young guard who has been on the job only four months. Hernandez has been closing down dormitory D-1 at the far south side, the unit for new admissions and short-term prisoners who are at the pen for diagnostic tests. He has seen and heard inmates on the loose in the wing, he tells Lucero, and he has locked himself in behind the central corridor grille that separates the rest of the pen from the two end units of both wings, and behind the door to D-1. Hernandez is now cut off from the rest of the prison by some five hundred inmates. He has not prevented his capture, only postponed it.

It is now almost two o'clock. Lucero calls Valentin Martinez, an older, more seasoned guard stationed in the north wing. He tells Martinez a disturbance is happening and to shut and lock the corridor grille (a twin to the one Hernandez has just fled behind), which will separate from the central hallway both cell block 4, the protective-custody unit at the far north end of the prison, and the adjacent and empty cell block 5 at the far north end. Just as the inmate radio man has caught the political essence of the takeover in his first message moments before, Lucero knows immediately the danger to cell block 4. This cell block is known as the home of the snitches, the pen's hated informers, as well as the child molesters and mentally ill and the weaker men who are vulnerable to homosexual assault or other abuse, all victims and outcasts of rigid, punitive prison society. If a tide is gathering in the south, Lucero knows, it will sooner or later crash northward. The control center officer hangs up on Martinez and immediately dials outside to Koreneos in his residence on the penitentiary grounds. He tells the security chief what he knows, that a riot seems to have started in the dormitories and that Roybal is apparently a hostage. Koroneos then hangs up to call Deputy Warden Montoya and Warden Griffin in their neighboring houses. At the same time, Martinez in cell block 4 is calling his old friend Ross Maez in the prison infirmary. Maez is yet another twenty-two year man on the staff; he is almost fifty years old. After Martinez's anxious call, he swiftly locks himself and seven invalid inmates in the hospital lateral just north of the control center.

Meanwhile, the growing crowd of inmates mills for a moment in the dim, forbidden territory of the central corridor and then begins to roll up the hallway toward the center wing. The momentum of the revolt now takes over: "Everybody out! Everybody must participate." Inmates will remember hearing in their south side bunks the first cries of the riot: "We've got it! We have the prison!" Some of the early leaders from E-2 call out the units with the same mix of threat and bravado they used on each other only an hour before. But not everyone is persuaded. Many in cell house 1, an honor unit in the southeast nearest the administrative area, stay cautiously in their cells. And down the corridor, just below where it started, the men of E-1, many of them young and sexually preyed upon by stronger cons, successfully barricade themselves in their unit the moment they hear the men loose in the hall. Already there is a small gathering of rioters at the door of E-1, promising, cajoling, menacing the scared young inmates inside.

The men who have leashed Bustos have decided definitely now what to do with him. They begin to kick the guard ahead of them as they move up the corridor, holding him out as a shield against the counterattack most of them expect any minute. As Lucero in the control center is telephoning Martinez and Koroneos, guards Larry Mendoza and Antonio Vigil are sitting in the officers' mess. Mendoza is finished with his morning meal, one of the few perquisites for officers on the graveyard shift, and Vigil is starting to fork his institutional food without enthusiasm. It is perhaps a minute before two. They hear unusual noises in the hall, men's voices and a din of too many footsteps. The two guards look vacantly at each other for an instant, then push back their chairs and walk to the mess hall door. From there they see something worse than they have even guessed from the ominous sounds. Down the corridor a crowd of men, and it could only be inmates, is pushing what seems a near-naked figure up the shadowy corridor. To Mendoza, an intelligent, respected guard who is thirty and has worked at the pen less than three years, the crucial south corridor grille, the bars that will stop the marchers, seems roughly halfway between the crowd and the door to the mess. And the grille is open. Too late, he thinks, to close the grille before the procession and its sacrificial naked man get there. Mendoza and Vigil then run diagonally across the hall, some 50 feet, to the control center window, where they pound on the glass to alert an already wide-eyed Lucero, and tell him to unlock electronically the near north grille a few feet from the window. Lucero opens the grilles slowly, and Mendoza and Vigil rush through, looking behind them at the oncoming flood. Vigil, age forty-seven and a ten-year veteran of the pen, then stands uncertainly behind the grille, watching the riot advance toward him, as Mendoza runs down to a telephone at cell block 3 to call Koroneos. Finding the security superintendent already alerted and on his way to the pen, he then calls the officer in tower 1, tells him to sound the alarm for the rest of the outside guards, and to shoot anyone attempting escape.

In the control center Lucero has watched the north grille clang shut and now turns to see through the window the angry faces of the first inmates in the corridor. As the rioters rush up to the window, Lucero is joined in the center by fellow officer Louis C de Baca. Only twenty-four, with scarcely a year's service at the pen, C de Baca carries one of the most venerable names in New Mexico, a shortened form of Cabeza de Baca, "head of the cow," and he has just performed one of the early acts of genuine official heroism in the riot. On foot patrol outside the pen, C de Baca hears the developing riot on his two-way radio and comes hurrying through the front entrance, past the administrative offices, and into the control center, because he knows Lucero may need help. Like other units in the shoddy, decaying building, the control center is being renovated, and for now its back door can be opened only by reaching through bars and blindly feeling to fit the key in the lock. C de Baca opens that door and stands with Lucero as more than a hundred inmates congregate about the newly installed window.

One of the rioters demands that Lucero open the gate grill just south of the center, letting the horde into the administrative offices and out the front door of the prison. When he refuses, standing there with C de Baca, they begin to beat Bustos with rods and pipes, shouting that they'll do the same to Lucero. The guards in the control center do not recognize Bustos, but when he sags unconscious from the blows and is dragged away back down the corridor to the south, they assume he is dead.

Lucero and C de Baca now stand inside the center; Mendoza and Vigil, all but unnoticed, are 15 feet away behind the north central corridor grille. All of them watch transfixed as the inmates begin to beat at the glass with pipes and with a canister fire extinguisher the inmates have found in the halls. The cons hurl the canister against the glass, and it bounces off harmlessly. They throw it again. Nothing. It is 2:02 A.M. With the third heave, the window glass begins to crack. And on the next two blows, to the accompaniment of cheering inmates, shards of glass begin to rain into the center. The glass does a "fine job…in a lot of offices and institutions all over the country," a corrections consultant will say later. "The main thing is, you just don't let a riot get up to that point."

C de Baca and Lucero now back up slowly, in disbelief, and turn to run out the repair-stiffened door toward the pen's front entrance. In their fear, they have left behind the equivalent of their regimental guns—all the keys on the center keyboard, a teargas launcher, fourteen teargas grenades, twenty-four riot-control batons, and a pair of helmets. At the prison's front entrance the two young guards pause for a moment and return through the office area to see if the inmates have really broken in. They have. A few feet back in, the guards glimpse inmates near the visitors' area, well beyond the control center. Inside the center, though the guards cannot see them, cons have clambered through the shattered glass and now stand over the control console with its electronic locks and keys to the entire institution. Lucero and C de Baca run back out to tower 1, the first guard refugees from the riot.

"If rioting prisoners ever were loose inside the institution," a reporter had written when the pen opened in 1956, "they still could not get to the man in the main control room." The reporter's confidence, like the prison's design and intention, had not reckoned with the men who run the institution or with the politicians, judges, and public who so obliviously let them. It is roughly 2:05 A.M. The inmates have seized the Penitentiary of New Mexico in less than twenty-five minutes.

Witnessing the debacle at the glass window, watching incredulously as the control center is overrun, officers in the north wing limber up for flight like an army rear guard whose front lines have been fatally breached. Mendoza runs back to cell block 3 and calls the main tower one more time, now finding Koroneos there and telling him that without help the entire institution will soon fall. "We're doing all we can," Koroneos answers. Griffin, Montoya, and Koroneos are all in the front gate house by the tower. Through the windows they can see inmates running wildly along the corridors, and they hear Lucero and C de Baca give a breathless report that the control center is gone. Koroneos orders the men in the towers to arm themselves with ill-maintained, undependable riot guns from the ramshackle armory beneath tower 1 and to shoot anyone going for the perimeter. But the men in the towers are not expert marksmen, and a mass assault on the gate, a mass escape loosing hundreds of prisoners into the Santa Fe night, is entirely possible. The State Police have been alerted, but their first units will not arrive for another quarter-hour. There is, in fact, almost nothing that Koroneos and his superiors can now do. In those first few minutes of the riot, Deputy Warden Montoya has sent his wife and children off the prison reservation entirely.

While Mendoza calls the front tower, Vigil telephones tower 3 and tells the guard there that he and Martinez, two older veterans, will hide beneath cell block 5, near the gas chamber, in a crawl space between the basement and the main floor of the pen. Vigil shrewdly tells the guard not to transmit the hiding place over the radio, where the inmates might hear it. And the alert guard waits to throw a note to a State Policeman below the tower, who in turn will give it to Griffin. Vigil and Martinez now run to the basement of 5 and push themselves into the dirty crawl space where they will listen to the rioters come ever closer. Meanwhile, as Maez, the medical technician, remains locked in the second floor of the hospital, Mendoza finishes the call to the tower and is joined by two other guards assigned to cell block 3: Ramon Gutierrez, age twenty-five, with a year's experience as a penitentiary officer, and Edward Ortega a twenty-three-year man who is fifty-four. The three then run back down to lock themselves in the basement of cell block 3, site of the maximum-detention strip cells and many of the pen's past horrors. The moment he is locked in, however, Mendoza realizes he has left the main key to the cell block in the vestibule at the front of the unit near the central corridor. Anxiously he crawls back to get it and somehow is not detected by the inmates then rampaging in the corridor, though, in mounting terror, he sees them. From the control center they have now unlocked the entrance grille to the north wing and are running to and fro down the hall toward cell blocks 3 and 4. It is only minutes after two o'clock.

Outside, in the women's prison annex nearby, one of the tower guards has alerted officer Susan Watts to a disturbance in the south wing, and Watts, like Koroneos's wife, has called the State Police, asking them as well to alert the pen SWAT team; the head of the women's prison, Joanne Brown; and Eugene Long, the corrections department adviser. It is, incredibly, Watts's first night on the job. She monitors closely the radio transmissions, and moments after 2:00 A.M. she and another woman guarding the annex hear the control center fall. The other female guard, perhaps more aware of the thin line of defense offered by the towers, begins to finger her rosary.

Rushing into the north wing, some inmates pause to

break into the hated psychological unit. In rage they break furniture and pillage files. And at roughly 2:15 A.M. they set fire to the ward. Diagonally up the corridor to the north another group of convicts huddles impatiently at the entrance to cell block 3, trying to find a key to the grille among a pile of keys taken from the control center. The right key has been hanging there on the board, but they have missed it, and their anger grows with their bungling at the lock. Inside 3, of course, are the objects of their liberation, now yelling and clamoring to be set free, the hardest, most recalcitrant men of the prison. "When they told me that people in cell block 3 were free," a corrections official later tells an investigator, "I said, 'There's death.'"

For some reason Mendoza now returns from the basement to the main floor while the cursing men are rattling at the grille. They see him and tell him to open the grille or else die when they break through. Mendoza coolly refuses and goes back downstairs. Moments later, as the psychological unit begins to smolder, inmates drag a trembling Captain Roybal all the way from E-2 to the entrance of cell block 3. There the rioters yell to the officers in the basement, "Open up or we'll kill this son of a bitch." Cons in cell block 3 hear Mendoza say to his fellow guards that maybe they should open, maybe they *will* kill the captain. But again, consistent with pen policy, they refuse to unlock the grille. In the next few minutes, however, the inmates find the right key and open the grille, though only for another brief cat-and-mouse game. Once through, the inmates demand that the officers open their grille to the basement; the guards refuse; and when the rioters eventually find the key to that grille, the guards scurry back behind one more grille and refuse to open this one despite more threats to Roybal. Finally, the inmates unlock the last barrier, and the three officers are captured, ordered to strip, and locked in another basement room of cell block 3. Meanwhile, upstairs the prisoners have had more trouble opening the two upper tiers of cells where doors are released or "unracked" by a control panel. They beat and threaten Roybal until he tries to help them operate the mechanism. Even then, though, the tortured captain is too shaky to do much, and a con from another area of cell block 3, who knows the controls as well as the guards do, joins them to work the panel and roll open the cell doors. It is nearly 3:00 A.M. The maximum-security men of cell block 3 are now free, little more than an hour after the lone con from E-2 fought his brief life-and-death duel with Curry.

At this hour the penitentiary is a panoramic stage, the freed men moving back and forth, busy in this corner and that, still largely oblivious to each other as if they are mingling actors following different plots in some theater of the absurd. In the plumbing shop under the kitchen they hurry off with a heavy-duty acetylene cutting torch, and they promptly cut through the grille sealing off D-1 and the educational units at the far south end, releasing eighty-six newcomers and diagnostic inmates and seizing guard Hernandez, the twelfth hostage. They then roll the torch ahead of them on the floor as they run up the central corridor to cell block 5, where they cut through, plunge to the basement, and take two more acetylene torches left there by construction crews doing the renovation. But somehow in their frantic grasping for the torches, they do not find Vigil and Martinez hiding in the crawl space nearby. At the same moment, other inmates ransacking the hospital somehow do not find Maez and his seven inmate patients upstairs in the infirmary. Afterward, the dial and the handle of the vaultlike door to Maez's hiding place are found torn off, as if rioters had tried halfheartedly to enter and then moved away. For the technician and the sick men inside, it is a moment of terror as the door handle is wrenched off—and then nothing. Maez, like the men in the crawl space, will stay hidden. The last hostage has been taken.

Several yards up the corridor, outside the entrance to cell block 4, there is already a crowd of inmates, and they will not go away. The corridor grille blocking 4 and 5 has been breached, but the grille at the entrance to cell block 4 is jammed, and neither key nor electronic controls will open it. Soon they bring the torches to eat at the bars. Inside are the supposed snitches, the members of other untouchable prison castes, and scores to settle. At the entrance, their faces lit in fiery pallor by the flame of the torch, men stand in a line, waiting patiently to kill.

At about 2:30 A.M., as Roybal is dragged northward to a spot in front of cell block 3, inmates have him speak on a radio to Griffin, Montoya, and Koroneos outside, repeating a convicts' ultimatum that if the prison is assaulted, the hostages will perish. The inmate on the radio tells the officials at the gate house that no one will attempt to escape—a promise that could only come as the first encouraging news of the riot to listening tower guards and to officer Watts and her colleague in the women's unit. But the inmate spokesman also repeats the demand made a half-hour before, that the rioters soon meet with Governor King and news reporters. Like the first message heralding the riot to the control center, this initial transmission to the outside is again plainly political.

Elsewhere inside, there is a gathering frenzy, punctuated by drugs, sex, and an inbred fear now bordering on panic. As the riot spills past the near north grille, inmates burst into the hospital to pillage the drugs—barbiturates, antidepressants, antipsychotics, and sedatives—left there in huge supplies by the obliging bulk-purchasing policy of the state. The prisoners tumble down the stairs as well to the paint shop and shoe-repair store in the basement beneath the kitchen, where they can sniff the paint thinner and glue available in similarly ample quantities. The sniff will make them high and violent, while the drugs—soporifics—supposedly sedate them. But pharmaceutical distinctions will not matter very much here. In angry, suddenly free men, even the most powerful downers may produce a "paradoxical rage," as experts later label it. In the hospital, rioters devour handfuls of capsules and then stuff more in their pockets. Their loot catalogues the reliance of this penitentiary, like so many prisons and asylums, on drugs in lieu of policy and social competence: Demerol, Talwin, and methadone; Valium, Miltown, Serax, and Dalmane; the ever-present phenobarbital; Elavil and lithium; Thorazine, Mellaril, and Sparine; Etrafon, Dilantin, and Parafon Forte. They are the place names of the cloudy, maddening hallucinatory world the rioters now superimpose onto the prison. And outside in the central corridor there is yet another extraordinary scene in these first moments between 2:00 and 3:00 A.M. Up and down the hall men are leaning against the wall or kneeling on the floor, bandannas tied in tourniquets on their arms, injecting morphine, liquid Valium, Demerol, and other drugs. Others stand by waiting eagerly for a bandanna. After the injection, some rise and reel away, some simply stand there in a stupor, some vomit and curse yet pronounce the drug wondrous and urge fellow inmates to try it. One con from cell block 3 wanders down the corridor into the administrative area, stops in front of the barbershop as if fascinated by something there, and then instead of forcing the door simply jumps through the barbershop window in a hail of shattered glass, opening a large cut near his right eye. In a moment he emerges from the window armed with the barber's largest scissors.

Back in the south wing dormitories, some still dark, some illuminated only by random blue night-lights, men are in bed with their homosexual lovers—"punks" in pen nomenclature, often prostitutes kept at the price of protection and favors by their stronger patrons. Outside the barricaded door to E-1, a crowd of men still alternately tries to coax or coerce the inmates of the dorm into coming out. Some are at the door to talk soothingly to their punks inside, to see after their welfare. Others brandish a teargas launcher, and there is talk of smoking out the frightened inmates.

Everywhere, destruction has already well begun, wanton, spontaneous, fueled by a pervasive loathing. Sinks and urinals are bashed, wall fixtures and fuse boxes torn out, bulletin boards and inmate photos before each dorm obliterated. The control center is destroyed; inmates pass by and jump through the shattered glass just to smash furniture or radio sets already ravaged. Yet in this orgy of revenge on the sheer physical furnishings of the place, as if the lifeless paraphernalia were responsible for their torment, the rioters also pause and methodically make telephone calls. In the first minutes of the takeover, before officials can control and disconnect the lines, inmates place a flurry of long-distance calls throughout New Mexico and the nation, speaking to relatives or friends or the media, trumpeting the news of their exploit and then bashing a desk or chair on the way out. But there is also purpose, crude purpose, to the devastation. They hurry to the administrative offices and to the psychological unit in large part to burn the files there. "They wanted the paperwork....They wanted to get the paperwork burned up before they got rushed," one con told State Police later, "because they felt that if they burned all the paperwork…there'd be no records." Yet along with the ransacked files they find as well in various officials' offices large stores of cash—by some accounts several thousand dollars, according to one eyewitness statement at least twelve hundred dollars. Whether this was a legitimate fund or a reservoir of the pen's rampant corruption—payoff money, a "snitch fund" of taxes or rewards for informers, an accumulation from the institution's dubious bookkeeping—the theft of this cash will never be reported. Like many of the missing files, including penitentiary personnel and land records as well as inmate folders, tales of the money cache—true or fictitious—will be discreetly ignored in the inquiry that follows. In any case, by 4:30 A.M. the paper in the records area and warden's office is brightly ablaze.

In spite of their intoxication as a result of narcotics, cash, and vengeful mayhem, however, the rioters are soberly obsessed with the frailty of their seizure. They are certain, despite their threats of reprisal and their drugged bravado, that they will be stormed. Every disturbance before, after all, has been harshly and quickly put down. Now they post guards with some of the eight radios they have captured, and they fear that the State Police will come in through the end of the south wing at the educational unit, sweeping south to north in some great dragnet of clubs and bullets. They hastily pull bunks out of B-1 and barricade the far south grille to block the attack. But they are not optimistic. At one moment early in the takeover, before cell block 3 is opened, someone yells in typically mixed Spanish and English, "*Juras* [guards] are coming, *juras* are coming!" And the cry sets off a stampede back to the dormitories. The men run like frightened children caught out in some classroom indiscretion and now scampering back to their desks. "There were people falling down, people walking on each other, elbowing each other, kicking each other, trying to get south," one witness describes the panic afterward. The rioting inmates expect the assault only minutes after the takeover. They expect it under cover of night. Then they expect it at dawn's first light. They expect it for the first several hours of the riot, just as the men of E-2 expected it momentarily when they jumped the guards. And even after watching the lax security and misrule of the pen for so long, even after seeing the control center glass put in as a veritable invitation, they cannot quite credit the completeness of their triumph, and the disarray of the administration. They assume a violent counterattack, almost as if the riot were a setup, a provocation to make them vulnerable, because, as one con will earnestly tell State Police agents a month later, "they [pen officials] had to know a riot was goin' down." The nervous inmate guards posted with their radios, the barricade at the south end, the stampede back to the dorms, the widespread sense of doom and swift retribution from the beginning—all mark how truly extensive the administrative blundering has been. But now, when the attack does not come, the inmates settle into the developing anarchy until the rage and debauchery have run their course.

Though the State Police and the riot squad are for now only fearsome phantoms, the inmates feel another deepening dread abroad in the corridors in these first minutes, and it, too, has always been there. They are increasingly afraid of one another. "Everybody into the gym. Meeting in the gym," someone yells up and down the south wing around 3:00 A.M. The purpose of the meeting is political, an effort by a few of the inmates, some of whom have worked on the Duran suit, to fashion a united front and agree on a negotiating agenda. But the meeting is chaotic, twenty men or so drifting in and out, and little is accomplished. To many the summons is instantly suspect. They worrry about being caught in the gym, subjected to some kangaroo court, at the mercy of too many penitentiary madmen now loose. The fears and lethal divisions in inmate society, to be confirmed in blood in the next few hours, haunt the takeover from the start.

For a time, however, the bloodshed and suffering belong mainly to the captured guards. Their fate hangs on the moment and the changing cast of inmates watching them. Some are savagely beaten, stabbed, reportedly forced to perform fellatio on their captors, and by inmate accounts brutally sodomized, now with an ax handle or a riot stick, now by prisoners. Naked and bound, they are under a hail of humiliations and threats, and in the process are dragged from place to place. Yet the torture is interrupted from time to time as other cons come and go and chide the captors for mistreatment and even sympathize with the guards. In Roybal's case, the small captain is kicked and prodded and choked up the corridor to cell block 3, threatened there with murder, then brought back down for a while to the officers' mess where he is given a cup of coffee by other inmates, and still later taken into the weight lifters' room off the gym where he is subjected to more abuse. At 3:15 A.M. Roybal is again put on the radio to stress the inmates' demands, but there is no sign, save his shaking voice, of the nightmare he is enduring. At one point inmates sacking the control center set off teargas bombs, and as the fumes flood the corridor and administrative area, furious rioters believe they are under attack and scream over radios that if Deputy Warden Montoya doesn't stop the gas they will kill the guards. For moments it seems the guards will be butchered as a result of the mistake, until the gas begins to dissipate and men realize the bombs have gone off inside the pen.

At 5:25 A.M. Herman Gallegos has crept out of his hiding place in F-2 and, dressed in inmate clothes, has walked up the long main corridor, crawled through the control center, and come to the main gate. He has been helped and escorted by sympathetic inmates from the dormitory, but the flight has been harrowing; he has passed by scores of rampaging cons who might have recognized or stopped him at any instant. Yet when Gallegos gets to the door, and apparent freedom, there is a last heart-stopping obstacle. A prison official outside recognizes the fugitive officer but thinks his release has somehow not yet been negotiated properly, and tells Gallegos to "wait a minute...go back." But Rodriguez quickly sees the situation and shouts for Gallegos to come ahead. The older guard runs stiffly through the entrance just ahead of angry inmates who have discovered his escape. Gallegos is the first free. Then Curry is dragged out at daybreak, slashed and mauled, five and a quarter hours after the decisive overpowering on the tier at F-2. Hernandez will be the third—and the last for another torturous twelve hours.

In the north, Mendoza, Gutierrez, and Ortega are luckier than the other hostages. They have been stripped yet given blankets and mattresses, and their captors clearly see them as insurance in any attack on the pen. "We'll at least be sure that we've got a way out, you know," one of them explains his thinking later to investigators. Periodically, inmates come through the basement to cell block 3 where they are held and threaten them, but their convict guards stand fast. One even gives Mendoza keys to the area where the officers are locked, and Mendoza quickly stuffs them under a mattress.

Near dawn, a battered and bloodied Hernandez is brought to the basement keep for the guards. At first he is thrown into a cell with a murdered inmate; then he is taken out by other prisoners. "Are you a guard?" one convict asks him. The young Hernandez does not reply. "Are you a guard?" the con repeats.

And the officer with his few months in the profession answers, "I used to be."

Mendoza and the other guards there are told to tend his wounds. But Mendoza tells the captors that the injuries are too serious. "Look here," a con remembers him saying, "he's not making it." The inmates then clothe Hernandez in a pair of convict overalls, make a stretcher out of a blanket, and carry the wounded guard out into the frosty air at the front gate after eight o'clock Saturday morning, more than five hours after his capture behind the grilles in D-1.

Outside, at the gate house, Griffin and his aides decide shortly after Lucero and C de Baca flee that they will not attempt to retake the penitentiary, or so they tell a subsequent inquiry. The decision is absurdly academic. No State Police or other officers will begin to arrive here for several minutes, and even then there will be only a handful of troopers to plug the perimeter. The forces necessary to recapture the building and quell hundreds of uncontrolled, unpredictable felons will not be here, or remotely ready, until well into the following day. For these first hours the question is not whether officials will storm the prison, but whether inmates will burst out of the thin, unprepared line between this pen gone berserk and the sleeping countryside and town around it. Fortunately, neither side senses the weakness of the other. Neither is organized enough to exploit this early moment, with all the bloodshed an assault or breakout would have brought.

Griffin tries to call Rodriguez immediately, even before he calls the State Police to tell them the full magnitude of the riot. But between 2:15 and 2:30 A.M. there is no answer at Rodriguez's phone after repeated rings. Joanne Brown will arrive an hour later, saying she, too, has tried to call Rodriguez, to no avail. Meanwhile, State Police Chief Martin Vigil, a longtime power in his own agency and an old associate of King and Rodriguez, has called the governor to inform him of the riot. King then calls the commanding general of the National Guard, whose five hundred citizen-soldiers of local units will be roused out of Saturday morning beds over the next two hours to take up helmets and arms to lay chill, uncertain siege to the prison south of Santa Fe.

Montoya has just taken a course in San Francisco on "crisis intervention," and a diffident Griffin defers to the aggressive deputy warden to negotiate with the inmates by radio for the time being, at least until Rodriguez can be found. Griffin tells King at 3:00 A.M. that negotiations are under way, and the governor agrees that they should talk rather than try to retake. He, too, has no choice. Using a two-way radio in his car, then a hand set from the gate house, Montoya begins a vague, broken dialogue with the rioters, alternately subdued and harsh, trying to stall and attempting by his recently acquired classroom prescription to put an insulating layer between the inmates and the ostensible decision-makers, the warden and governor. But soon Rodriguez and Montoya will do the negotiating and the deciding, theory aside. Montoya talks with a jumble of voices from within the walls. The eight captured radios often pass from hand to hand. The night air is tangled with competing spokesmen, two or three inmates talking at once, messages garbled and gone. Yet for all that there is still a common theme. The insurgents want to talk to King and Rodriguez along with representatives of the news media. They insist on making public the mismanagement and abuses at the pen. If the prison is rushed, the hostages will be executed. And in these predawn talks on Saturday the demands also begin to make a new, more precise point. The inmates want the resignations of Montoya, Associate Warden Adelaido Martinez, Koroneos, and two guard officers, Captain Daniel Benevidez and Lieutenant Benito Gonzalez, known among the prisoners as Green Eyes. As the names of the officials are rasped over the receiver in the gate house, smoke has begun to climb into the black sky over the center of the prison. The psychological unit, the offices, and soon the gym are aflame.

A little after four, Santos Quintana, a corrections department aide whose diary chronicles a parole scandal embroiling the first King administration, finally reaches Rodriguez on the telephone. The acting secretary gets to the pen about 5:00 A.M. and immediately takes command of his longtime staff now mostly assembled there, telling Griffin that the governor has put him (Rodriguez) in charge henceforth. Apparently, King and Rodriguez have spoken sometime earlier that night, but in all the elaborate official tracing later of phone calls and transmissions for the investigative record, that call—with its content and rich history—is nowhere recounted.

Minutes after guard Herman Gallegos narrowly makes good his escape amid the official confusion at the front gate, Rodriguez meets with State Police officers in Griffin's house and hears about the precarious front of troopers, Santa Fe Police, and sheriffs drawn up around the prison. A half-hour later, a State Police SWAT team will arrive, the second on the scene. But there is still no serious question of an assault.

As they talk, the officials are joined by Ernie Mills, a local radio commentator and longtime friend of State Police Chief Vigil, who has briefed him and driven him onto the grounds after the newsman got an early call about the riot. Mills is the vanguard of a crowd of reporters and anxious relatives who begin to gather before dawn outside the highway entrance to the prison reservation. Strung out along the narrow two-lane highway, the families and journalists can monitor on car scanners some of Montoya's talk with the rioters. Otherwise, they are told little. Griffin, now having been replaced by Rodriguez and effectively cut out of the decision-making, becomes by the usual bureaucratic logic official spokesman. His mixture of misinformation and ignorance, the product of his deliberate removal from developments, will plague the waiting crowd throughout the vigil. Griffin comes out to the highway to give a briefing just before daybreak, but he tells the media and relatives nothing they have not learned from the scanners. The onlookers can get a more accurate, and ominous, sense from what they see. SWAT teams, their weapons and orders cracking in the night, are assembled before the institution. The National Guard is setting up a command post just east of the pen in a corner of the parking lot near the highway, preparing a staging area for the arrival of troops. Whatever is going on inside, the hundred square yards in front of the prison is increasingly a mass of lights and sounds in the predawn cold, a battle that seems waiting to happen.

From six to seven o'clock, the radio negotiators jockey. Inmates ask for a doctor to treat injured guards, repeat demands for the media and the governor, propose Montoya's resignation, and threaten to "throw heads out" if the police rush them. No one knows it then, but they will soon have a head to throw out. Montoya refuses the doctor, asks for the release of wounded hostages, ignores the demands for a media parley and for his resignation, and plays for time. Dawn lights the sky with a pale glow and briefly dyes the few clouds with its ruddy tint. Inside, the floor of the cell blocks is already blood red, and the killing is beginning in earnest.

"I guess the penitentiary inmates know the operation better than we do," Bruce King will later tell reporters. "I guess the prisoners just acted before we did." Afterward the governor will keep a shard of the control center glass in his office as a reminder. "I guess the biggest contributing factor," he will say to reporters asking about the fragment, "was the architect and the construction guys putting that darn plate glass out there."

Then I, and you, and all of us fell down,
Whilst blood treason flourished over us.

Shakespeare, *Julius Caesar*

My son, God wants you to be a snitch.

Minister to inmate,
New Mexico State Penitentiary,
circa 1979

As I was going up the stair
I met a man who wasn't there.
He wasn't there again today.
I wish, I wish he'd stay away.

Hughes Mearns,
"The Little Man Who
Wasn't There"

hen two or more inmates gathered anywhere, Rodriguez would boast during his tenure as warden and afterward, half of them belonged to him. Snitching—informing in exchange for power, for revenge, for survival, for fear, occasionally even for justice, for most of the motives that drive men—was a way of life at the New Mexico pen. As the prison of the black and brown sixties became more difficult to govern, as the traditional guard reliance on old inmate "heavies" and prisoner subservience grew less effective, as the sheer veneer of the penitentiary wore through as a result of decay and overcrowding, the administration of the institution was suddenly laid bare. Its resort, like that of any regime losing its grip, was to the keeper's Faustian bargain: betrayal to ensure loyalty, disintegration to achieve stability.

The system began simply enough as the quest for information by insecure, isolated management, and inevitably fed on itself. Knowing no other way to command or simply to hold on, the pen's overseers became more and more dependent on the snitches' reports and less able to distinguish between the real and the fraudulent. As the power of the system grew, so, too, did the potential for its abuse. Inmates with enemies real and imagined could be sure that the prison's hated disciplinary committee would use a kite or whispered accusation as "confidential information" against which there would be no defense. "There isn't much said about the committee on the outside, but there isn't a prisoner who doesn't know about it," an experienced lawyer told a reporter after the riot. "The authorities call an inmate in, tell him there is an unnamed informant who said he committed a particular offense, and the inmate is then told to present any evidence he has in his own defense. The inmates are always found guilty. It's the prison's little court. The prisoner never wins and never learns who accuses him." It would be a description repeated and confirmed again and again by classification officers and other officials who watched the star chamber proceedings of the system over more than a decade. On the strength of such petty show trials, and often to the amusement of the officials passing judgment, men were variously thrown in solitary, given extended sentences, deprived of privileges both small and significant from mail to visits to enrollment in programs. Meanwhile, the informers were rewarded with favorable housing and classification, furlough, disciplinary leniency for the same offenses, canteen privileges, money, drugs, and even early parole. Not surprisingly, some traitors flourished and the victims, actual and potential, a vast majority of inmates, hated the system and its beneficiaries with a passion frequently unfathomable to outsiders.

But in reality the anonymity of the snitch was sacrosanct only for purposes of the accusation. An essence of the practice was that informants must be identifiable to some extent, that the infamous "snitch jacket" cast a visible aura. Officials could then threaten to label inmates as spies if they did *not* inform on fellow prisoners. Or venal guards and administrators might simply use the same coercion to extort cooperation in bribery, drug traffic, or other corruption. With the loathsomeness of the system and the often lethal consequences of having the "jacket," the threats produced a steady supply of more betrayal, more division and suspicion and murderous venom in inmate society, more dubious intelligence from agents who knew that invention served their purpose as well as reality—and that their largely uneducated handlers hardly knew the difference anyway.

Inquiries and testimony after the riot brimmed with examples of how this cutthroat management practice might work. In one case documented by the attorney general, an inmate was asked by a captain to provide information on drug supplies; when he refused, another man in the same unit gave the guard a list. When the cons on the list were swiftly thrown into maximum security, it was made obvious who supplied the names. The informant had his throat slashed in the riot. In another recorded history, an inmate was falsely accused of making home brew. When he denied it vehemently and refused to inform, he was thrown into segregation with another prisoner, whom friends then believed was named by the first inmate. The innocent man who would not spy for the administration was stabbed to death in the riot. In yet another variation, a new Anglo con was recruited to snitch, and because he refused, several Hispanic men in his unit were locked up amid the rumor that the young white had "snitched them off." Targeted to be stabbed in a mess hall line soon afterward, the Anglo escaped, and the case came to light only after he was caught and pleaded "duress" in fleeing the pen.

The viciousness of it all reached a climax in the sheer and common stupidity of officials who could not seem to protect the anonymity even of inmates they did not intend to betray, or who might be sources of legitimate prison intelligence. Typically, one guard captain left a note from an informant in his uniform shirt when it went to the pen laundry. The snitch was promptly identified and stabbed. One of Rodriguez's longtime informants, a respected con among the prison toughs (and the source of precise information on a post-riot inmate murder officials would ignore) would be code-named in pen files by his initials! Leaving little to the imagination of officials and inmate clerks who saw the memoranda, the security blunder soon made the man a target and forced his transfer to other prisons, placing his life in jeopardy for years to come and depriving the prison of authentic intelligence.

Snitches are not an inevitable disease of prison life. "People who have the most knowledge and who have been professionally trained in criminal behavior and penology don't use them," a former warden and corrections commissioner in other states told the *Santa Fe Reporter* after the riot. "It's more the amateur and the undertrained who have to resort to snitches. . . . They've always caused trouble, as far as I'm concerned." But in New Mexico the system flourished as the convict society's dread, frustration, and hate built toward 1980. On top of the usual rage of the caged was heaped the pervasive sense of treason and fear. And its fount, the visible leper colony of the contagion, would be there in the far northwestern lateral, along the tiers and behind the filthy, streaked windows of cell block 4. There the snitches were sent for protective custody when they were exposed or used up. There they were gathered, their curse nakedly exposed, their photos on the wall outside the unit color-coded in red, pink, and white to mark for all who passed their rank as informers and outcasts.

And there, too, were the other men, the weak or victimized or unjustly branded, or simply the mentally ill felons in a state with no proper facilities for their treatment save an already over-crowded, nepotism-riddled, and nightmarish asylum. But in the end the truth about the administration or about individual men would hardly matter. The faceless informer held the New Mexico pen together. Whether he snitched for protection or malice or conscience, whether he was himself betrayed by administrative stupidity or design, whether he was innocent, whether he was a snitch at all except in the fevered folklore of the corridors—he would be there at dawn on February 2 when they broke through at last. "The place always had an aura of death," said Dr. Warren Wilson, a psychologist who worked briefly at the pen and who knew some of the men in cell block 4. When it was over, the butchery seemed almost natural. At about a minute after seven that Saturday morning, the bars to the last grille at cell block 4 began to melt under the flame of the torch.

CARNAGE

We arrested them because they had nothing.
We jailed them because they threatened the
bounty of our existence. We forgot about
them because they had been banished from
our presence until they paid their debts
and learned our rules. When they complained,
our guardians protected us with billy clubs,
dungeons, tear gas, false testimony and bullets.
Some men died because they were black. Others
died because they were white. But that angered
the men more and they rose, like a brotherhood,
with one voice. Roaring from their cages, they
protested, damned us, and died. We stirred....

Finally, we realized *we* had killed them,
killed them all, and we cried.

Min S. Yee,
*The Melancholy History
of Soledad Prison*

the killing begins sometime after 3:00 A.M. in the basement of cell block 3. As the hostages and their convict captors look on, a group of rioters comes down armed with steel pipes; they gather in front of cell 67. "We got to kill this son of a bitch, man," one of them announces to a con watching the hostages, pointing to a trembling inmate inside the cell. "He's a snitch." The con tries to argue, but he's outnumbered. "No, fuck it," the executioner says, and they start unlocking the cell from the front control panel. They go in swinging the pipes, and there is the thud of heavy metal on flesh and a shrieking Spanish voice reverberating through the cell block out into the corridor until scores of men hear it in distant corners of the wing. *"No era yo....No lo hice"* ("It wasn't me....I didn't do it"), an eyewitness remembers him "screaming and screaming and screaming." Then suddenly a tower guard is flashing his searchlight toward the screams in the basement, Deputy Warden Montoya is talking on the radio about "staying cool," and the men watching the hostage officers there are worried the tower guard may start "popping caps," may shoot toward the basement. A con tells the attackers the tower guard is "going crazy," and they leave the cell and stand a few feet outside, away from the window.

Inside cell 67, the beaten man is still whimpering, "I didn't hurt nobody, man. I didn't snitch on nobody, man." In moments the attackers come back into the cell again, begin the beating once more, and the tower light plays back and forth across the walls and floor of the basement, searching for the source of the screams that are now trailing off. The beaten man pleads for help from a nearby con, but he turns and walks away, scared the men with the pipes will assault him if he intervenes. But again, other cons in the basement tell them to stop the beating before the tower starts shooting; they emerge from the cell for another pause and seem to leave the basement. A few minutes pass. Then one of the attackers comes back and asks around the basement for a shank to finish off the job. No one gives him a knife, but one drugged onlooker holds up a pair of scissors, dangling them in a wordless offer. He takes the scissors, goes into the cell one last time, and comes out with blood on his hands. He grabs a towel from a nearby cell, tries to wipe the blood away, curses when it won't come off on the dry crusty cloth, and leaves.

This first casualty of the pen's self-mutilation takes with him apt symbolism. He is a young thief from a superstitious northern New Mexico village renowned for its apples, red chiles, and a lovely old hacienda restaurant celebrated by tourists and the *New York Times*. He has escaped the Rio Arriba County sheriff so many times that some of the villagers think he changes himself into a dog to get through the cordon. He is called the Dog Boy of Chimayó, but Anglos and outsiders scoff at the tale. Later, his body will be dragged out the entrance to tower 1 and eventually driven away in an ambulance. There are several police dogs in patrol cars drawn up along the road to the pen. As the ambulance with the Dog Boy passes, the police dogs, disciplined and quiet at every other coming or going, begin to howl. Their handlers have difficulty calming them.

Back in the basement of cell block 3, the hostage guards are now huddled together in new fear at the reality of what is happening. In a segregation cell nearby, yet another accused snitch is beaten and stabbed to death amid screams that end in a sudden, final silence. Minutes after that, there is the dull champagne-cork popping sound of a teargas launcher fired close to a convict's head in another cell on the lower tier of the block. The official inquiry will call it simply "head trauma." But now in cell 12, it is not so tidy. The air is choking with gas, and the man's forehead and one of his eyes no longer exist. They had derisively called him

Pancho Villa; he was a Mexican national who had been involved in fights and was obviously in need of psychiatric care. The victim has appealed for help to the Mexican Consul in Albuquerque, and the consul has written the pen. Orner has replied that the man is dangerous, that he has visions of the devil and Jesus Christ, and that officials are "endeavoring" to transfer him to the state mental hospital. Later there will be a dispute about whether Orner's letter was written before or after the riot, but the psychologist is cleared of any manipulation of the record. It scarcely matters; there are no adequate facilities for such men at either the pen or the hospital. He dies now, in the middle of this February night, because his illness brought him to one fight too many, because he is different. His last vision is of the barrel of the teargas launcher, point-blank.

Meanwhile, like a Bosch or Bruegel panorama, now terrible, now pedestrian, the riot unfolds in feverish, contrasting little scenes, often close by yet strangely sealed off from one another. As the murder is being done in fitful cadence in cell 67, several inmates are using cell 65 to have sex with one man, and one of those among the attackers has a "kid," or punk, in number 63, to whom he returns to speak soothingly during the execution. The hostage guards are being reassured, too, by their captors that no harm will come to them, despite the mounting violence. They are still terrified. For a while, when he is first brought down, the wounded Hernandez is thrown into the cell with the murdered Dog Boy. In the crowded hallway outside cell block 3 men are roaming back and forth, watching the progress of the blowtorch eating away at the grille that protects cell block 4 and all the supposed snitches. The convicts keep drifting in and out of 3 and cell block 6 directly across the corridor. Almost everyone now, at nearly four in the morning, is armed; most are consciously traveling in pairs. The murders in 3 have communicated themselves throughout the prison. There is a growing sense that the riot will go on for hours, perhaps days. They are still bound up inside this institution, surrounded by guns and tower lights, or so they imagine, yet they are also free here inside with their rage and their scores to settle. Men begin to put on improvised masks when they leave their units.

The violence is both random and planned. As two convicts walk along the north wing, they meet another with a kerchief about his face. One of the pair watches the lone man's eyes intently, then lunges at him to strip away the bandanna. Recognizing an old enemy, he chases the fleeing inmate back up the corridor, beating him with an iron rod torn from one of the beds.

Down in the south wing, where it all began little more than two hours ago, there are still inmates around the barricaded entrance to E-1 with its frightened young men inside. One of those at the door is from B-1 across the hall. He has a punk in E-1, a kid he sends coffee and cigarettes to and talks to as they lean against the grilles of the facing units, a lover he protects and keeps in return for sex. Earlier in the night, a passing con sees this man in bed with yet another young inmate. But now, in the minutes before dawn, he tries to help his lover and others in E-1 by slipping a wrench through a broken window to enable them to break a hole in the dayroom and flee into the yard. He gets the wrench in after waiting patiently for his chance, but he has lingered too long. He, too, is known as a snitch—to some of his enemies as the King of the Snitches—and he has already come close to death for his involvement with the pen's savage narcotics trade. Now several men have come for him, and they know where he will be. They find him in the corridor between B and E, beat him with pipes as he screams for mercy—"I didn't do it, I didn't do it"—and then begin to use a Phillips screwdriver. Afterward they drag him down near the control center, an eyeless corpse with fifty stab wounds. As he dies, the frantic residents in E-1 are using the wrench to smash a window and pry a hole large enough to escape. The young men, eighty-four of them, get out at dawn and are taken back into custody by authorities in the yard, the first inmate defectors from the riot.

At daybreak, too, the men are nearly through the grille at cell block 4. The murder and atrocity are about to begin in earnest.

There are ninety-six men in cell block 4 tonight. Some are parole violators recently returned to the pen. Some are said to be there for failing to pay kickbacks to guards. Some traffic in narcotics. A few have killed or molested children.

Most are weak or physically frail, or mentally ill. Many are there by accident. A handful are genuine snitches or informers. But all wear the bluish green coveralls that bear the Cain's stencil mark, SEG, that will make them fair game. "Before the riot started we knew all about it, where it was going to start and everything, and that they had sent word down there that they were going [to] go ahead and kill us all," one inmate from cell block 4 will explain afterward. It is unlikely that the outcasts of the protective unit are more aware of the coming riot than others, but they are no less so. For months they have seen the kites like everyone else, and know they are in danger of being slaughtered. Now, as dawn lights the sky, the segregated inmates have been watching and listening for hours as the riot crashes around them, breaking only against the jammed grille at the cell block entrance. Those on the south side of 4 have looked through barred windows across the small yard and seen the hard cons of cell block 3 released from their cells. They have heard on their radios the first news bulletins about the revolt. Worst of all, they can hear the sickly hiss of the acetylene cutting torch gnawing at the grille bars.

Still, for a time they believe that the riot will soon be quelled, that they are safe behind the grille. At three-thirty or four, some men begin to call for guards. But there are none. The officers in the north wing have long ago fled the cell block to be captured elsewhere or to hide in the basement crawl space. The guards have locked the corridor grille leading to 4 and 5, but that is opened soon after the control center falls. But, unlike the prisoners in E-1, the men in 4 are still closed in their cells. They cannot defend themselves, cannot barricade the entry or flee. They have been left caged and alone as their predators come for them. Then, suddenly, at about 4:00 A.M. the inmates in 4, still locked in their cells and hearing the constant whisper of the torch, become aware of headlights all about the outside perimeter. State Police cars and other patrol vehicles are pulling up along the fence outside. The trapped men in the cell block begin to flash SOS with lights and to yell, "Hey, they're cutting into...they're killing motherfuckers, man! Do something! Get the cops in here!" One of the inmates there would remember the moment bitterly in later testimony: "I mean all the state troopers that were parked all up and down the fence, man. You could see them driving inside the sally port, you know. Why didn't they come in? The back door was right there."

The back door is indeed "right there." On the far northwest side, an exterior entrance to cell block 4 lets out onto the yard and into a vestibule and stairway leading to the tiers of cells on both sides of the block. The outside entryway is a mirror image of the interior area where impatient murderers are now melting the bars. Grilles separate the vestibule from the catwalks, but there is a clear line of vision, or fire, from the outside grilles down the tiers to the interior grilles through which the rioters must enter. The riot-control plan—the plan officials have difficulty finding before tonight but that convicts mail out of the pen—requires that there be in tower 1 emergency duplicate keys to every part of the institution, so that even if all keys and the control center are seized, as they are now, officials can still have access to the pen. But tonight, typically, the emergency set of keys in tower 1, like the arsenal similarly stored there, is not complete. There is a key to the outside door, yet none to the grilles that lead to the cell area.

At that, however, the police gathering outside might still act. There are acetylene torches elsewhere on the pen grounds that can be used to open the exterior grilles. There are penitentiary locksmiths who might be summoned. One locksmith, in fact, will free inmates still closed in their cells after the riot. And even if the grilles remain closed, once inside the vestibule the troopers might command a field of fire straight down the catwalks and warn off anyone storming the unit. In the inquiry that follows, penitentiary officials will say they dare not allow such an entry for fear of what may happen to hostage guards, and that in any case they assumed the prison was completely in the rioters' hands. Yet for three hours, from 4:00 to 7:00 A.M., the men in cell block 4 signal frantically that they are still closed in and are in mortal peril. During those hours, the attackers with the torch methodically burn away and roll replacement fuel up the corridor to feed the blue flame. All the while, radio transmissions between the rioters and the outside make clear that the capture of cell block 4 is to be a massacre.

Afterward, an investigator for the attorney general's inquiry will be convinced that police could have entered the outer end of the cell block, held off the mob, and saved lives. But it will all be academic. At the end of a long train of neglect and negligence that has led to this instant, the last betrayal at the outer door to cell block 4 seems somehow inevitable. As inmates on the radio taunt the pen administrators with the imminent fate of their snitches, one older con listening nearby hears an official's voice remark of the men in 4, "It's their ass."

In the moments before the sun breaks the rim of the Sangre de Cristos, the men at the grille begin to yell into cell block 4 that they are almost through. They shout the names of their victims. Desperately, the men in 4 try to barricade their cells with their metal bunks. Some try, pathetically, to tie their bars shut with towels and blankets. Among the last sights and sounds men will remember before the onslaught are of inmates trying to chew or tear apart their dingy linens and gray prison blankets. Some are mute and limp with fear, and shrink to the back wall of the cell between the sink and toilet, where they will be found cringing. One young inmate reaches for a Bible and begins to read aloud.

Then at last, the sun streaking the walls, the killers are past the grille. "They came in hollering, you know, for certain motherfuckers that they were gonna..." one resident of 4 would remember. "And they came in crazy." Many of the attackers are masked somehow with stocking caps, bandannas, pillow cases, making their onslaught an even more spectral, sinister sight. There will be memories and accounts of an organized "execution squad" of seven or eight assassins, and similar tales of a wild horde of merciless killers. But most come in small groups of three or four men, men who stick together for their own protection, men with scores to settle who have lined up early at cell block 4.

Now, though they are through the entry grille, the control panel for unlocking the individual cell doors must still be torched open. And while some work on the panel, others run from cell to cell along the tiers looking for victims. When they find their prey, they stand there with knives and pipes and various other weapons and tell the man he is about to die. Even when the control panel is open, however, several cells remain jammed or barricaded shut. For some, the killers will wait patiently for as long as thirty minutes while they burn open the door. The delays will make a mockery of many of the later prosecution witnesses to such murders. In what follows, in the mounting chaos and horror, no one will stand around watching when they finally torch into a cell.

One of the first cells they open is on the second tier of the north side. "You son of a bitch, you'll never tell on me again," one of the killers says to the young inmate inside. He has a minute to beg for his life, and as the door grinds open they rush in swinging pipes. They beat him to death on the floor of the cell, kick the lifeless body, and eventually one drags it out, picks it up in raging strength, and hurls it over the railing of the tier to the cell block basement two stories below. One of the killers then runs back across the tier catwalk and plunges down the stairs following the body. When he finds it, he looks around, sees a shovel nearby in a maintenance area, and digs the shovel into the corpse, cutting off its genitalia. At the same moment, another inmate is being pitched over the tier above. But the man's neck is tied with a long rope, and his body snaps to a stop in the air above the basement, his neck broken instantly and his head nearly severed by the force of the plunge. This time the killers haul the contorted hanged man back up to the tier, where they slash the corpse with knives.

Impatient when some doors do not open right away the rioters at a few cells throw flammable liquids through the bars and onto their victims. Then they throw matches or shoot the blowtorch to ignite the screaming men. One cell goes up in flames, becomes an oven in which the remains will be a charred, blackened miniature of the man who lived there. In the next cell they cut a large hole in the door and come through one by one, stripping and holding the prisoner down for the last killer, who comes through with an acetylene canister. Outside, a prison official hears a whistling sound from 4, scans the block with binoculars, stops on an incredible scene through a window, and watches in horror as four or five inmates hold a man down as another burns his head and face with a blowtorch. When his eyes explode out of the back of his head, the inmates burn his groin, then mutilate the body with shanks, and torch him again. When they are through, one seared corpse, a man who weighed over 200 pounds, will weigh less than 50.

The killing ground is everywhere, on the tier catwalk, in the cells, on the stairs. Thick paths of smeared blood lead from the toilets and sinks where they have clung to the back wall, out through the shredded paper and pillow ticking and toilet paper and blankets on the floor. One man is let out unintentionally by another who is trying to open an adjacent cell, and he runs frantically down the catwalk. His killers see him from another tier, and there follows a strange cat-and-mouse game—north side to south, upper tier to middle to basement. Finally they trap him in a back corner of the block and bash him with pipes, his blood, as a fleeing eye-witness will remember the scene, "splattering all over." They find another man in a cell block washroom, and bludgeon and slash him there. They hack and incinerate a convicted child molester, a loathed untouchable at the bottom of prison castes. They kill one man, then drive a metal bar through his ears. In another cell they fire the teargas gun again point-blank. A body is heaved off the tier, bounces near a terrified inmate, and is then carefully wrapped in newspapers on the block floor and set afire.

Few men try to defend themselves. Most have no hope against the odds. As one man waits nearly a half-hour for his seven attackers to burn through the cell door, he sits quietly on his toilet. He has ripped the metal plate off his ventilation duct, and he holds it in the sink. When they come in, he swings it back and forth, holding them off for a while, hitting one in the face and sending him howling back out of the cell. But it is soon over. They catch him with a pipe. Stunned, he reels, and an attacker comes forward with a hammer and strikes his temple. He falls back, hitting the toilet with his head. For a moment he regains consciousness as they are bending over him with a torch. He screams. "I could smell it, man," an inmate witness will later tell the State Police. "They were burning him."

A few feet away, they cut and kill a mentally ill black man who usually lies on the cold block floor naked and who this morning is standing there, bewildered, as they come into his cell. They take turns beating him. Then they drag in another cell block 4 inmate and tell him he can save his own life by killing the "nigger." Then they cut off the dead man's head. Someone comes along in the madness, picks up the severed head, and carries it about on the end of a rod as a fetish of the slaughter. At one point, inmates brandish the head before the hostage guards in the basement of cell block 3. Later this grisly trophy is stuck on a little yellow maintenance cart used for repairing ceiling lights, the eyes, as one passing convict would remember, "kind of like [shut] half mast." And then, somehow, the head is returned to the original owner, placed between the legs of the corpse as it is eventually taken out the front gate.

Execution is by ax and rope, electric drill, and torch and sander. Witnesses describe one rioter walking through the carnage wantonly hitting victims with a large heavy paddle stirrer from the kitchen. By their account, he finds one young inmate lying in blood on the floor but still alive and cowering to avoid the debris falling from the tiers. He swings the paddle like a golf club, striking the wounded boy in the back of the head and raising his whole body off the pavement.

On foreheads and chests of some of the dead they carve "RATA," and on others they cut whisker-shaped gashes, the marks of the rat. As the murders accumulate, the killing takes on its own momentum. "Anybody here you don't like," says one con, inviting another to name a victim. And the slaughter comes in waves. First the rush through the torched grille, the old, long-sought vengeance. Then there is a second tide of torture and death, and men are killed less because of festering purpose than merely because they are there or are remembered for some actual or imagined offense or are mistaken for someone else. Some killers take their time. One has sex in a nearby cell block, hears the cries of terror, gets up from his bed, and walks over to 4 to join the rampage.

Meanwhile, in the bedlam, with men screaming and shrieking and cursing and dying, cell block 4 is like a battlefield of some great military disaster where men's fortunes are hauntingly random. Some intended victims shrewdly mask themselves, take up weapons, and follow in the wake of the roving gangs until they can slip out. A young Hispanic saves his own life only by agreeing to have sex with a black gang that offers its protection in return. Afterward, he hates his assailants but owes them a debt of gratitude. "Those niggers saved my life," he tells a Los Angeles newspaper. Others wander, dazed, in and out of the butchery without attracting notice or assault. One man carries a crucifix, holds it through the day, and then loses it the next night in an escape. A few inmates remain in their cells, paralyzed with terror and yet untouched, to be found there, quaking, thirty hours later amid the ghastly wreckage. There is no pattern to such fate. One resident is spared when attackers finally give up trying to open his cell, which he has not barricaded but which has simply failed to open from the control panel. Other inmates who have fortified or disguised or armed themselves are annihilated just the same.

The relatively few blacks in the prison band together, as they commonly do, and manage to rescue most of their brothers from cell block 4, in part by luck, in part by a rough bargain struck with Anglo and Hispanic leaders in the corridor before the entry grille is burned apart. But the escape is narrow. Some blacks must be dragged out to be saved. Another from cell block 6 walks about wrapped in an American flag he has found in the corridor, as if to ward off attack. "You mean, Stars and Stripes?" the State Police ask him incredulously when he tells the story afterward. "Stars and Stripes," he replies.

And the investigator says again in disbelief, "Our American flag?" As though the inmate should not have worn *that* flag. In their evacuation, the blacks make a deliberate decision to leave the severely disturbed man in 4 in his cell, reasoning that he will be safer locked up than wandering the corridors. But soon after they decide to leave him in that refuge, he is wantonly butchered.

Incredibly, while his fellow inmates in cell block 4 are being overrun and murdered, one resident will remember taking pictures of the killing with a Polaroid camera a friend has brought into the cell block from the administrative offices. According to his account, he and his friend stood there amid the wild savagery, snapping photos of each other, eagerly watching them slide from the camera and slowly take form, occasionally focusing on a murder in a nearby cell. Months later, almost inadvertently, he tells investigators about the photographs, but the pictures have somehow disappeared like so much other evidence of the riot. Though officials know there are cameras and film in the pen, they have by then decided on the targets of their indictments and do not seem eager to discover any new evidence that might complicate matters.

Minutes before eight o'clock, less than an hour after they have broken in, the killing abruptly ends in cell block 4. The stream of refugees flows down the main corridor, past the demolished control center, and into the front halls of the prison, from which the hunted men will eventually escape into the raw gray morning. "We hid everywhere we could," one will remember. Behind, in the cell block, there is the odor of seared flesh and of the feces of crazed men, and everywhere the broad smears of blood, spilled and worked into the floor almost like the paints on an artist's palette. Here and there a ravaged victim is still breathing as men leave. One corpse suddenly quivers and sits up in a death spasm, and lingering killers are chilled by the omen and beat it down. For months to come, old inmates and new will feel ghosts in 4, describe pockets of chill air and sounds in their cells at dawn. They have murdered thirteen men in the cell block, including one who has come there, or been brought there, from dormitory A at the other end of the pen. And the carnage is not over.

Elsewhere, over the next few hours, there is another wave of killing, some of it undoubtedly racist, some retributive, some vengeful and provoked by acts committed during the riot itself, some utterly senseless. Six men from F-1 are variously beaten, stabbed, and blowtorched, and they are splayed up and down the central and south wings. One is dumped in the Catholic chapel, his blood staining a crumpled silhouette into the floor. In dormitory B-1, known as the unit for the "screw-ups," perhaps the least popular place after cell block 4, three men are stabbed and burned, including two brothers and the inmate who is trying to protect his kid in E-1. Three more young inmates from dormitory A have their skulls crushed. Predators now seek out their prey as they did in cell block 4. They find one young Anglo in his bunk in cell house 1, passed out, perhaps from drugs. They bludgeon him with a shovel and later drag the body to the gym where it is cremated almost beyond recognition in a pile of corpses. A Hispanic the same age is alone in the far south dormitory D when they come in. His crushed head and shredded torso are left in the corridor adjacent to the prison classrooms. Two men get out of cell block 3, roam the halls for a time, eventually meet the wrong people, and are slashed to death or shot with a teargas gun. One is heaped on the pyre in the gymnasium, the other thrown into the officers' mess. A nightmare come true, after dawn there is for a time a kangaroo court in the gym where judges in gauze masks tied with shoelaces hand down their verdicts. A few men brought before them miraculously talk or bargain their way out. Most will be among the dead. An Indian from cell house 6 is burned to death at the other end of the pen. One slight Spanish man perishes of smoke inhalation as he tries to rescue others. Scores of men will barely escape—beaten, stabbed, tortured, one of them hacked with a meat cleaver.

And everywhere, north to south, bodies are mutilated, the killing and rage continuing long after men are lifeless. As an afterthought, they break the fingers of one hand on an already burned, dismembered body. Several corpses are mutilated, then sodomized, the torsos left at grotesque angles. As if the torches and pipes and teargas guns are not enough, some convicts this morning even search the gas chamber under cell block 5 for stored cyanide or acid. They come close to the hiding guards, Martinez and Vigil, but are distracted by their search for some more effective means of killing. When the murders are done, there will be wildly conflicting accounts of how many have died. Convict counts verge on fifty. Inmates whose testimony indicts fellow prisoners tell of bodies in the laundry, on a meat hook, in an oven— bodies where none is officially discovered. Yet there is no further investigation of the reports. The chaotic accounting of survivors during the ensuing days and weeks marks the beginning of unanswered questions about the actual number of those killed in the New Mexico riot.

Afterward, however, the toll for families will be vivid in the plight of individual men. Robert Quintela is one of those found in F-1. At twenty-nine, a natural artist, he is in prison for burglary; although he has tried once to escape, he is eligible for parole in the spring. The day before the riot he has mailed his parents a colored pencil sketch on a linen handkerchief. It shows Jesus nailed to a cross, engulfed in flames, with a grieving woman at his feet. A bar with the word "*pecado*" (sin) blocks the gate to heaven. Mario Urioste, twenty-eight, is the son of a former guard at the pen. Arrested often for drunkenness, he is not a violent offender. He has pleaded guilty to shoplifting clothes, record albums, and two fishing rods, and to receiving twenty-seven stolen shirts. The sentencing judge has ordered him confined to a minimum-security facility, but no space is available. He goes to the pen, where he is molested and beaten; he weighs barely 90 pounds when his family sees him last. He is in cell block 4 when the grille gives way. "They can't kill me in here," twenty-three-year-old Donald Gossens has written his family on January 31. Convicted on a drug charge, he is due for parole in August. Gossens, too, is in cell block 4, where he is one of the first to die. "I feel like he's gone to a better place," his mother tells the Associated Press the week after his murder.

James Foley passes his nineteenth birthday in cell block 4 in January. His cellmate does all the chores that day—"it was his day," the fellow prisoner recalls later—and Foley begins to read the Bible. "He just kept reading and reading it....I noticed a definite change in his attitude," the cellmate will tell a reporter. Two days before the riot, Foley is transferred to A-1. His cellmate survives the carnage of 4, but the rioters find Foley in the south wing and crush his skull. The Ortega family of Las Vegas, New Mexico, the father a disabled World War II veteran, loses two sons in the riot. Filberto and Frank Ortega are twenty-five and twenty, one eligible for release in September, the other for parole in October. Frank has complained to his parents about the lax security at the pen. "He said somebody could get killed before the authorities would do anything about it," Eliza Ortega says of her son after his slashed body has been carried from B-1. Frankie Sedillo is thirty and older than most of the victims. Jailed on a burglary charge, he has spent part of his youth in a reformatory and six vain months in the state mental hospital. He dies of carbon monoxide poisoning in the smoke of cell house 6. "I think they just put men in there and forgot them," his mother says later.

The inmates come, too, for Paulina Paul, the thirty-six-year-old black man who lies naked on the cement floor of his cell in 4, sometimes moaning, sometimes crying, "Get back, Gentile!" at passing white inmates. According to press accounts, one of his brothers gunned down five fellow American soldiers in a Saigon theater; another shot a policeman; his sister has been convicted of murdering her three-year-old infant. Paul robbed a motel in Alamogordo ten years ago. At his trial he howled "loud animal-type noises," as one witness described it, and leaped up to mutter religious incantations at the court. He is one of the half-dozen murder victims this morning who belong in psychiatric care. Paul is desperately ill and cruelly neglected, his plight a metaphor of the penitentiary at large, his head, with the heavy-lidded, quizzical expression molded forever on the face, a trophy of the massacre. And he will be betrayed to the end. In large part because of the state's bungling, his murder, perhaps the most witnessed and cold-blooded of the entire riot, will go unprosecuted.

And in cell house 1, the rioters have come to crush the life out of Tom O'Meara, a twenty-five-year-old blond convict who is still another of the pen's tragedies. On his way to Santa Fe, O'Meara has left a trail of robbery, assault, and escape. He has done time from Missouri to New Mexico. But his sister Kathleen is a probation officer back in Maryland, and with her encouragement and the support of friends and teachers he begins slowly in the hell of Santa Fe to reclaim his life. He studies, counsels others on making parole and succeeding on the outside. "If I can get you out of here, my life will have been worth something," he tells a friend a few weeks before the riot. O'Meara has consistently defied the prison regime and lately has tried to warn female employees about the coming violence. For his compassion he has been given a snitch jacket by officials. During the first few hours of the night, sensing the danger to him, friends try to guard O'Meara as he lies in his bunk sleeping off drugs. But they are gone when a gang of killers with shovels searches him out in the honor unit. Perhaps the most political, the most "administrative" of riot murders, Tom O'Meara's, too, will go unprosecuted. Afterward, his body reduced to ash and a few charred bones in the gym, his sister will fly to Santa Fe to ask why her brother had to die. And from the state once charged to keep him and now to find his killers, there will be no answer.

"There's a lot of people that did a lot of things in that whole riot that didn't make any sense," an inmate testifies to the post-riot inquiry. "Good people were killed and people that didn't have a meaning to be killed were killed. That's what the waste is."

Of the thirty-three officially counted dead, twenty-four are Hispanic, seven Anglo, one black, and one Indian. Though the prosecution will finger far fewer and bring to trial only a handful, eyewitness accounts will implicate over fifty-seven men—Hispanic, Anglo, and black alike—in the thirty-three murders and will name nine men in four or more killings.

Official explanations of the castrophe will be eloquent. Drugs will be blamed for the murders, yet it is clear, too, that sober men stood in line outside cell block 4. Narcotics trafficking accounts for some of the hate and revenge, but drugs also blunt and blur the minds of those who would kill more men otherwise. "If it hadn't been for the drugs," one convict negotiator will say, "every inmate in cell block four would have been dead." Yet another veteran of the riot will add, "If I was an inmate in cell block four, I would have been glad they found those drugs. The drugs saved their lives." It will be said that there are mutilations because no strong convict organizations exist, or that organizations and racial gangs feed the hate that leads to mutilation. Some will say that the Hispanic gangs took care of their enemies and left the most wanton slaughter to the brutal Anglos. Others will say that the Anglos of the Aryan Brotherhood killed to assert their status in a predominantly Spanish institution. Still others will insist that such groups do not exist, or that they play no real role and should not be given too much credit, whatever happened.

"To me a human life is the most precious commodity we have and I place no man's life above anybody else's," Rodriguez is quoted as saying later. "In fact I knew some of the people that got killed. I had known them for years. When I found out who had been killed, it was very hard for me."

Psychologist Orner would observe, "The depth of the

violence is incomprehensible to me both as a human being and as a psychologist."

As the bodies are later carried from the pen, a Santa Fe district attorney will mutter to a reporter, "They're just a bunch of fucking animals."

"The fact that nobody was killed in this major uprising," a prominent legislator says three days after the riot, "is certainly a credit to the governor of the state of New Mexico."

"They killed twelve of my people," a guard who works in cell block 4 will remark months later. He will be talking not of the rioters, but of the administration.

The trap having been sprung as scheduled for
the Delgadillo execution, Elfego Baca stationed
himself near the attending physician, busily
engaged at the time counting the murmurs and
pulsations of Delgadillo's heartbeat. The physician
whispered the results of his findings to Elfego,
who then anounced: "Gentlemen, the official time
is three minutes and sixteen seconds," speaking
grimly through clenched teeth. He continued,
"Gentlemen, this is one of the nicest hangings
I have ever seen. Everything went off beautifully."

William H. Keleher,
A New Mexico Item,
Memoirs 1892–1969.

... but if the efficiency of the prison in correcting
prisoners is yet doubtful, its power of depraving them
still more is known because experience proves it.

Alexis de Tocqueville

following the riot, a Justice Department study found the New Mexico pen, according to a summary, "one of the harshest, most punitive prison environments in the nation." This conclusion came as no surprise to the men who had been there for the last decade or more, on both sides of the bars. If the administrative method of the penitentiary regime was treachery, its moral was punishment, its ethos violence, its habit indifference to suffering.

The history of the Santa Fe pen was a steady drumbeat of brutality, of which the riot, however more ghastly and intense, would become an almost natural extension. In 1971 a minor disturbance was put down by forcing prisoners to run a gauntlet of ax-handle-wielding guards. Scores of men were left bleeding and injured. In the autumn of 1975 a College of Santa Fe professor teaching a creative writing class at the pen submitted some of the poems and drawings of his students to a local paper, the *Santa Fe Reporter*. Headlined "Voices behind Walls," the collection appeared with a convict's sketch of a giant eagle holding a mouse in its beak with the penitentiary in the foreground. Enraged prison officials threw the artist in the strip cell hole beneath cell block 3, where, he recalled years later, guards beat his testicles with a rubber mallet.

Bare windowless 6-by-9-foot cells, unventilated in summer, unheated in winter, the ten holes of the New Mexico state pen were used commonly in the sixties and seventies, save for a brief period when they were closed by Warden J. E. Baker, who was soon ousted by the legislature. According to successive waves of men who suffered there, the naked convicts were allowed only a filthy, threadbare blanket, a toothbrush, a metal cup, and a single roll of toilet paper. Guards threw in a thin mattress at night and took it away at dawn. Running water from a single spigot was turned on only three times daily for a few moments. Meals came once every three days. Light pierced the prisoners' darkness only when officials opened the steel flap over the small window in the door, no more than once or twice a day. The toilet was a small, lidless opening in the floor, flushed from the outside at the whim of the guards. Beatings, even attempted murder with guards carrying their own braided blankets to make it look like suicide, were said to be frequent. Men remembered their own stench from the open cesspool as clearly as they recalled the assaults and isolation and hunger. Appropriately, two of the cells were padded, for those who broke under the multiple agonies. It was apt, too, that these modern dungeons were just off death row at the Santa Fe pen. "Being in the hole," wrote one convict, "could make a man wish he were dead."

When some inmates filed federal suits aginst such medieval mistreatment, they were threatened with indefinite solitary confinement or, in one recorded case, with violence against the prisoner's family. "The only reason I got out of the hole was that I agreed to drop the civil rights action," convicted murderer Barry Courtright told reporters almost a decade later. "I used to sleep on the floor," he remembered of his time in the hole, "surrounded by a little dike made of toilet paper to keep out the sewage that dripped down through the ceiling." By his account, Courtright sent repeated letters to the Santa Fe grand jury about his plight and finally got a response after he enclosed in one smuggled envelope a live cockroach. When the grand jury representatives came to visit the basement of cell block 3, however, officials had been tipped off and had hurriedly cleaned and clothed Courtright and moved him to an upstairs cell.

According to several eyewitness reports, brutality was by no means limited to cell block 3 and its hard cases. In the early seventies, a prison hospital administrator watched in horror as a senior officer strode into cell block 5, singled out a young redhaired Hispanic inmate as an example, took him to a nearby guard's station, and jammed his index finger more than once into the inmate's eye socket. In July 1976, following a work strike and damage to dormitory furniture, cons from E-2 were stripped naked and run nearly a hundred yards down the central corridor through another gauntlet of officials, who beat them with the ubiquitous ax handles. Called "the night of the ax handles," the incident was corroborated by several eyewitnesses, including some officials themselves, and resulted in serious injuries as well as a federal lawsuit, still pending in 1982, naming a deputy warden and a senior guard captain among the assailants. Both men would deny the allegations and would remain securely in their positions following the bloody reprisal. Nor was the reign of violence always direct or in the open. Inmate goons, or enforcers, were often bribed or forced to intimidate other prisoners. Violence by proxy was commonplace both behind the walls and outside where inmate families faced threats, vandalism, or worse when their sons or husbands somehow challenged the regime.

New Mexico did not carry out a legal execution after 1960, yet the system retained its own form of capital punishment. Between 1968 and 1977, in addition to several murders, seven inmate deaths were listed as suicides. Most of those incidents were suspicious; many more suicide attempts were unsuccessful; and a number of men tried to kill themselves in the eighteen months before the riot. Before the prisoners were murdering and castrating one another with what officials regarded as such puzzling abandon on the weekend of February 2–3, 1980, they could be condemned to death by official abuse and negligence. In the autumn of 1978 Ronald Thompson, a black inmate, was recommended for transfer from the pen for safekeeping by both the Santa Fe district attorney and a district judge. Because he was a witness to a pen murder and had also testified about official misconduct, Thompson's life was "in danger every minute he is at the penitentiary," as the judge wrote the warden. In January 1979 orders were posted outside Thompson's cell block that he was never to leave his cell unescorted and in particular was never to shower with other inmates. On February 16 a guard ordered Thompson to shower with a group, and in minutes his throat was slashed three times from ear to ear. Despite being then thrown into a disciplinary cell and given minimal medical treatment, he managed to survive and was finally moved from the prison by court order. Nearly three years later, the state avoided a public trial by settling a Thompson lawsuit out of court for $40,000, with no independent investigation of the official negligence or subsequent cover-up in the cutthroat near-murder.

For those who survived the beatings, the strip cells, and the attempted assassinations, there remained other assorted tortures of penitentiary life at Santa Fe. Prison records showed that in 1978–79 mentally ill inmates were often immobilized in grotesque plaster body casts with holes that allowed them to urinate and defecate.

Even if they were not put in casts, the 10 percent of inmates who were psychologically disturbed—hundreds of men over the course of a decade—rarely received more healing treatment. In their torment, they were left to gouge at themselves or at fellow prisoners. Between June 1978 and May 1979, an investigation by the *Albuquerque Journal* revealed, there were twenty-six self-mutilations. And over a longer period, psychotic prisoners were perpetrators of or victims in nearly half the violent incidents inside the penitentiary. A *Journal* reporter, Craig Pyes, described vividly the plight of the mentally ill prisoner: "Raving lunatics screaming behind bars. Inmates with unfocused eyes who never spoke a word. Self mutilators doing radical surgery on their bodies with razor blades, and friends who give them razor blades to do it." The officially sanctioned barbarity went on in defiance of several court orders in a prison that was minutes away from the courts. "Everybody knew the problems were there," said a New York psychiatrist called in by the ACLU to examine pen records after the riot. "Everybody, all the way up to the governor."

Medical or dental ailments received little better care. In one case, old and ineffective spinal anesthetic was administered to an inmate undergoing surgery at the prison hospital. When the incision was made, the patient sprang off the operating table, wild with pain. Guards were called to hold him down, and the surgery continued with only partial local anesthetic. Similarly, inmates told of tooth extractions without anesthesia. A dental assistant saw one convict bolt from the dental chair in agony and collapse on the floor. Medication, though ostensibly provided by the prison pharmacy free to those in need, was said to be a major item on the pen's active black market. Pain killers for bad teeth or migraine headaches, if the sufferer was desperate enough, sometimes went for ten dollars a capsule in the years just before the riot.

But for many men incarcerated at Santa Fe, the institution's worst abuses were the daily psychological torments—the furloughs granted and then canceled at the last moment by guard captains, the ever-present danger of rape or coercion or theft by pen toughs whom guards gave free rein, the "loss" of personal belongings, the denial of canteen privileges for no reason, the score of small punishments that loomed so large for men caged away. Years later men remembered with tears of rage how guards taunted them by reading personal mail from loved ones, promising to sleep with a convict's wife or sister on the outside, toying with their women in the visiting room, often telephoning or visiting the wives of men whose only rejoinder could be self-defeating rage. Generations of cons, men who had been in other prisons and who prided themselves on their cynicism, would uniformly describe Santa Fe as one of the hardest places in which to do time, less because of the dramatic brutality than because of the routine mistreatment. "A convict's code of honor," said one, "is to tend to business and not to lie, steal, cheat, or screw another's woman. The officials at that pen did it all."

"I hope you don't ever think you're getting out," a prison administrator once said to Lloyd McClendon as he was struggling to earn a college degree and get other cons into educational programs.

"Don't let the sensational abuse hide the daily horror," McClendon was to tell a writer more than a decade later. "It's the little stuff that finally gets you."

The official brutality at the New Mexico penitentiary could never excuse the butchery of the riot, the cannibalism of the inmates who were themselves prey to the same abuse, the torture of guards who were caught in the larger machinery. Nor could the snitch system justify or explain fully the wanton killing and mutilation of the dead. The murderers and torturers clearly brought their own dark fear and rancor and dementia into Santa Fe. But to each man's lethal inner imprisonment of hate and craven violence this pen—most pens—would offer no contrast, no alternative. And from both prisons that bloody Saturday morning, there was no escape.

SIEGE

Man, there's blood all over this
damned floor...up to your ankles.

> Convict radio transmission
> from New Mexico
> State Penitentiary,
> February 2, 1980

He just told me they wanted
to be treated like men.

> New Mexico Governor
> Bruce King, after speaking
> with convict negotiator,
> February 2, 1980

Survivors would describe
the penitentiary that Saturday morning in terms that evoke
Dante. "The things that I saw," one stammers to a state policeman later, "were just unreal—I—a nightmare." Toilets,
sinks, and pipes are smashed; the main corridor is an inch
or more deep in the flow from the ruptures, and the mixture
of sewage and tap water in many places is stained bright
red. Mingled with the seepage, too, is the debris of nearly
total devastation: broken glass and furniture, shredded mattresses and clothes, and paper everywhere, paper of every
description from toilet rolls to official files to photos of children. Almost every floor of the institution is covered with
this gruesome man-made muck. Smoke from fires in the control center, psychological unit, administrative offices, gym,
and elsewhere gathers in the main hallway until men can
hardly see or breathe. The day outside is clearing and bright.
Sunshine from small barred windows filters through the pall
in sharp rays etching lines of gray light along the long, dark
passage north and south. But the light does not keep men
from stumbling over the mauled, still hemorrhaging bodies
that are strewn the length of the prison. Walking the corridor
this morning, witness after witness will be aware that there
are corpses "everywhere." Santa Fe's pen is a dank, bloody,
smoldering battlefield, a "war zone," a region of some inferno,
and it is still hellishly dangerous.

Gangs armed with knives, tools, and pipes rove the corridors or wait in the entryways just off the hall, challenging
the lone or the passive wanderer. Those whom they do not

kill they beat or try to dismember, hacking at arms and hands, or simply taunt and terrorize. In the south wing the strong are still raping the weak, taking dormitories A and F like an occupying army ravaging the women of a conquered village. They are raping, too, in the north, even in cell block 4 where the smell of burned flesh and hair and blood makes some men wretch. And the sodomy victims will joke later with flared eyes that they wonder about their rapists, about "how they got it up" amid carnage that causes others to vomit. In the basement of cell block 3, with its hacked and faceless bodies, the brothel that opened moments after the seizure is flourishing. Occupied by two young inmates and a proprietor, it will do business for what witnesses call the "entire time" of the riot, and men count at least twenty customers "going in and out."

As accompaniment to the savagery, radios and television sets blare from every unit, some tuned to the coverage of the riot itself. It is as if the inmates, children of the television era, are watching Albuquerque stations to find out what is happening to them—as if what flickers on the screen is somehow real while the smoky, flooded corridor just outside is not—though they alone are part of it, while the reporters around the prison have only the first vague pictures of the catastrophe. Someone has brought a stereo into the gym and plays raucous music as smoke billows, inmates are dragged in and out, and bodies are piled on the small stage at the end of the basketball court. One September, Santa Fe sent the cast of its fiesta melodrama to perform on that stage a parody on local politics and pretense. The penitentiary audience sat there, polite and quiet, not entirely understanding straight society's jokes on the current vogues of the Holy City, and inmate stagehands flirted with women in the cast. Now another drama, whose cast has been waiting in the wings all the while, is playing in the gym to some of the same audience.

Through it all, drugged men stagger and reel around the chaos, finding safe corners in which to give themselves over to stupor or sleep. One wanders about the ravaged control center and falls through the trapdoor into the cellar where Lucero and C de Baca left the teargas grenades and riot-control gear. Already another inmate is lying unconscious in the cellar, apparently dead or overdosed, and the fallen man, too disoriented to climb back up, calls out for help until other convicts wander through hours later. Meanwhile, there is one strange oasis of order amid the devastation. Dormitory E-2, where it all started, is almost undisturbed. While killing and screaming, pillaging and burning go on a few yards away, while the corridor fills with smoke and the riot's bloody silt, convicts move in and out of E-2 with bags of chips looted from the canteen, eating and drinking coffee almost casually as they watch television. "E-2 was kind of like a command post," one con would remember. None of the unit's men, leaders or subjects, will be among the riot dead, and after the seizure of the guards there, the mayhem unleashed in the rest of the prison will never cross its threshold.

Then, too, the nightmare has its incidents of humanity and genuine heroism. Cons guarding the three hostage guards in the north wing this morning give the officers food, coffee, and cigarettes and continue to protect them from assault. While most inmates cringe from the madness and plan their escape into the yard, some begin to help their fellows who have overdosed on drugs or have been attacked and left for dead. In several cases, inmates defend friends, or strangers, with their own lives, stepping between them and their attackers. One convict, a trained paramedic, braves murder or later retribution by treating both inmate victims and guards. "I'm over here checking this Lieutenant Anaya," the paramedic will radio officials later in the morning. "I think Anaya's got a concussion, and I think he's got a busted rib, and I know he's got a heart condition," he goes on, "and he needs to be moved....He needs to be taken out of here." Elsewhere, convict radiomen report overdoses and ask for medical help or evacuation. Surrounded by the most horrible inhumanity, fear, and lust, men summon mercy and courage and save lives no one can count.

Although the paramedic is trying to care for Anaya, although the rioters have allowed the wounded officers, Curry and Hernandez, to be surrendered in these first hours, not all the captives are so lucky. Cons visiting sites where other hostages are held will describe their brutalization and will remember the heavy fecal aroma of men who have been sodomized; one blindfolded and handcuffed officer is forced repeatedly to perform fellatio on his captors. Another guard is beaten, tortured, and reportedly impaled on a night stick. The hostages are still scattered throughout the prison; some are in the south; one or two are led from place to place in the central offices; three are still in cell block 3, and three are hiding: the two officers in the crawl space and the medical technician behind his locked door, all three within a few feet of discovery. The hostages' dispersal makes rescue impossible and any storming of the pen obviously dangerous. But negotiating their release will be difficult, too. An inmate voice just after dawn reports that Officer Anaya is "pretty bad." When rioters offer to give up the stricken fifty-two-year-old lieutenant in exchange for Deputy Warden Montoya, however, Montoya, in the understatement of the subsequent attorney general's report, "rejected the plan to switch hostages." Later in the forenoon, when a trembling and savaged Captain Roybal appeals to officials outside to send in a doctor or medical technician in some kind of exchange, Montoya again tersely refuses, insisting that the wounded officers be brought out without a quid pro quo. There will be no self-sacrifice among officials to match the convicts' valor and compassion on behalf of fellow prisoners inside. "Montoya, you better come in, sucker," one rioter tells the deputy in a conversation overheard by an inmate on Saturday morning. But when trades are later made for hostages, it will be journalists, not prison officials, who are bartered and whose lives are risked.

Roybal's is not the only radio plea by a captured guard. At daybreak other hostages are put on the air to beg that the prison not be rushed. To their strained voices Montoya answers, as a later inquiry puts it, that the guards' "well-being" is his "utmost" consideration.

"At this moment our lives are in your hands," Mendoza tells him from the basement of cell block 3 a few minutes after seven o'clock as the screams from the next block echo down the corridor. "What else can I say?"

As Mendoza breaks off, the Protestant chapel catches fire, adding to the black cloud of smoke now suspended over the center of the institution in the still, cold dawn. Camouflaged army vehicles draw up in the parking lot in front of tower 1. By 7:30 fifty National Guardsmen have arrived in full combat gear, with flak vests, M-16 automatic rifles, and bayonets. As the anarchy mounts inside, more convicts have spoken on the eight two-way radios they now control, filling the air with a jumble of rasping transmissions, threatening, asking for medical help, sneering at Montoya. Before first light, one of the negotiators has begun to call himself Chopper One. Although there will seem to be more than one convict using the name and the radio, the distinction is respected by the other operators and introduces some order into the broadcasts. At about 7:40, in hope of reducing confusion further, Chopper One asks for a field telephone to replace the phones destroyed by rioters after their first flurry of outside calls announcing the takeover. He wants direct communication with the outside.

A half-hour later Chopper One repeats the demand to speak to the media and threatens to kill the hostages and fifteen inmates if reporters are not produced. By 8:15 a field phone has been placed near the front entrance and has been snatched inside. Minutes later, convicts call the nearby State Police headquarters just off the Albuquerque–Santa Fe Highway and demand to talk to Governor King.

Already on his way from his mansion in the hills above Santa Fe to be briefed at the headquarters, King arrives there at about 8:40 while the convict negotiators are still on the line. He hesitates, stalls for time by talking to aides, finally agrees to speak to the rioters. Now and later, there is a kind of bravado about the governor's attitude toward the negotiations. "I know these boys," he has said. "I can talk to 'em." Before the depth of the disaster is known, before anyone learns of the ferocity inside and the uncertain strength of the encircling forces outside, there is almost the implication that King can somehow solve the problem and return the "boys" to their cells, with a few twanged assurances. It will not be so simple.

On the line King hears the voices of angry, embittered men who supposedly say, as he relates the conversation later, that they have started the riot "just to get somebody's attention" and because they are treated "like a bunch of kids." Sometime that afternoon the governor will tell a reporter of the conversation: "He just told me they wanted to be treated like men." But the demands to King are also specific. The negotiator repeats the demand that E-2 had first made more than seven hours before—a meeting with King and Rodriguez, and now Montoya, in the presence of the news media. One con tells King that the hostages will not be killed and that the pen will be peaceably surrendered by "three or four o'clock" that afternoon if the demand is met. The governor promises to provide a table for the parley in the prison yard within an hour and says that police and troops will not charge the building. Yet such agreements do not reckon with the realities of power. The governor will not honor his morning telephone commitment. For the next ten hours, amid growing evidence of murder and lunacy in the pen, as wounded and tortured hostage guards remain captive, and while Anaya is said to be seriously ill, Rodriguez and other officials in effect overrule King's promise and refuse any contact between the rioters and the press.

For their part, the convicts apparently take the governor's promise seriously. Minutes after talking with King, they radio Montoya and report having second thoughts about including the deputy warden at the table. "I talked to Bruce a while ago and he said he was going to come down here," the negotiator tells Montoya, "and I would appreciate it if you didn't come down here with him." A few moments pass, and another inmate chimes in to address Montoya, "You've got fucking uncles, you've got brothers, and you've got cousins working here and that is bad." The statement is not true of the deputy warden; it is a reference to the hated nepotism in a regime Montoya symbolizes for many.

While King speaks to the convict negotiators from State Police headquarters, twenty desperate inmates have banded together, stolen an acetylene torch left in the entryway to cell block 4, poured into cell block 5 across the corridor, and cut their way through the exterior door of 5 to the yard on its northeast side. It is an extraordinary escape, one of only two recorded instances in the riot of refugees using the predators' tools to escape; the other instance involved the wrench given the men in E-1 by the doomed lover. Most of those who flee out the door toward the police cordon are residents of cell block 4, and they begin to relate their tales of the slaughter. By helicopter and ambulance the wounded among them are taken to Santa Fe's Saint Vincent's Hospital, and others are hurried off to the county jail, a prison annex, or State Police headquarters to be questioned. But before they are dispersed, officials assemble from the stories the twenty blurt out a list of fourteen dead inmates. The count is ready for King when the governor arrives at the pen around 9:15 that morning. Also greeting him is a still more specific list of the rioters' negotiating demands. Minutes before King drives up, Rodriguez and Montoya have talked face to face with con Don Stout and an unidentified convict negotiator on the walk halfway between the tower 1 gate house and the pen entrance. Stout has also talked to the officials through a broken window in cell house 1, and in the wake of these brief meetings an inmate runner brings Rodriguez a list of demands. This first document of the negotiation is clear: "reduce overcrowding...comply with all court orders...no charges to be filed against inmates...due process in classification procedures...10 gas masks...2 new walkie talkies." Almost immediately Rodriguez gives the prisoners the gas masks. The other demands go unanswered. And compliance with court orders and due process in classification, ostensibly routine legal and administrative obligations of the prison regime, will never be explicitly promised during the negotiations, and never fully implemented for more than three years following the riot.

Besieged by journalists and anxious relatives, now hundreds strong at the highway gate to the penitentiary, King can tell them almost nothing. He enters the grounds to find near chaos at the base of tower 1, the officials' headquarters. There is no control over access to the gate house, and anyone in or near the adjacent fence can witness the negotiations. Policemen, National Guardsmen, prison guards and administrators, and passersby who have somehow entered the reservation swarm about the small building. At one point Rodriguez orders someone to "get all these people the hell out of here," but the area remains crowded. In addition to Rodriguez and Montoya, with his radio, there are two corrections aides recording the transmissions; later two lawyers from the Santa Fe district attorney's staff arrive; Orner and a State Police captain are debriefing refugees; still later a state senator and the lieutenant governor appear; and finally, after midnight, the newly appointed corrections secretary arrives, having flown in from Washington. Some are Rodriguez's men, some King's men, and some utter strangers whom no one seems to know. But there is about the siege command team one common element: all, including King, seem to understand that Rodriguez is in charge. He is *el jefe* once more, the chief here as always, as the prison implodes before their eyes.

In these minutes after King's arrival, the transmissions begin to grow increasingly ominous. Convicts demand that the tower be emptied, but officials ignore them. At 9:19 A.M. one voice from inside tells the gate house throng, "All them guys in cell block four that you've been using, well, I've got some of them in the sack just in case you don't cooperate. Eyewitnesses that you call the snitches over here...they are going to start getting shanked." The threat, officials know by now, may be all too real, particularly in light of the gruesome accounts of murder just related by the men fleeing from cell block 5. Just before 11:00 Montoya picks up a report from inside that there are two more bodies in cell block 3, one of them the Dog Boy. Almost ten minutes later, Mendoza's captors put the guard on the air to assure officials that he and the other hostages in the basement of 3 are still unharmed. Though inmates have asked for aid in putting out the several fires burning fitfully around the institution, when firemen approach the administrative section at about 11:30 to help douse the flames from the outside, inmates pelt them with debris from open windows and drive them off.

Meanwhile, Orner has compiled interviews with the first defectors his own list of suspected killers in the dawn's butchery, and an inmate radio message seems to confirm his conclusions. "There [are] a couple of groups of lunatics running around that just want to get into violence," says a voice before noon. "It has been creating some problems." By 12:15 Orner has a roster of the ten-man "death squad." As the attorney general's inquiry will later conclude, however, "knowledge of inmates being killed did not change the negotiation process." Montoya and Rodriguez, with King looking on, continue to stall, apparently in the belief that they will eventually talk the rioters into releasing the hostages. Nor does the story of the torture of the captive guards, now recounted by refugees no less vividly than the murders, cause administrators to alter their tactics. Again before noon a convict paramedic has reported Lieutenant Anaya's condition as critical. Yet the rioters' enduring demand to speak to the media is refused. At midday Chopper One offers to trade Anaya for Benito Gonzales, "Green Eyes", and when that is rejected, he offers Anaya and two other hostages for Gonzales. As Montoya refuses that, too, the convict voice threatens to "chop heads off." But the deputy warden insists that Anaya be released unconditionally before the media are allowed to go in. Forty minutes later, four convicts come into the yard briefly and ask again for Montoya in return for hostages. From the gate house there is no reply.

In the early afternoon, as negotiations sputter on to no effect, more and more inmates desert the riot. Thirty clamber out the hole in E-1 at a little after one o'clock. A half-hour later twenty more follow. By 3:30 almost another eighty have surrendered, including twenty who come straight out the front entrance to the surprise and fright of some officials. These men—many of them dazed, wounded, or drugged—are searched and herded into the yard or sent off for medical care. And they, too, bring out fresh testimonials to the terror in the pen, reports that guards have been sodomized, that Anaya is badly hurt, that there is a "stack" of bodies—perhaps six or seven, perhaps thirty—in the gym. Four of the refugees, either victims themselves or simply witnesses to the horror in cell block 4, will be sent to the Forensic Mental Hospital in Las Vegas.

Back on the highway the waiting families and journalists hear of the refugees, can even see clusters of them huddled in the cold about the yard. The scream of ambulance sirens and the blunt staccato of evacuation helicopters overhead raise their fears. The swelling crowd surrounds every entering car to no avail, and official briefings, after Griffin's initial appearance, are few and frustrating. A corrections department spokesman and a former King press secretary talk to reporters, but they know little. At one o'clock, a Santa Fe county undersheriff comes to the highway to announce with no further explanation that twenty inmates are dead, producing still more tears and anguish among hundreds of relatives who fear that their loved ones are among the twenty. At another point Griffin emerges to offer the information that the dead were badly beaten but not mutilated, though by then officials have heard scores of accounts of ghastly atrocities on the dead and dying. By nightfall a rumor, which has spread like a plague through the families huddled in cars and around bonfires, has people believing that the death toll stands at eighty-five.

But if ignorance and neglect torture the relatives of inmates, there is equal and senseless agony for the loved ones of the guards. Left to watch television or listen to the radio, they are not kept abreast of the 2-way transmissions that show their husbands and sons still alive. "He came in last night and was supposed to leave today, but he never got out," one mother would tell a reporter Saturday night after keeping a vigil in the cold since midafternoon. "I thought they would at least call and say something," she says choking back tears. She is Pina C de Baca, and her son is Louis, the foot patrol guard who helped Lucero from the control center and fled the pen nearly twenty hours before. He is safe, and both the officials and rioters know it, but no one has told his mother.

Whatever the families imagine, however, is probably less bizarre than the reality inside the prison this Saturday afternoon. As inmates flee through the hole in E-1, the torched door in cell block 5, and the front entrance, enraged rioters post armed sentinels at each opening. A dozen blacks try to get out through 5, are turned back, and make it into the yard only by sneaking around a convict guard who momentarily leaves his watch at the door of E-1. Incredibly, after this narrow escape, some of the blacks will later wander back into the nightmarish prison in search of food and drink, and the yard will be dangerous for them, too, but for the time being they are safe. Meanwhile, to their potential victims, the strong and the dangerous in the pen seem more organized, more powerful as the day wears on. One eyewitness will remember a convict leader "like a general Saturday afternoon, leading his troops, directing traffic, and telling people, 'Don't let anybody leave. Nobody is to leave. Too many people have left already!'" And the orders soon produce one more surrealistic image of the riot. At about 1:30 inmates notice a strange, lone figure in the corridor, a con nicknamed Mighty, who with rods and a torch and a small wheelbarrow in which to transport his equipment is methodically welding back together the holes torched in grilles and doors. He's sealing up the escape routes, binding up the riot's own fissures. One witness will remember Mighty fusing shut the bars in E-1, and then those near the control center, "just standing over the bodies like they were nothing, you know, just spread-eagled over the bodies...just wel—welding away."

Just before 3:00 Montoya meets three convict negotiatiors at the front entrance, and for an hour or so there seems genuine progress in the bargaining. By 3:15 the cons have handed officials another list of demands. This one numbers eleven and presumably, though the talks never make it explicit, includes the conditions for surrendering the hostages and the pen. Montoya and Rodriguez then retire to the warden's residence, just to the northeast across the pen grounds, and discuss the demands with Griffin and State Police commanders. They prepare answers quickly and hand them back. Apparently Governor King, who by midafternoon has left the pen and returned to the statehouse office, has no say in the official replies. In any case, the list of requests and responses, as well as the results of the promises, will be typical of the two sides. In their own shifting, violent politics, the rioters are trying to address specific grievances. In time-honored tradition, the officials merely dissemble. To prevent retaliation the cons want federal officials summoned to the pen. They also ask for reclassification of men in cell block 3, many of whom have been in maximum security for too long without due process. The convicts also stipulate that, until the uprising is over, all inmates be left in the units to which they were assigned. The official answer to the question of units, reasonably enough, is that the condition of the pen must be determined before housing can be set. But to the demand for a federal presence, Rodriguez and his adviser say merely that they will "ask for the assistance of the FBI." (The promise leads to a brief visit to the pen by a Bureau agent from Albuquerque but no monitoring of any kind, state or federal, of retaliation.) As for cell block 3, the officials answer only that "security risks will remain" where they are. (Both classification and conditions in the maximum-security unit will be a lethal problem at the pen, as well as the subject of a million-dollar court battle, for years after the riot.)

Convict envoys similarly ask the regime to end over-crowding, improve visiting conditions, serve better food, and provide decent recreational and educational facilities. Officials reply that 288 more beds will be ready in July (they will not), that visits are already "worked out" (this, too, will remain a festering dispute for more than a year), that they will hire a nutritionist (prison meals remain scandalously unsanitary when an ACLU food expert visits the pen a year later), that they are "negotiating" with the ACLU on recreational facilities (there will be no new facilities and no replacement for the burned-out gym for eighteen months), and that they are "discussing" education with the legislature ("discussion" will lead to little change and will even result in cuts in some programs).

The convict negotiators persistently repeat their demand to talk with the media, to which Rodriguez again answers, "Not until all the hostages are released." And the list concludes with rehearsal of two major issues at the penitentiary of New Mexico. The prisoners want "a different disciplinary committee" and an end to "overall harassment." "We will take a long, hard look at that," the officials reply regarding the disciplinary committee. On the demand to stop harassment, they promise to train additional guards, and they say that the corrections commission, a figurehead body appointed by King and subject to official guidance, "is also looking into this problem." (The ACLU will subsequently charge that postriot disciplinary reports are blatantly falsified by officials while brutality will continue, in some cases worse than ever, for nearly two years after the riot.) In a manner typical of the riot negotiations, the eleven demands of Saturday afternoon and the official answers drafted at the warden's house now fall into the bureaucratic and political maw. The replies are greeted contemptuously and cynically by the convict negotiators, who let them go unacknowledged. Despite the stakes, despite the plight of the hostages, the regime never meets these eleven demands, and the negotiating record is never monitored by the press or by higher authority in state government. Some convicts involved in the bargaining believe that more positive responses to the demands might have served to hasten the release of the hostage guards and the general surrender of the pen, staving off another day of suffering on all sides. But Rodriguez's answers are too transparent, and the standoff continues.

While the demands and answers are being exchanged, another more violent drama is being acted out in secret. At about 3:00 P.M. officials at the gate house suddenly hear a fragmentary but lurid report that four hostages have been killed. The report does not produce more serious negotiating tactics, but instead sparks pen officials to recommend, and King to approve, a storming of the institution. Griffin and Orner believe they dispose the forces necessary for the assault at dawn, but the State Police chief announces that he will not be ready until 9:00 A.M., and still cooler heads counsel waiting until nearer noon the next day.

Now, however, with two SWAT teams, over a hundred battle-outfitted National Guardsmen, and a sizable contingent of State Police, command is divided and planning nonexistent. There are still nearly a thousand uncontrolled prisoners inside the penitentiary, and the authorities' ability to retake the pen is uncertain at best. Nonetheless King calls his State Police chief and authorizes an attack. For twenty minutes, while inmates' demands are being given to Rodriguez, troopers and police stand ready for their hurriedly planned invasion. Officials cannot be sure where surviving hostage guards are being held at this moment, and inmate refugees have related some wild stories of rifles among the rioters. The men of the assault force are told to be prepared to be fired upon, but they are given only the roughest outline of an institution most of them have never been inside. The minutes count down.

Then, suddenly, Rodriguez tells King the report of hostage deaths has been discounted by eyewitnesses and by radio transmissions from inside, and the attack is called off. "You better bet that if we had confirmed any deaths we would have gone in right then," King later tells a reporter. "I'm not going to do anything to threaten the safety of the hostages, but I'm also not going to do anything that will allow them [the prisoners] to get out." The governor does not explain how an assault would protect the remaining hostages or why it might be necessary, as he seemed to suggest, to prevent escapes from the besieged penitentiary. "There's no point," King says at another moment on Saturday, "in having more bloodshed than we absolutely have to."

Despite the three o'clock scare and the obvious confusion of the attack preparations, an assault on the smoking pen continues to lure the siege officials in the fading afternoon light. Rodriguez convenes another meeting at Griffin's house at 4:00 P.M. to review intelligence about the location of the hostages. A quarter of an hour later, King talks with Raymond Procunier, a former California corrections secretary and prison consultant, who recommends that the prison be retaken immediately. At around five o'clock one inmate reports that at least eight of the hostages are alive, but another inmate gets on the radio and threatens to kill the captive guards if convict demands are not soon met.

Meanwhile, as Rodriguez convenes his intelligence meeting, State Police, Santa Fe city police, and National Guard commanders gather between three and four o'clock to discuss a State Police SWAT team's plan to seize the prison at four o'clock the next morning in a surprise attack. The result of this meeting will be chaos. Rodriguez and Montoya never consider the pre-dawn attack plan seriously. The State Police chief, who is ostensibly in command of the paramilitary forces at the pen, never hears of it. Other State Policemen believe the plan is to be executed at first report of a dead hostage; Griffin thinks it will be carried out sometime if talks do not "start progressing." A SWAT officer assumes it has been canceled because of raging fires at points of attack. Another prison guard believes it is not implemented because there is substantial progress that night in negotiations. A high-ranking police officer thinks the plan has been abandoned because it would put his forces at a disadvantage. And the National Guard commanders reject the plan at nine-thirty that night because their men have no keys, no lights, and not enough firearms. At the same time, one policeman prepares for the assault until one hour prior to the planned time before he is told it has been canceled. One SWAT leader is never told the attack is off, and simply waits at the ready at 4:00 A.M. to be ordered in. Some National Guard commanding officers expect the attack up to minutes before the designated hour. And army helicopter pilots stand all night by their assault craft at the Santa Fe airport a few miles away across the Albuquerque Highway and are never told the plan has been scrubbed. Afterward, Rodriguez will tell a reporter that "knowing the mentality of some of the inmates" he has been sure they would kill the hostages "immediately" if forces moved on the prison. Montoya will discount the disarray in the attack preparations but will point to the effects on the rest of the guard corps if an assault had led to the death of a hostage. "Fifty percent would have quit," he will say to *Corrections* magazine. Was that a consideration in an attack? he is asked. He will reply, "Sure."

Far to the southwest below the Jemez, the winter sun settles onto the wavy, barren mesas beyond Albuquerque and soon disappears over the rim toward Arizona and the Gulf of Baja. It is 5:30 P.M. The strange, humming siege camp on the plateau is overtaken by a cold darkness. As the temperature plunges from 40 degrees into the teens, a National Guard helicopter wheels and throbs over the recreation yard to the southwest, dropping tents, jackets, and green GI blankets for over three hundred inmates now huddled outside the pen. The forces arrayed around the occupied building are a heavily armed investment, and with the continued exodus of inmates from the riot despite efforts to seal them in, the power of the revolt is gradually but perceptibly ebbing. Men feel the shift both inside and out, in the dank, defiled cell blocks, in the knots of guardsmen and police along the perimeter drawing together against the chill. But there is this night left.

In the enveloping darkness the mood turns ugly on both sides. Before sundown an inmate on the radio has threatened to kill the hostages, and at 5:26 P.M. Montoya finally agrees to allow the media to go inside the prison if all the hostages are proved to be alive. As some cons run through the corridors preparing to put the hostages on radio to prove their survival, another radio message repeats once again that the hostages will be executed if the demand to meet with King and reporters is not met. This warning is broadcast again in thirty minutes. These are the latest of half a dozen snarled death threats to the captive officers, and they are not the last, as officials deliberately stall negotiations despite the governor's early morning promise of a conference table in the yard.

Outwardly, the pen now seems subdued. Inside, it is again bathed in an eerie twilight of smoldering fires and fear. A convict curious about cell block 4 walks over to the unit and climbs in the shadows to the upper tier, but then he moves quickly up and down the catwalk past the open cells and their trails of clotted blood, and leaves without looking down at the horror now shrouded by darkness on the floor below. "Why wouldn't you look down? Did you know there was something there?" a State Police agent will press him later.

"I figured there had to be something."

"Why? You didn't want to...you didn't want to look down?"

"I didn't want to look at any more fuckin' death."

"You knew there was death?"

"I could smell it."

At 6:30 that evening Chopper One assures Montoya, "We got no dead staff members in here." But then another voice breaks in on their conversation from another radio, "There are dead people all over this damn floor."

"Attention all units," still a third convict voice crackles over the prison band. "Attention all units. Stop killing each other, stop killing each other. I repeat. No more killing. No more hurting each other." Then a pause, and the same man speaking to no one and everyone, "Man, there's blood all over this damn floor...up to your ankles."

Minutes later inmates drag out two corpses, dump them near the gate house, and disappear back inside. Then several overdosed prisoners are carried or helped out, some babbling that there are fifteen dead in one dormitory alone. Drug-crazed men are still prowling the corridors and dormitories in the dark. And tonight, eleven or twelve hours after some of the killings, passersby are still beating and hacking in rage at some of the bodies. As the lights of the siege vehicles and helicopters play outside, younger, weaker inmates are still seized in A-1 or other south wing units. They are tied in a fetal position, then gang-raped until they scream and finally pass out. Other men, even the so-called stand-up cons, the tough Hispanics and Anglos, now seek out the darkness, not for aggression but for their own refuge. In the corridor, a Hispanic inmate begs two of his fellow homeboys to protect him, crying that "they" are coming for him. But before his friends can respond, he bolts away down the hall. "Everybody," a survivor of Saturday night will remember, "was just trying to stay alive."

At about 6:15 P.M. their nervous captors move officers Mendoza, Ortega, and Gutierrez from the basement of cell block 3, where they have been increasingly menaced by rioters drifting in and out, to the dayroom of cell block 6 across the corridor. Ten or more convicts carrying pipes and knives have been roaming the north wing, their homemade shanks dripping with blood. Other cons crouch in the smoke-filled hallway as they go by, then rush to tell the men watching the three hostages to move them quickly. The guards are then allowed to radio Montoya that they have been moved and are still unhurt.

But in the minutes and hours after that call, there is new terror. One of the roving gangs discovers the new keep for the hostages and threatens to come in and kill them. For several minutes the two outnumbered inmate sentries warn and posture, and the predators eventually move away with taunts that they will return. One of the sentries now gives Mendoza and his fellow officers broken fragments of a broom handle as makeshift weapons.

"This is the least I can do for you people if they rush us," he says to them, by his own account. "If they rush us, they rush us. We're just all going to have to go for what we know." The con then tells the guards he would unlock their handcuffs if he had a key, and when Mendoza produces one he has been concealing for such a moment, the sentries gratefully let the hostages free themselves for the common defense. Then they sit together near the dayroom door, the officers huddled under blankets clutching their broomsticks, waiting. Elsewhere, a Spanish-accented voice barks over the radio once more that guards will be killed soon if King or the media do not come in.

Back at the front gate, at 7:12 P.M., over ten hours after Bruce King promised a meeting between press and rioters, officials finally allow convict negotiators to see reporters. Ernie Mills, the longtime Santa Fe radio commentator who was first on the scene that morning with his friend the State Police chief, is sitting in a vehicle outside the gate that evening when Montoya quickly summons him. Mills is joined by John Andrews, a young television anchorman from the CBS affiliate in Albuquerque, and the two newsmen along with Rodriguez and Montoya meet two convict representatives for a brief exchange.

The cons ask for a television camera to be brought in the next day, and Mills agrees to get one from the Albuquerque public broadcasting station. After a day of terror and evasion, the bargain is astonishingly direct and simple. "They just wanted to tell their story," Andrews would remember. An hour later, suffering what the hospital report will daintily call "multiple traumas," Lieutenant José Anaya is brought out by rioters on a stretcher, more than eighteen hours after his capture. Convict paramedics have worked to keep the beaten and fading Anaya alive for more than a day, although his release might have come much earlier, had officials allowed rioters to speak to a reporter.

With Anaya set free, eight hostages remain in the pen, and three staff members remain hidden—Maez with his patients in a hospital vault, and the two veterans, Martinez and Vigil, still lying stiff, chilled, and frightened in the basement crawl space as the screams and thumps of the rioters reverberate above them. Moments after Anaya is evacuated to the hospital, officials hear from two other captives. Close to 9:00 P.M. a tortured Schmitt tells Montoya that if the building is attacked that night or if teargas is used, "I've had it." Then one of the convict negotiators who has met with Mills and Andrews speaks on the radio with the equally abused Captain Roybal to show that the fifty-two-year-old shift commander is still alive. As if to remind everyone of the continuing horror, however, before Schmitt and Roybal begin to speak, three more mangled inmate bodies are brought out and left near the gate house by their masked bearers.

The corpses are moved to a field morgue set up by an associate medical investigator and her staff on the prison grounds. By nine they have tagged five bodies for identification. Although the condition of the murdered men makes identification difficult, the doctor and her staff do not yet realize that these atrocities will seem relatively minor compared with what they will discover inside.

Bonfires now dot the siege camp as the tower searchlights sweep the darkened prison. Refugee inmates are herded to one side of the yard under guard, and the institution is the focal point of the hundreds of troops and police who surround it. Yet at this moment on Saturday night, the riot produces yet another bizarre, almost unimaginable event. Between the radio transmissions from Schmitt and Roybal, a strange inmate voice has radioed a demand that the tower lights be turned off and that siege forces be removed from the south side of the prison. Officials have ignored the order. In the glare of the siege fifteen minutes later, three prisoners make their way out of the beleaguered penitentiary, across the yard, through the heavily guarded perimeter fence, and into the prison industries building to the northwest of the institution. At the last moment they are seen entering the prison industries building by a deputy sheriff near a far tower, and he instantly reports the escape to prison officials at the gate house. They do nothing. Whether the report is lost in the confusion, discounted, or simply ignored, no one can later confirm. Despite the governor's assurance that there have been no escapes, the three men have indeed gotten out. They will stay in the prison industries building that night, however, and flee no farther. When the three are finally discovered and arrested two days later, they will have soaked the interior of the building with kerosene, clearly intending to burn it down and perhaps escape in the commotion that would have surely followed.

At ten that night convicts again broadcast that the hostages are "doing fine," though in truth some of the guards are about to suffer a new round of beatings and sodomy by baton. A half-hour later there is an offer to release Roybal in return for another meeting with the media. Apparently these are not the same negotiators who have met Mills and Andrews, though officials cannot be certain. The mood of the men at the gate house in any case is still hostile to any involvement of journalists. When a former gubernatorial press secretary, now a ranking state official, drives three reporters onto the grounds earlier in the evening, one of the siege commanders, as a later inquiry puts it, is "infuriated." But now the prospect of getting Roybal out moves Montoya to send back an apparent concession. There will be no "retaliation" against the rioters, he says, and they can meet reporters. Minutes after this message is sent, two convicts parley briefly with Rodriguez, Montoya, and newsman Mills. Mills reiterates that a camera will be taken inside the prison the next day and that the convicts' interview will be broadcast at least locally and perhaps beyond the state. In return for this concession, the rioters free another hostage. Tied to a chair, freshly cut and bruised from an assault moments before his release, Juan Bustos is carried out the front gate at about 11:20 P.M. To Lucero in the control center Bustos looked as if he had been beaten to death twenty-one hours earlier when the cons dragged and kicked him up the corridor collared by his belt. Those first minutes of the riot and his final beating were among his worst. He will now be treated at Saint Vincent's and soon released, luckier than some of his fellow officers of the graveyard shift. But he will not go into the prison again.

While the exchange of Bustos is being negotiated, the officials' apparent readiness to allow a press conference has brought still more eager officials into the decision-making. At around eleven o'clock two local assistant district attorneys begin to assemble reporters from among the crowd on the highway, arbitrarily ranking them according to the "prestige" of their affiliations and contemplating a "one on one" exchange: one interview for one hostage released. The plan has no basis in the negotiations, however, and a fellow district attorney from Albuquerque warns the elbowing reporters about the rioters: "They're stoned, screwed up, they'll be talking trash. You're liable to be there for the next nine thousand days listening to these guys." Nonetheless, the journalists are assembled at 11:30 P.M., and among them are not only local reporters but also representatives of the three television networks as well as reporters from *Time*, *Newsweek*, and the Denver and Dallas newspapers. Santa Fe's riot is by now news of national, even international magnitude, though the local siege command does not quite practice effective press relations or negotiations to match that grand scale. At midnight the improvised plan for an interview-hostage exchange is canceled altogether, and most of the newsmen return to the highway vigil with the relatives.

Like the soldiers and police officers still preparing for the 4:00 A.M. assault, however, not all the reporters get the word, nor are they all herded back to the road. Around midnight Michael Shugrue, an NBC cameraman based in Los Angeles, is still standing beside the gate house with a portable camera and videotape recorder, awaiting what he assumes will be a news conference at a table somewhere in the yard nearby. The table will never materialize any more than did the conference table King promised that morning. But as Shugrue waits alone, apparently unnoticed by officials or by his colleagues who are sent back outside the perimeter, some of the cons near the pen's front door, men who have carried out Bustos or negotiated with Rodriguez and the others, watch him for a few minutes and then yell out, asking him to come inside and tape their grievances. Shugrue shouts back uneasily that he will go in only if the officials give him permission, and he then walks over to ask Montoya. Again, incredibly, having denied media contact with the rioters for nearly twenty-four hours, having prolonged the captivity and torture of wounded guards by their policy or lack of it, the men of the siege command now treat Shugrue's request almost casually. "If you want to go in," Montoya tells the NBC cameraman, "go ahead."

Shugrue tells the cons that he is coming and shoulders his video equipment. Almost instantly, rioters appear with Officer Schmitt on a stretcher and half carry, half drag the heavy young guard along the front walkway toward tower 1 as Shugrue and the officials look on. Then suddenly the stretcher-bearers hesitate, pull Schmitt back toward the pen. The men at the gate house now at last see the inmates' point—they are releasing Schmitt in return for Shugrue's interview—and hustle the newsman through the fence onto the walkway. As Shugrue disappears into the pen, the inmates bring Schmitt out. The young officer lies there in the agony caused by severe internal injuries from one assault after another during his first hours in E-2, his rescue purchased at last by a ransom that has been available since dawn, yet which officials seem to have feared as much as the rioters coveted it—a television camera.

Shugrue stays inside for less than an hour. Trembling with fear, he triggers his camera to catch a changing collection of cons in a room in the visiting area. Some masked with bandannas or stocking caps, some unmasked, they carry clubs, baseball bats, and pipes, but no visible knives. The devastation of the pen is plain; nothing seems unbroken or unscarred. But nowhere does Shugrue see the guns rumored to be abroad in the riot. Outside Montoya monitors menacing radio transmissions between prisoners. "Be careful, take somebody that's armed and ready to fight," one con tells another in a far wing. "There are two groups in there that are going wild." Yet the Shugrue press conference is uneventful. The convicts chime in with complaints about food, the tyranny and injustices of the disciplinary committee, the harassment by and cruelty of the guards and administrators. Then the talk trails off. The cons thank Shugrue and escort him back out into the glare of lights bathing the front entrance. The cameraman is scarcely through the fence when officials brusquely say they want his film for intelligence reasons. He gives it to them, and they take it to the warden's residence.

A few minutes after one o'clock in the morning on Sunday, February 3, a convict radioman signals the other sets: "Attention all units. We're going to hold off till tomorrow morning. Make sure those guys [the remaining six hostages] are fed and nothing happens to them....No hostages will be hurt." He repeats carefully, "No hostages will be hurt." They will resume negotiations at eight o'clock the next morning, the rioters tell Montoya, and the prison radios fall silent.

The siege camp, too, is quiet now, and nervous guardsmen begin to relax. Would he hesitate to shoot an inmate if he had to, a reporter asks a soldier. "Not a bit," the guardsman replies. "I figure these s.o.b.'s would shoot me."

"We're planning a long stay," a guard officer breaks in. The camp stirs briefly at around 2:30 A.M. when a car whisks a new official onto the scene. A jowly man with a creased face and graying black hair, the newcomer is driven around the perimeter and, for a moment, moves importantly about the gate house before going off to the warden's residence to view Shugrue's grainy black-and-white videotape of the convicts. He is Adolph Saenz, a native of Las Cruces with powerful friends in New Mexico's state government, a veteran of seventeen years as a U.S. police adviser in Latin America, and King's new $40,000-a-year appointee as corrections secretary; his nomination was announced the Thursday before the riot.

For now, however, the relatives on the highway are concerned only about the next few fateful hours, and the survival of their loved ones. A small, crudely lettered sign has appeared late in the day on Saturday. "No More Attica," it reads. Mercifully, the families in their anguished ignorance are unaware of the frightening disarray and confused orders surrounding the putative 4:00 A.M. assault. From the highway the prison still appears to be faintly aglow from its inner fires, the rising smoke a sharpening gray against the clear, star-filled night sky. Inside many inmates sink into exhaustion. A group of convict leaders sits near the entrance in dazed silence at the memory of the madness of the last twenty-four hours. But in the south wing, other inmates are pinning a teenage boy to a bunk and beginning to take turns raping him. In the corridor outside cell block 6, the convicts have left the hostages alone, but they are beating a young, mentally ill Hispanic who has wandered too far down the hallway.

"The situation," the attorney general's report will say later, "is relatively static until dawn." Above the hum of the siege camp, above the chug of Saenz's car circling the perimeter, the families strung out far down Highway 14 begin again to hear the screams from inside.

The misery suffered in gaols is not half their evil. They are filled with every sort of corruption that poverty and wickedness can generate.... In a prison the check of the public eye is removed; and the power of the law is spent.

John Howard, *The State of Prisons* (1777)

t

he Hobbesian world of the riot mirrored the rampant corruption of the New Mexico State Penitentiary over the previous decade and more. If murder and brutality were part of the official regimen, so too were theft, blackmail, extortion, and graft. "That prison was the most corrupted place on earth," a former aide in the warden's office would tell two investigative reporters after the riot. The ex-official, a veteran of the 1970s, looked out the window of a small Santa Fe house on a quiet summer evening and added, "I lived in fear of dying, because I knew that if I died while I worked in that place, I'd go straight to hell."

Whether viewed from the higher administrative offices or from the cell blocks, however, the official criminality seemed to flourish with few such worries about a reckoning, divine or otherwise. The corruption ran from petty employee thieving to major misappropriations of public funds. At least since the early seventies, the pen had been a plump commissary of cut-rate or free goods and services for officials at all levels. Among the unadvertised fringe benefits for guards, according to a former corrections secretary and other eyewitnesses, were free use and then sale of the prison dry-cleaning services to paying customers in Santa Fe; free automobile repair, upholstery, and body work; free shoe repair; haircuts by convict barbers; the use of paint supplies and other uninventoried material, including pen cinder blocks and lumber; fill-it-up privileges at state gasoline pumps at the prison; and, not least, dental and medical care at the pen infirmary, complete with discount injections and medication. Officials also reportedly helped themselves to prison food supplies, from bits and pieces taken out in brown paper bags, to eggs purchased from inmate cooks at fifty cents on the dollar, to sides of beef. The cooks would remember the pilferage, the profit, and the resulting watered-down eggs and hamburgers in the chow lines. So would the officers. "We raised the only nine-neck chickens in captivity," a pen lieutenant said bitterly of the theft from the prison farm and stores. Generations of cons would relate accounts of officials backing their pickups to the loading dock by the kitchen, usually on Monday nights, and driving off with beef. Whole truckloads of dressed meat and livestock allegedly disappeared on a regular basis while in transit to the pen from the Las Lunas honor farm south of Albuquerque. Dwight Duran, who worked for a time at the farm, would describe to ACLU lawyers the "seven–fourteen rule"—prepare fourteen meat shipments one day in the slaughterhouse, return to prison dormitories for the night, go back the next morning to find only seven shipments ready to be sent out.

No property, state or personal, was beyond reach. Convict Barry Courtright, who had sent the cockroach to the grand jury from the hole, would later describe to investigators the lucrative kickbacks to officials who sanctioned and facilitated prosperous inmate rackets in extorting valuables from incoming prisoners and from weaker inmates whose families might pay protection money. According to the testimony of Courtright and others, officials simply looked the other way while inmates stole and resold watches and other valuables routinely surrendered by incoming felons, the proceeds to be split later among the salesmen and the turnkeys. According to these accounts, inmates were allowed to scan official files to find potential extortion victims among men with drug addictions and other weaknesses or among those from apparently affluent families. The victims were then variously "set up"—enticed into drug deals or trapped in some prison rivalry or betrayal—and their lives were threatened if they did not pay blackmail. Sometimes collected in bank accounts in Santa Fe, sometimes blatantly brought into the prison, the racket money was then divided among the inmates and their official collaborators. "I never made money so easily as I did in the joint," said one participant. "It was no little thing. At one point I was sending five hundred dollars a month to Mom and Dad's checking account."

Not all the money was sent home. It multiplied unnaturally in what convicts would later describe as a reasonably professional counterfeit operation in the prison industries printing shop, an enterprise whose plates were said to be still secreted in the prison after the riot, and whose function, like the printing of private invitations or business announcements for officials, apparently went on under a suitably tolerant administration. Either U.S. Treasury bills or homemade cash might be used as wagers at nearby Santa Fe Downs in a flourishing bookie operation. Summer race days at the nearby Downs tended to reduce the pen's water pressure. "You could get a bet down, but you couldn't get a shower," remembered one prison staff employee. Nor did all the ready money originate inside the institution from official voucher, resident extortion, or counterfeiting. Throughout the 1970s liquor and other contraband were allegedly supplied to inmates by well-paid official distributors. By some accounts, prison guards or administrators took orders for whiskey from certain cons, interviewed the men in pen offices, were paid $25 to $30 a bottle, and then vouched for the prisoners as they went back through the control center to the cell blocks and dorms, their bottles hidden.

By far the single most profitable trade, however, was in narcotics. "You can turn around drugs for a fifty percent profit," said one experienced guard. "It's a lot of money. You can probably make five thousand dollars a month." Inmates in the heroin trade did well, too. "The big money was in heroin and extortion," Courtright told investigators. "I knew one inmate who made fifteen thousand dollars in eighteen months, and he was only a monkey, a go-between. The officials were raking off a lot more."

A State Police investigative report recorded a typical story. On the night of September 1, 1978, a con named Larry Cruz Hill was stabbed to death in cell block 5 when he refused to share with three other cons the marijuana he routinely received from guard Patrick Vigil. Vigil confessed to the State Police that he regularly brought in baggies of marijuana to several cons and received payment in gold wedding rings or watches. Before Hill was killed, the guard had taken in payment from him "two more watches . . . and about one more watch and four rings." The baggies were ubiquitous at the pen, as were the official pushers. Vigil confessed and was fired without charges, and the case was reported to the Santa Fe district attorney, who pressed no further investigation into the obvious drug trafficking at the penitentiary.

Only weeks before the riot, a board member and staff manager had blown the whistle on alleged cocaine trafficking, official cover-up of falsified urine tests, and even gunrunning at Albuquerque's Aspen House, a drug rehabilitation halfway house for both federal and state felons. Referred to the attorney general, the charges were then shunted to the Albuquerque police and went largely unpursued.

Earlier, in another controversy, the state's Organized Crime Commission had looked into the Aspen House facility, a former motel off Interstate 40 in the decaying inner city, and reportedly found "undesirable conflicts of interest" in the composition of its board of directors. In 1979 the board included an Albuquerque city councilor, a federal probation officer with power to parole offenders to the institution, a state senator and brother-in-law of another board member who was administrator of a related, publicly funded drug-screening program, and psychologist Orner, who also could recommend pen inmates for parole to Aspen House.

While specific cases and charges were buried in official files, at least the silhouette of the corruption at the penitentiary was publicly visible in the state auditor's perfunctory annual reports. Year after year, from 1976 through 1980, the reports documented repeated and glaring discrepancies in the prison's financial books, making the institution vulnerable to widespread graft. No financial controls or outside audits prevented the corruption; the state auditor and his contract accounting firms only amassed the signs. But behind such accountant's terms as "qualified reports" and "lack of accountability," the annual audits bore the classic earmarks of mismanagement and fraud in a public institution—for those who cared to see it.

Inventories of prison supplies—from guns to vehicles to furnishings, items valued all together in the millions of dollars— could never be audited because the pen invariably scheduled its inventories prior to the state audit, leaving the examiners to complain each year that their inability to observe the inventory was a "serious exception in the audit." The auditors found, too, chronic mishandling of cash, from failure to balance income with deposits to consistent refusal to use numbered receipts. Missing completely were records of money paid in and out of funds held in trust for employees as well as inmates.

The annual audits showed dramatic and mysterious inconsistencies in the finances of prison industries, costs fluctuating all the way from 40 to 80 percent of sales for no apparent reason. Failure to account for raw materials by cost-per-item and failure to maintain records of food stores on a cost-per-meal basis allowed precisely the kind of theft, waste, and resale of commodities that convicts have been describing for years. Similar distortions, involving thousands of dollars at wholesale or retail prices, marked prescription drug accounting at the pen.

Despite the same irregularities year after year, corrections officials largely ignored the auditors' recommendations and complaints. Nor did they allow other auditors near their books. The pen's masters shunned readily available federal grants in the early 1970s, money that could have provided badly needed programs but which required U.S. Justice Department audits. No auditable federal money was sought under either administration of Governor Bruce King.

Over the decade from 1971 to 1981 there would be those who tried to lift the veil for a moment. There would be periodic scandals, some amazingly well documented, that seemed about to break it all open. But each time the disgrace would disappear again behind the walls of official self-protection. By the weekend of the riot, corruption, like brutality and incompetence, governed the pen with brazen impunity, the thieving a mocking fulfillment of the New Mexico state motto, adorned by a stern American eagle sheltering under its wing the smaller Mexican eagle: *Crescit eundo*—It Grows as It Goes.

We felt that the Governor should be the
first to see this report because it would be
dynamite and could only hurt the Governor....
this could become a little Watergate.

The Governor was very concerned and he
said that if this kind of thing went to the
Grand Jury it might make him, especially
the Governor's Office, look bad.

The Governor said that he wanted all copies [of the
memo].... He again thanked me for the report
and said that he would be destroying them.

Excerpts from a New Mexico
Department of Corrections
memorandum, "Confidential
Information on Granting of Paroles"

†he pre-riot history of New Mexico corrections was shrouded in official cover-up. During the seventies it had often been a bizarre saga, studded with interesting characters and sordid politics. The cast included a Presbyterian minister who was shot at after testifying about conditions leading to a 1971 riot; a frightened but conscientious probation official with voluminous documentation of a pervasive scandal in parole sales and bribery; a governor of the state who reportedly sought to confiscate the official documentation; and a governor-to-be who as a statehouse aide was depicted in these documents as repeatedly using his influence to secure paroles. The scenes included Felix Rodriguez's survival and vindicating promotion even after an official report publicly revealed widespread wrongdoing during his wardenship and after the governor announced his removal; the firing of the warden who conducted the pen's first genuine shakedown; the dismissal of one corrections secretary who was known as "the nigger upstairs"; and the hiring as his replacement an unknown figure with little corrections experience. This decade of thwarted reform and buried evidence began with gunfire in the night on the Albuquerque–Santa Fe Highway.

Harry Summers, the pastor of La Mesa United Presbyterian Church in Albuquerque and a leader of the state's Council of Churches, was driving home from Santa Fe in his daughter's new Mustang late one night in 1971. He had just testified before the legislature about official abuses at the pen prior to the October 1971 disturbance, and he noticed a car that seemed to be following him along the desolate desert road. When he slowed, it slowed;

—149—

when he speeded up, it kept pace. It even stopped when he pulled over to the side of the road to let it pass. As he screeched away from a stop to outrun his pursuer, there were one, two, three flashes of gunfire, and the usually composed Reverend Summers, known for the ornate turquoise cross he wore around his neck, flew the new 1972 Ford the remaining distance into Albuquerque at an unceremonious 125 miles per hour.

It was not Summers's only encounter with prison politics. Earlier he had been approached by a newly released convict and a young Hispanic writer for a radical paper, *El Grito (The Scream)*, who said they wanted to expose several penitentiary scandals and could document their charges. Summers invited them to appear on his weekly Sunday television show. But the night before the scheduled program, the ex-con and the journalist were killed, supposedly by police in a mysterious incident. Their deaths went unreported for some twelve hours, and the circumstances were never fully investigated. In yet another, less lethal episode, Summers and other reformers, despite constant spying and harassment by officials, arranged for a dozen dissenting guards to see Governor King to explain conditions at the pen. If the officers were telling the truth, Summers remembered King assuring them, he "would take care of it." Six months later all twelve guards had been fired. Summers and other reformers, both clergy and lay, would continue their lonely efforts to change New Mexico's prison despite more tailing cars, threatening calls in the night, and more false promises from authorities.

Early in 1972, under pressure for reform, the corrections department instituted with fanfare regular press conferences for inmates at the pen. Officers were not to be present, and ostensibly the prisoners could discuss any subject. Applications bearing the prisoners' names were filed with the warden's office, however, and interested reporters chose five at random. For a time, the local newspapers carried stories of abuse, and the press quoted the inmates along with the routine administration denials. Then, six months later, the press conferences were ended. The media had found the inmates' accusations "unfounded and ridiculous," pronounced a chairman of the New Mexico Corrections Commission, whose agency had never independently investigated the pen.

Lloyd McClendon would recall later that the cons themselves came to deplore the conferences for indulging the perennial petty grievances of inmates and not addressing "the more substantive things... the inequality of sentencing, the inequality of treatment."

"They were interesting sessions, but they could only go over so much ground before they became repetitious," recalled an *Albuquerque Journal* reporter. "We didn't get a public response one way or the other—and what more could the inmates say?" she added in an interview with *Corrections* magazine without asking whether public response was a condition of news, or what more the reporters might have done. Except for sporadic shallow features, neither the *Journal* nor any other news medium in the state would conduct over the decade authentic investigative journalism about the penal scandal. Only months after the riot did reporter Craig Pyes's *Journal* series on psychological abuse and maltreatment in the prison break the gentlemanly reticence, albeit then with no lasting effect on Pyes's generally lax colleagues.

Ironically, despite the intimidation of reformers and the abdication of the press, the October 1971 pen disturbance was eventually to trigger the most serious challenge yet to the larger structure of New Mexico prison politics. A grand jury impaneled after the disturbance had called among its witnesses Santos Quintana, the young director of the state's parole and probation office, which served as bureaucratic staff to the parole board appointed as political patronage by the governor. The jury had asked Quintana about political interference in paroles, one of the convict grievances that had sparked the 1971 uprising. And though he replied that he had "no specific information" on such pressures, the questioning obviously touched a raw nerve. Quintana resolved to protect himself in case of future investigations, and he began, on October 14, 1971, to keep an exhaustive diary of almost every encounter he had over the next two years bearing on improprieties in the parole process. Or, as Quintana himself put it at the beginning of his narrative, "I decided to take notes concerning things that were out of the ordinary in matters concerning granting of paroles." The result was "Confidential Information on Granting of Paroles," a ninety-page archive, most of which was composed of Quintana's tightly packed, single-spaced, dated entries chronicling a parole system awash in allegations of bribery, political manipulation, favoritism, assorted chicanery, misconduct, and deliberate cover-up at the highest levels of state government.

Quintana was to record case upon case of improper paroles. He preserved the story of twenty-one inmates who had committed "serious parole violations" and were nevertheless "reinstated or reparoled without justification." He recorded the bartering of Indian jewelry as well as cash for paroles. His journal contained numerous allegations and what seemed to be mounting evidence of malfeasance by the parole board. But perhaps his most interesting entries for posterity would involve Toney Anaya. Anaya was then a young aide to Governor Bruce King during King's first term. He was later to be elected state attorney general. Eventually, in 1982, Anaya became New Mexico's governor, the highest ranking Hispanic elected official in the United States.

According to Quintana's meticulous notes, Anaya was implicated repeatedly in pressuring what the probation offical regarded as questionable paroles. Quintana's record showed that one inmate was paroled "not on [his] merits" but rather "at the request of Mr. Toney Anaya" and other political figures. In another case, Quintana recounted that the son of a local politician was twice denied parole only to be placed again on the board's agenda by Anaya. The parole was finally granted under "pressure." In this case, "The Board gave no real consideration to this man's record. Parole was granted on the basis of the request made [by Anaya]." For yet another inmate, Quintana recounted that "There was a poor psychiatric report, but parole was granted because of request made by Governor King's Administrative Assistants and the Lt. Governor's Office."

In late June 1973 Quintana recorded a meeting with Corrections Secretary Howard Leach, at which he and Leach discussed "Ymelda Salazar [another King aide] and Tony [sic] Anaya's involvement and that they were using their job and the Governor's name in the granting of pardons, paroles and commutation of sentences." Later that same summer, the probation staff director was discussing with the chairman of the Corrections Commission "in general the problems encountered with . . . Tony [sic] Anaya when Tony [sic] was on the Governor's staff reference paroles, pardons, commutation of sentence, etc."

At the beginning of 1974 Quintana returned in his chronicle to a case that had long agitated the handful of bureaucrats and

Attempts to elicit comments from Governor Toney Anaya regarding the Quintana memo and the subject matter relating thereto were unavailing.

—152—

politicians who knew about it in the early seventies. This case involved a convicted murderer who, several stories went, had allegedly been granted parole after a substantial amount of money had been apportioned among various figures outside the Governor's office. The inmate had indeed been paroled and subsequently sought a pardon. Quintana recorded a discussion with Warden Rodriguez and Corrections Secretary Leach: "The Warden then stated that . . . the Governor had mentioned to him and Mr. Leach that Toney Anaya at one time had tried to pass a whole batch of papers for the Governor's signature. Included in this batch of papers was a pardon for [the ex-convict] but that Governor King had seen it and he had called Toney and asked him, what the hell is this, and that the Governor had taken no further action concerning the pardon."

Yet Anaya's were scarcely the only parole indiscretions alleged in Quintana's journal. In March 1973 he documented a call from King's office instructing parole officials "that the Governor wants this man out." In May Quintana noted a request from the governor's office for "no reason" to place on the parole board agenda a case rumored among officials to involve bribery. At the same time he recorded a request to commute the sentence of a convicted murderer who had served "only 18 days" of his sentence. As the bribery allegations surrounding one case became widely known inside state government, however, Quintana wrote in his diary that the governor "had thrown a fit" when the request for parole was presented, and that "the Governor did not want to consider this request for a year." Another time Quintana quoted King as saying of a questionable parole, "Let him go."

Throughout his extraordinary narrative, Quintana seemed confident that King would act responsibly on the festering scandal. In June 1973 he noted that other officials had three times warned King of "parole board doings" and that the governor "had promised to do something but never had." Nevertheless, Quintana decided to give the governor his own detailed chronology of cases and conversations. "I would give one to the Grand Jury. . . . I was a professional and I felt that it was about time someone stood up and be counted," Quintana wrote about what he told fellow officials at the time. Yet he was instructed at one point, according to the journal, not to give a copy to the citizen chairman of the Corrections Commission, who might use it for "his own personal political gain." The scandal, they agreed, as the Nixon administration began to fall in Washington, was "dynamite...could only hurt the Governor...could become a little Watergate."

In the next entry, Quintana described a call to him from the governor himself. King thanked him for bringing the problems to his attention. "I told him...he should be the one to see my report as he was our leader," Quintana wrote of his conversation with King, "and that it was very lucky that I had not been called before the Grand Jury." King apparently told Quintana, according to the director's log, "not to pay much attention to what his [the governor's] staff was requesting [on paroles]."

A day later, on June 26, 1973, Quintana noted that "The Governor said that he wanted all copies" of the report. According to the archive, Quintana and an aide went to King's office and handed over copies of what the probation official had compiled thus far. "He again thanked me for the report," Quintana recorded in his continuing diary, "and said that he would be destroying them." (See page 161 footnote.)

Six months passed. By January 22, 1974, Quintana had apparently become disillusioned with King's old promises to act on the record of wrongdoing in his regime. "The Governor should shit or get off the pot in matters of parole, commutations, etc. He tells us one thing and someone else something else," Quintana chronicled a conversation with Corrections Secretary Leach.

On February 10, 1974, Quintana entered the minutes of a meeting with King, Rodriguez, and Leach at the governor's mansion just north of Santa Fe. Leach and Rodriguez were "a little easy on their presentation," the parole official noted, but again Quintana warned King of the widespread improprieties. "The Governor was very concerned and he said that if this kind of thing went to the Grand Jury it might make him, especially the Governor's Office, look bad," the archive went on. "The Governor realized that we have the information and we could get the information necessary for indictments on some of these people," Quintana observed. "I think the only problem with him is that he doesn't want to give this information to the Grand Jury because it will make him look bad." But the governor "realizes," Quintana wrote, "that something has to be done." He wanted to "straighten this thing out in the next few months that I have," Quintana recorded King as telling him two days later. "Then after I leave, if somebody messes them up again, it's their fault."

By July 1974 the Quintana archive was at an end, and the scandal it recorded never to be probed by the King regime. Despairing officials did eventually go to the FBI, however, triggering a ten-month Bureau investigation of bribery and other crimes that supported most of the Quintana record. The inquiry and federal grand jury testimony "revealed evidence," read an FBI Airtel to Washington from Albuquerque on July 25, 1975, "of political and economic pressure, questionable conduct and peculiar behavior among parole board officials in granting paroles to New Mexico State Penitentiary inmates." The investigation had come to involve, said a November 6, 1974, FBI teletype, "many prominent members of the Criminal Justice system for the state of New Mexico" and "many politicians and political appointees." But by the time the FBI probe got under way, the delay in pursuing Quintana's record had proved fatal. FBI files showed the local U.S. attorney advising the Bureau late in the summer of 1975 that the crimes "occurred outside the Statute of Limitations and therefore no further investigation... is warranted."

Meanwhile, the ambitious Anaya had left King's staff in a dispute the governor would later describe as "political." That summer of 1974 he ran for attorney general and was elected in the larger Democratic victory of November, while the FBI investigation was under way. After taking office, Anaya began his own ten-week probe into the parole system in conjunction with the governor's Organized Crime Commission. In effect, he was looking into alleged improprieties in which his own name was prominent in the Quintana record. But when the inquiry report was released in May 1975, there would be no trace of Anaya's own embroilment in the affair as detailed by Quintana. According to the Anaya report, there had been "apparent attempts" to influence parole decisions, "excessive leniency," and "some inconsistency." Certain parole board members were "favorably influenced by political pressure, business pressure, or inmate family pressure," and the inquiry disclosed "questionable conduct." But a former high-ranking official and a former aide to King had refused to cooperate altogether, and the investigation failed to develop the evidence "necessary to sustain any successful criminal prosecution." In addition to those who declined to cooperate, the report noted, some other sources "suffered acute memory failure at certain points." Among the victims of amnesia was Quintana, who apparently told investigators about portions of his reported archive on corruption "that he couldn't understand why he would ever write such a thing." In July 1975 the old patronage parole board was replaced by a new full-time, paid agency—a reform forced by the legislature and the new gubernatorial administration amid the publicity surrounding the release of Anaya's report. But the deeper story of the involvement of and possible cover-up by the past governor and his staff, and any legal reckoning for the history Quintana wrote so stenographically over nearly two years, would disappear swiftly into the political mists of Santa Fe, one of the principal actors in the seedy drama, Bruce King, to go on unquestioned to sit another term in the governor's chair four years later and another, Toney Anaya, to succeed him there in 1983.

The new parole board had hardly begun to meet and the FBI investigation into bribery and abuse of office had scarcely ended when another scandal erupted over New Mexico's corrections system. Frank Stockham, the penitentiary hospital administrator for thirteen years, had campaigned for Jerry Apodaca in the 1974 election. After Apodaca's election as governor, he moved in the summer of 1975 to promote Stockham to "administrator four," a relatively highly paid, senior state rating for which the pen usually had only one position, the deputy warden's. Whether fearful for their prerogatives and of Stockham's eventual appointment as deputy, whether righteously opposed to such external patronage, or whether simply convinced they had discovered official peccadillos in the ranks after all these years, Rodriguez and the current deputy, Horacio Herrera, moved in turn to set Herrera and Rodriguez's brother-in-law, then the prison intelligence officer, on an internal "investigation" that would end by charging Stockham with selling drugs to inmates, loansharking, placing bets at Santa Fe Downs, altering drug addiction screening tests, and making derogatory remarks about the pen administration. When it was over, the charges against Stockham, the resulting political furor, and Rodriguez's manifest power over a governor of the state would constitute a virtual parody of prison politics, played out briefly and, this time, openly.

The situation turned rancid, and public, faster than any of the participants seemed to have expected. In August 1975 Rodriguez cryptically raised the charges against Stockham and refused to promote him. Apodaca's envoys told the warden to prove the allegations and dismiss Stockham, or else give him his raise. Apodaca then asked Corrections Secretary Leach for the pen's "confidential" file on Stockham, and when Leach refused to hand it over, the governor promptly fired him. At the same moment, Attorney General Toney Anaya launched his own investigation of the Stockham affair. By the end of August Stockham had been dismissed as well, but Anaya's agents were also swarming over the pen.

By September 20 Anaya was ready with a twenty-seven-page report that largely exonerated Stockham and excoriated the prison regime. Anaya found "no written memoranda, reports, letters, or any other documents" to show previous wrongdoing on Stockham's part. Stockham had helped an inmate to get money from his mother to pay a pen gambling debt, Anaya concluded, but the other charges, all based on inmate testimony, were "highly questionable." An inmate had admitted to Anaya's investigators that he had been approached by Herrera about "the need to develop a case against Frank Stockham," and the con in turn had enlisted others in the effort with "vague indications that cooperation would not go unnoticed" by the authorities. Four of the five inmates who leveled charges had received preferential treatment after making their statements, Anaya found, and all had known they would be rewarded. The attorney general's probe even uncovered that Rodriguez himself had phoned an inmate's mother in Texas and offered to take her son from the pen to eastern New Mexico to visit the mother's invalid sister if the mother would agree to meet them there and give a written statement against Stockham. The mother subsequently told Anaya's agents that she felt the warden was trying to "use her," but she would go along with the "deal" if it meant her son could visit her sick sister. In addition to all this, Anaya discovered the brisk pen traffic in heroin, cocaine, cash, and liquor. He learned of the livestock thefts, the inmates with access to confidential files, and the drug peddling from the pen pharmacy. And he revealed a derelict Corrections Commission. All echoes of convict charges for years, now recorded on official stationery. The fate of this report, however, was typical of the system.

According to the account in the *Albuquerque Journal*, the chronology unfolded rapidly. With Anaya's report in hand on

September 20, Apodaca said he would ask the Corrections Commission and Michael Hanrahan, his new corrections secretary, to fire Rodriguez and Herrera. Anaya announced that he would take his evidence to a grand jury.

On September 21 the Corrections Commission chairman, who was privy to some of the earlier parole-pressure charges against Anaya, defended Rodriguez publicly as a man "with a spotless record of twenty-three years" and "a very fine warden highly respected throughout the United States." Apodaca still indicated he wanted Rodriguez dismissed.

The next day Deputy Warden Herrera was fired for "ineffective management" in controlling contraband and "improper conduct" in the handling of the charges against Stockham. Hours earlier Frank Stockham resigned quietly despite his exoneration. Rodriguez announced that cattle thefts were "nothing new" in the prison system and said that he had been trying to stem the flow of contraband. Meanwhile, Hanrahan told reporters that the evidence against Rodriguez was less "numerous" and "detailed" than that against Herrera and that Governor Apodaca had assured him he would have a free hand in deciding Rodriguez's fate.

"Let's investigate further," the *Albuquerque Journal* editorialized on September 23. The same day Anaya talked with District Judge Santiago Campos about presenting his pen evidence to a grand jury, an Apodaca aide told the press that there was sufficient evidence to fire Rodriguez, and Rodriguez reportedly told the governor's office that as warden "he had no knowledge of some of the things Herrera was doing."

On September 24, less than seventy-two hours after the governor had last indicated that Rodriguez would be fired, New Mexico had indeed hired a new pen warden, an ex–federal warden from Dallas. But Felix Rodriguez, far from being dismissed, had been promoted to state director of adult institutions, a position in which he would be the new warden's superior. Asked about the promotion, Corrections Secretary Hanrahan said simply, "No comment." Shocked, the state branch of the National Council on Crime and Deliquency called for an independent investigation of the prison and of the whole affair. "I would have hoped," said an otherwise silent Anaya, "that after nine months of demonstrating the independence of the office there would be no need for these types of comments made by the Council." There would be no grand jury indictments, no further probe, and Anaya's files on the pen would be neatly locked away. Stockham, the former hospital administrator, went on to sell real estate. Herrera, the former deputy warden, went on to run a laundromat in Santa Fe. By the end of 1975 the state had effectively buried its *Affaire Stockham*.

The new warden, Ralph Aaron, toured the pen that autumn of 1975 and pronounced it "depressing." "It is not maintained to the standard of institutions I've worked in," he told reporters, adding prophetically, "I think if you no longer meet the needs of the staff or ethnic groups . . . if you don't keep it up physically, and there's a breakdown in the needs of people, then it could blow up."

Aaron was gone in eight months. He was succeeded by the deputy he had recruited, Clyde Malley, a twenty-seven-year veteran of the federal prison system. Malley would remember the New Mexico pen he first encountered as a "national disgrace." "You know, we used to judge prisons by how they smelled," he once told a reporter, "and that one smelled rotten. It looked rotten too." Malley swept through the pen in the institution's first authentic shakedown, hauling in a vast array of ice picks, knives, hacksaws, and other weapons and contraband. Though marred by the July 1976 inmate strike and ax handle reprisals, Malley's tenure as warden was consistently praised by outside observers for increasing inmate contact with case managers and for reducing the number of cons in segregation. But Malley was increasingly excluded from policy decisions by the corrections department headquarters staff where Rodriguez was ascendant, and the old guard corps at the pen remained largely intact. By 1978 Malley, too, was gone, leaving the warden's office again a local sinecure, and later to be called "a liar" by Rodriguez when the longtime federal officer finally told his story to the Santa Fe *New Mexican* months after the riot.

In June 1976 Attorney General Anaya, Assistant Attorney General (and future judge and corrections secretary) Michael Francke, and an inmates' attorney signed a consent order in a New Mexico district court supposedly compelling the pen to improve classification practices, legalize disciplinary procedures, reduce overcrowding, and significantly improve food, water supply, plumbing, heating, ventilation, and electrical wiring. Ordered by District Judge Edwin Felter, the decree went largely ignored and unenforced for more than three and a half years prior to the riot.

Over the same period, under both Anaya and his successor, Democrat Jeff Bingaman (who, like Anaya, would go on to higher office, in this case U.S. senator), the attorney general's lawyers would vigorously oppose civil rights lawsuits filed by New Mexico pen inmates. At the same time, the state's chief public defender in the mid-seventies, Jan Hartke, son of a U.S. senator and later to be state treasurer and a Democratic congressional candidate, reportedly reduced much of the still meager public defender's access to state pen convicts with legal complaints. Officials similarly ignored some thirteen grand jury reports from 1971 to 1980 detailing major problems at the pen and calling for special audits and investigations. Like the incriminating state auditor's reports, the grand jury warnings were filed away. "What effect did these actions have on the feelings of desperation felt by the prisoners?" a local attorney would ask in a letter to the *Journal* after the riot.

By 1979 corrections department headquarters was in political and bureaucratic disarray. Hanrahan's successor after two years, Charles Becknell, a Ph.D. and former professor of Afro-American studies at the state university, had been retained by King after Becknell helped rally black votes in the southern half of New Mexico during King's 1978 reelection campaign. But the corrections secretary was deplored by the pen's old guard, viciously called "the nigger upstairs," and attacked as well by conservative members of the legislature. In spite of their racial slurs and jokes, Becknell's opponents went to lengths to prove their lack of prejudice. "My wife's very best friend is a black woman," one Republican state senator assured Becknell in a committee hearing.

After the December 1979 mass escape from the prison and the obliging investigative report by Francke, formerly one of Rodriguez's lawyers at the corrections department, King was able to rid himself of Becknell. The way seemed open at last to name Rodriguez corrections secretary. This was the highest penal position in the state, and the title carried the career-crowning prestige to match the de facto power Rodriguez had wielded for years. Just as the governor was ready to move, however, a group of powerful Anglo legislators, both Republicans and Democrats from some of the state's older families, met with King and warned him that Rodriguez's appointment could touch off a new investigation. Hurriedly, the governor looked elsewhere for a corrections secretary.

On the recommendations of New Mexico Supreme Court Chief Justice Dan Sosa, who knew the candidate back when they were growing up in Las Cruces, and State Purchasing Director Joe Baca, who knew the appointee when they worked together recently in Latin America, King named Adolph Saenz, age fifty, a former federal official whom the governor's press release called "a person of such excellent quality and expert experience" that it was "a great pleasure" to have him running New Mexico's prisons.

What the public did not learn until later was that Saenz had passed a seventeen-year career in the Office of Public Safety (OPS). This U.S. government program was established in the late 1950s to advise foreign police forces in Latin America and elsewhere. It was abolished by bipartisan congressional action twenty years later amid a controversy over foreign police abuses.

After the OPS was disbanded, Saenz went through four federal jobs in as many years. The first he took at barely half his OPS salary. Along the way he applied on a merit basis for a junior position in the New Mexico criminal justice system and failed to get the job. Then, when his last position as deputy director of the U.S. Customs Patrol was about to be abolished in 1979, his patrons in Santa Fe recommended him for the open secretary's chair in corrections. Saenz had no experience in administering a modern penal system, and his background in the controversial OPS was apparently unknown when King offered him the $40,000-a-year cabinet appointment.

Asked about the Quintana memo, King responded on August 29, 1983, "These guys get things a little out of proportion. As I remember it, Quintana brought the information. He had already given it to the head of the parole board, the corrections commissioner, and Judge Moise. We were trying to shore up the setup. I had no intention of suppressing it. That's the way it was. I think this thing was given to the local papers and even the district court. I didn't think it was so damning. It was hurriedly put together and not so damning. I saw trends but nothing criminal. This was the first time anybody has approached me about these problems."

Asked about parole board improprieties, King responded, "My concern was obvious. They (King's aides) were acting without authority. I immediately removed them from any participation with the parole board."

SURRENDER

Lector, si monumentum requiris,
circumspice.

> Inscription on the tomb of
> Sir Christopher Wren,
> St. Paul's Cathedral, London:
> "Reader, if you seek a
> monument, look around."

"I vomited."

> New Mexico National Guardsman
> asked what he did while
> retaking the penitentiary,
> February 3, 1980

half-hour before sunrise on Sunday morning, Rodriguez and Montoya are back at the gate house for negotiations. The gray light of the coming dawn seeps into the prison, and the men inside begin to stir. One con checks on a hostage guard and finds him cold, trembling, silent. Through the windows and the front entrance, convicts can see the clusters of National Guardsmen and State Police huddled about their bonfires. Helicopters have begun to whir overhead; more truckloads of soldiers are pulling into the reservation. In the siege camp there is the nervous rustle and dull crack of readying weapons. On the highway, anguished dark-eyed women are begging the drivers of passing vehicles for some news of what has happened, what will happen. Their pleas turn to vapor in the sharp morning cold. One con will remember afterward in testimony that he looked out in the Sunday half-light and saw the dark truck of the State Police SWAT team, parked there by the yard like La Muerte, the death figure of New Mexican *penitente* folklore, about to begin the procession. One of the troopers near the gate house apparently seems too close, too eager, and a radio transmission rasps out of the pen: "Don't get any ideas, Montoya. We're not asleep."

Now, more overdosed inmates stagger out of the escape holes, past sleeping or deserted sentries. As the sun breaches the mountains, Montoya asks Chopper One how many bodies may be inside. The officials, he says, need to know how many stretchers to provide. After a pause and a quick survey, Chopper One replies simply, "Fifty-one." Montoya does not answer.

"Sunday morning," another convict will tell State Police, "there were bodies everywhere." When cons later ask for more stretchers to help clear out the bodies, Montoya curtly tells them to use what they have, that no more will be provided.

Minutes earlier the cons have taken some of the hostages to the information booth at the front of the prison, prepared to negotiate. They now radio Montoya that they want assurances that their chief negotiator and spokesman for the coming talks and press conference will not be harmed. After the shifting negotiators of Saturday, the designated envoy is to be Lonnie Duran. Thirty-one years old, serving a lengthy term for armed robbery, Duran is a coauthor (though no relative) in the Dwight Duran constitutional suit for prison reform, a bright, respected convict advocate with some higher education and a past record as a spokesman for grievances. He will be one of the unacknowledged heroes of the riot negotiations, a man of sanity and candor amid the madness and deception. And for his role he will be misled by officials who falsely portray him as a traitor to his fellow rioters. As a result he will be distrusted by other cons, later shunted from prison to prison until assigned again to Santa Fe to wait for a promised commutation that never comes. But now Duran is preparing to negotiate an end to the horror and perhaps some sort of vindication, and the gate house politely assures him of diplomatic immunity, for the moment.

Before the talks begin, however, the trickle of refugees out of the unguarded orifices of the institution becomes a torrent. "What the hell is going on?" one con asks another on the radio. "Where's everybody sneaking out of this place from?" Many pour out through an exit in a southside dormitory. As officials use loudspeakers to instruct the refugees to throw down any weapons and hold their hands over their heads, a small group of convicts stands at the front entrance yelling curses at the surrendering inmates. But the exodus continues. Some bodies are now carried out the front entrance, and some of the rioters screaming at the defectors turn to laugh contemptuously as the corpses are dumped near the gate house. Nearly eight hundred men have now fled the riot.

Inmates are not the only ones freed this morning. In the first hours of the riot Victor Gallegos, the young southside guard, an ex-marine with only three weeks on his job at Santa Fe, has been blindfolded, stripped, bound with his belt, and separated from the other hostages. Rioters run past him, kicking and threatening to stab him. Then for a time he is back with Captain Roybal in a cell, the injured shift commander on a bunk and Gallegos shoved under it. Smoke is filling the cell house as they are locked in, but as their captors depart they somehow leave the cell door locked on the inside with the outside latch broken off. After an interval the convicts return. Furious that they cannot get in, they beat at the door, finally cut it with a torch, and in the smoke and their frustration rush in and drag Roybal away without noticing Gallegos under the bunk. Gallegos lies there in terror through Saturday and the long dark night into Sunday before he is taken in hand by sympathetic inmates and given water, coffee, potato chips, and little cakes from the canteen. They then dress him in inmate clothes taken from a dead man and, near 8:00 A.M., take him to join the refugee stream. Gallegos is young and relatively unknown. He walks anxiously, eyes down, past angry cons in the corridor hurling epithets at those who are fleeing. Then, at last, he is finally outside the fence in the daylight, identifying himself to disbelieving guardsmen. Long afterward, Gallegos will remember the last lockup that Friday night when they were standing there in front of F-2, and "this guy dressed in a guard's uniform" came up the stairs.

Minutes later comes the event that the officials have been awaiting since the previous evening. A badly beaten and abused Captain Greg Roybal is released in return for the scheduling of a news conference. His skull is fractured. The fifty-two-year-old veteran bursts into tears as soon as he is outside the fence and is swiftly evacuated to Saint Vincent's by helicopter. The talks now begin seriously. Rodriguez and Montoya are joined intermittently by Saenz, reporter Mills, and Manny Aragon, who is a state senator from Albuquerque and one of King's informed envoys at the parley and who grew up with Lonnie Duran. On the rioters' side are Duran and two other Hispanic representatives, Kedrick Duran (again no relation) and Vincent Candelaria, both respected cons. As Mills videotapes the proceedings, the two Durans sign a written agreement with Rodriguez and Montoya guaranteeing that there will be no retaliation against the rioters. Officials also give the cons an acetylene torch to cut free prisoners who are trapped in a burning dormitory.

While they talk, the National Guard medical field hospital and Saint Vincent's are trying to cope with the casualties among the morning's refugees. Guard medics treat a man whose hand is nearly severed and "hanging on by just a couple of fractures [*sic*] of bone." Another man has been stabbed through the heart. Some surrendering convicts, high on sniffing glue or paint thinner, violently fight off medical assistance. The commanding physician will estimate that half the casualties are suffering from psychological problems. One dazed inmate mutters over and over, "They killed him like it was nothing, they killed him like it was nothing." At Saint Vincent's the wounded keep coming by ambulance and helicopter until one emergency room doctor will remember a "sense of endless casualties." Their faces caked with blood, freshly stabbed or beaten as they file out that morning, one inmate having been hit in the head with a meat cleaver, the men are in shock from injuries or drug overdoses. They lie in the crowded hospital hallway groaning incoherently as a nurse goes from stretcher to stretcher marking with a felt-tip pen on their naked chests, "John Doe #13...John Doe #14..." The tense, weary hospital staff members, thinking they must have seen the worst, are told at midday Sunday to prepare for "heavy casualties at any time" as the pen is about to be stormed.

Back at the pen entrance the talks have begun constructively, but soon the old hatreds erupt. Lonnie Duran begins to tell his boyhood friend, Senator Aragon, about Montoya's practices as deputy. Another convict emerges from the building in a group of refugees, and as he passes the negotiators he yells out, with tears in his eyes, "Montoya, you chickenshit, you're the one who caused all this."

According to one published account, Aragon would remember Montoya snapping back, "You wait till this is over. I'll show you what shit can really go down."

With retaliation a central issue in the release of the remaining hostages and the surrender of the pen, Aragon moves to cut off the exchange. "Hey, Felix," he yells to Rodriguez, "Bobby's losing it; you ought to get him out of here."

Rodriguez seems to agree, and Montoya leaves the gate house and walkway for a time.

Meanwhile, Mills is promising the rioters that their long-awaited televised press conference will begin soon. He will also pledge to do a five-part series about prison conditions. Mills will have seen perhaps more of the riot than any other reporter—inmates with throats slashed, the rage and devastation, the despair in the convict negotiators' litany of questions, their fear of reprisal. The prisoners this morning trust him and other reporters to tell their story and to probe behind and beyond the riot. But to the cons waiting for Mills's series afterward, this promise, too, will seem lost. His post-riot reporting will not be the exposé in depth they envision during these tense negotiations.

Meanwhile, young Ronnie Martinez, the eighteen-year-old novice guard at the door of E-2 thirty-three hours before, escapes out the back of the prison at about 11:00 A.M., helped by some inmates who have shepherded him, as they did Gallegos, down the smoky, still dangerous central corridor from his southside captivity. And moments before noon, Officer Edward Ortega, the oldest of the three guards held in cell block 6, is released by his sentries and taken out dressed as an inmate. In part, Ortega's freedom is a response to the imminent press conference, in part an effort to lighten the sentries' responsibility in a prison still in spasms of violence, where the hostages cannot yet be surrendered entirely, yet where no one can be sure there will not be some last-minute crazed assault on them. Only seconds before Ortega comes out, a convict reports on the radio a stark reminder of the massacre. There are four or five bodies in cell block 4, says the voice, two in another cell house, one by the school, several in a dorm. Ortega's release leaves Mendoza and Gutierrez alone in cell block 6. The only other officers inside are the three still hiding in the hospital and in the crawl space.

By Sunday morning the tension has been transplanted to the yard along with the crowd of refugees. Some Hispanics begin to menace a cluster of about a dozen black inmates who are standing by themselves on the south side of the grounds. Shouting "Kill the blacks" and still equipped with shanks, although they were ostensibly disarmed when they surrendered, the men chase the blacks up against the perimeter fence by the sally port at the northwest corner of the yard. There by the fence, policemen on duty tell the fleeing blacks to drop to the ground, and a county deputy sheriff orders some twenty National Guardsmen near the perimeter to "lock and load." The guardsmen level their weapons at the oncoming Hispanics. The deputy shouts that the attackers have five minutes to disperse. He looks at his watch. At that moment Koroneos, the pen security chief, suddenly appears out of nowhere and steps between the gang and the guardsmen. The deputy sheriff tells him to get out of the field of fire or take the consequences. Stunned, Koroneos moves back. The minutes tick off. The deputy orders the guardsmen to take aim. At the last instant the Hispanics retreat, cursing. The guardsmen lower their weapons, and a hole is cut in the fence to evacuate the blacks.

"This is one of the least, least, least racially tense institutions I've been in," Rodriguez's protégé Joanne Brown will tell a reporter the next week. "We had to escape to save our lives," a black inmate will remember of the guard incident Sunday morning. "We've been segregated for years and it still hasn't done any good. As soon as the police and National Guard leave, we're dead." Little more than an hour later, cons near the front entrance will hear Rodriguez and other officials gasp as the corpse of Paulina Paul is brought out and the covering blanket taken off the stretcher, revealing the slashed, decapitated torso, with the head lying between the legs. Someone has finally closed the eyes. Witnesses will recall vividly Paul's last moments and, later, the beheading by kitchen knife. "Die you nigger, die," they remember his murderers screaming.

Elsewhere in the yard, the teaming POW compound of the siege, there are other scenes at this hour. Some Hispanics seek out an educated young Anglo inmate clerk and ask him to read into a battery-powered cassette recorder a letter they have written to federal authorities about the conditions that led to the riot. The letter describes the nepotism, the official manipulation and provocation of convict factions, the setting of race against race, the trumped-up charges and punishments by the disciplinary committee, the widespread official violations of civil rights. The clerk reads it all, almost filling a ninety-minute tape. Careful to avoid prison officials or local police, they then give the tape to a National Guard officer who says he will pass it on to his commander. The cons never hear of the tape again, and their letter is confiscated. That morning a frustrated young con has started throwing rocks at one of the guard towers. "Hey, shoot me! Shoot me now!" he invites the rifleman on the perch. "I mean, you're not going to do anything to change anything."

By high noon the first floor of dormitory B is aflame, and the smoke pours out as Mills, his cameraman, and four print reporters at last meet the two Durans and Candelaria for the televised news conference in a tiny office in the gate house. It has been thirty-four hours since the fall of the control center, twenty-seven since Governor Bruce King promised the rioters a press conference. The camera purrs, and pens scratch across small notebooks.

"Right now while we're sitting here," Lonnie Duran tells them, "there's probably killing going on."

Candelaria adds, "I think there's been enough of this. I don't want to see no more killing."

The negotiations began hours before with convicts defiantly demanding the resignation of the official clique as well as other sweeping changes. Now, though the envoys still talk of grievances—"all this harassment, harassment, harassment," Lonnie Duran says—the coveted interview wanders. The inevitability of the old politics outside has become all too clear to the cons, along with the exhaustion of the riot. They now refer respectfully to "Mr. Rodriguez," who moves in and out of the office during the interview. Essentially, they have narrowed their specific demands, the price of surrender, to post-riot protection and a few procedural improvements.

They complain about "permanent segregation" in cell block 3, false disciplinary charges, the absence of programs and psychological care, and the official drugging of inmates. "Under Mr. Rodriguez, when he was foreman, this penitentiary ran smooth," says Lonnie Duran of the coalition of the early seventies. "Under Mr. Rodriguez's rule they had school release, work release, rehabilitative courses [and] this is what the penitentiary lacks, rehabilitative courses." They need someone of Felix's caliber again.

"It's a total disaster," they report of the prison. Their

own friends have been killed. As for these three envoys, they are from cell block 3 and have been "brought out" by others. They have had nothing to do with starting the riot. Their speech is slurred with sleeplessness and narcotics. Someone in the room is hiccuping audibly as the videotape records it all for posterity.

Do they believe the official assurances that there will be no retaliation? "Yes, I believe I have Mr. Rodriguez's word and Mr. Montoya's word for no retribution...whatsoever," says Lonnie Duran, "and I'm gonna take it at that." At that moment Rodriguez enters the room, and one of the negotiators slurs a last-minute reservation. "Is there any possibility we can get a lawyer in here, make this all legalized?" They are worn out, almost desperate, but they have lingering doubts that they can trust the administration. "That way, if something comes down..." he goes on. "I'm not saying that maybe you'll go back on your word, because I doubt it, or Mr. Montoya. But it always looks better in black and white where we can say, well, look at here, this is what they gave us. It's not just hearsay. You know what I mean? If you could arrange something like that."

But there will be no lawyer, no written contract or settlement here. Rodriguez is intent on freeing the hostages. "Whatever we negotiate at this time," he says vaguely, "then you guys will release hostages?"

Lonnie Duran says they will do their "damnedest." But another convict worries that without the hostage guards they will have only Rodriguez's word.

"Felix hasn't gone back on his word with me yet," reporter Mills interjects.

But Mills was not here "last time." A con tells him of the 1976 disturbances when men were lined up and clubbed brutally.

The videotape is running out. The Durans ask for medical aid for wounded inmates and request stretchers to carry out the dead. Five hours before, Montoya has refused to provide additional stretchers. Now, on camera, Rodriguez tells the cons they can have all the stretchers they need. At 12:30 P.M. two more cons join the filmed talk, and the negotiations now transfer with reloaded video tape onto the walkway in the Sunday afternoon sun. The new men are Michael Colby and Jack "Two-Pack" Stephens, feared men from cell block 3, whom one reporter will call modern Vikings. These are cons who have been convicted of the baseball bat murder of another inmate in the yard, men whose three-piece suits and courtroom poise often unnerve onlookers, and who now worry about reprisal and transfer. Colby and Stephens, whatever the evidence, will be major targets of the post-riot prosecution—cast by the state as conspicuous villains of the drama, yet eventually acquitted of the riot charges. All five negotiators will be moved out of the state immediately, Rodriguez now assures them. Suddenly, the drama, the carnage, the tumult seem to be ending in talk of a few convict transfers. But Colby still asks about "those who stay behind."

"Won't be hurt," Rodriguez promises.

"No segregation," Colby persists.

Rodriguez answers, "Not at all....You have my word that no one will be beaten up or shot up."

And no one seems to question the naturalness here, the necessity and rationality in front of the New Mexico penitentiary, of a ranking corrections official offering a pledge, like some extraordinary and hard-wrung concession, that his employees will not commit criminal acts as soon as the institution is back in their control. Rodriguez tells the five inmate spokesmen to release the two remaining hostages, and then the men of each unit may return to their bunks to pick up their belongings. The negotiators go back inside. It is about one o'clock. Back in the flooded, smoking building, Duran and the others explain the agreement to a few men near the front door and to the sentries guarding the hostages. Their authority goes unquestioned. Twenty-five minutes later, Lonnie Duran emerges with two small sacks of personal effects. He puts them down and goes back inside yet again. A moment passes; then Duran and another convict, followed by Candelaria, come out with officers Mendoza and Gutierrez. Blindfolded, their hands tied behind them, the two guards are told to sit on the ground by the front door, and are soon surrounded by more masked, armed convicts. As the hostages sit there, a National Guard helicopter suddenly thrashes onto the scene just overhead, and the convicts panic, fearing some betrayal and thinking they are about to be gunned down. They harshly drag Mendoza and Gutierrez back inside.

But officials radio the copter away, explain that it was a mistake, and gradually the hostages are brought back outside.

The riot is at a climax and now it will end with a small act that is symbolic of the world that has made it. Seeing the two hostages, Rodriguez tells Colby and Stephens to go back inside to get their gear for the prompt transfer they want. As soon as they are gone, Rodriguez seems to pull himself up to his full height. He barks an order to Candelaria and the Durans to bring the hostages all the way out. To those watching, Rodriguez is clearly counting on his physical authority over the Hispanic prisoners. The three cons hesitate for a time, then take the hostages from the circle of armed men and bring them to Rodriguez. As Mendoza walks out unhurt, a reporter asks him, "What's it like in there?" The guard starts to answer, cannot speak, and breaks into tears.

When Colby, Stephens, and others return to the door moments later, they are enraged to find that the hostages have been freed. "You lied! You lied," they yell. They turn to go back in, and for an instant it seems that the surrender will collapse. But State Senator Aragon tells them, "It's over," and Rodriguez finally threatens to have the guards at the fence "blow your heads off" if they retreat inside to make a stand. Once more Colby and Stephens are assured of their transfers, and they sit down in the yard. As they surrender, fifty more inmates pour out of the pen through other exits. Yet there will be more than a hundred men inside when the prison is stormed.

Afterward officials will say the negotiators betrayed the rioters and will even tell a national corrections magazine about the alleged treason. As for the bargaining for the release of the hostages, Mills will say later that "at no time did the inmates go back on their word." But if the bruited charge of betrayal will endanger the convict envoys in *their* world, no one will seem interested in the fidelity of official assurances. No district attorney, no warden or corrections secretary, no governor or legislator will ask to view Mills's videotape. In spite of Rodriguez's assurance that it will happen "not at all," within weeks men will be again back in the harsh segregation of cell block 3 as soon as the riot damage in the unit is repaired. Maximum security punishment at

Santa Fe will continue to be arbitrary, indefinite, and in violation of rights recognized in most of the civilized world. There will be no gauntlet reminiscent of 1976, but the pen will be shaken over the next eighteen months in a new outburst of brutality. Men suspected of being leaders in the riot will be singled out, punished, often indicted on flimsy charges. And too soon Lonnie Duran and others who have been promised out-of-state sanctuary will be quietly brought back to Santa Fe, back into the grip of the system they have publicly denounced. "It was the administration," Mills will remember more than a year afterward, "that broke its word."

With the release of the last hostages, legislators, corrections employees, and some relatives crowd around the gate house to watch the assault on the pen. Inmates are still streaming out of the building. One stops in the yard and yells his name three times, as if to tell the world, or himself, that he has survived.

The siege forces have been contemplating the assault all night, and most of the commanders are eager if not ready. King has variously given authority for ordering the attack to the State Police chief, the National Guard commandant, Rodriguez, Saenz, and a state patrol captain. There is a confused meeting at eleven o'clock Sunday morning to discuss assault plans. The attackers are to fire only in case of an inmate charge or danger to an officer, and guardsmen are not to use their weapons unless their commanding colonel fires first. But otherwise the nervous, heavily armed men will storm the pen with uncertain orders, no real contingency planning, and small crude maps. Some think there are still hostages inside; almost no one knows what is happening inside the institution, though hundreds of escaped inmates could have provided detailed intelligence during the last twelve hours. At the moment of attack, 1:30 P.M. on Sunday, there is even a dispute over which unit should enter the front entrance first.

The State Police chief now gives the final order to retake the pen, but it is Saenz who tells National Guard and SWAT units to ready themselves. He shouts, "Move out," to men who have no idea who he is. With helmets, flak vests, and gas masks, the twenty-two members of the State Police SWAT team go through the main entrance, disarm two cons with knives in the reception area, wade through ankle-deep water, and climb through holes in the walls to the demolished control center. At the center they find three mutilated bodies. One trooper steps on a corpse as he climbs through the shattered control center window.

On the north side, with Rodriguez and Eugene Long, the twelve police of the Santa Fe SWAT team come in the yard through the sally port. They stop first to persuade a National Guard platoon to give them cover; the platoon leader has no such order and agrees only hesitantly. Now the Santa Fe SWAT officers, with Long and Rodriguez, first try to get in through the exterior door to the basement of cell block 5, where the two fugitive guards are still hiding. But they discover no one has keys to this door. Next they try the outside entrance at the west end of cell block 4. And just as they might have done Saturday morning before the massacre, they get inside but cannot get past the locked grille to the cells and the full horror within. Long tells them, though, that the grille can be forced, and they hesitate. Then the team commander decides on yet another means of entry and takes the team back outside and around the west to the loading dock at the kitchen. There they finally enter the pen, and there Rodriguez decides to leave the team and stay outside for the time being.

Once inside, six police officers sweep through the ground floor, surprising two inmates there, while the six others search the shops, laundry, and maintenance plant in the basement beneath. Then the members of the team are reunited and move through the mess hall into the main corridor. But at the door they run into the State Police SWAT team, which is moving slowly south through the bloody, debris-filled corridor from the control center. The State Police expect the city team to be in the north wing according to plan, and mistake them for armed convicts. In a frantic instant weapons are leveled and the city officers are nearly shot. Only shouted warnings prevent a tragedy. At that, Long has trouble identifying himself as a non-inmate. Pen officials are supposed to wear white armbands, but none are worn during the assault.

The state team now continues to pick its way down the corridor, past bodies in the officer's mess, in the otherwise untouched Catholic chapel, at the entrances to A-1 and D-1, and inside A-1. Looking into the burning gym, they see a pile of charred corpses. Three bodies will be conclusively identified only by anthropologists who reassemble the bone fragments.

And as they move south, officials at the gate house hear one last riot radio conversation in Spanish. "The stupid asses gave up the hostages. Now they're going to come in and shoot us," one voice says.

"I'm up to my neck in this. If I'm going to die, I'm going to die like a man." There is a pause, then the same convict sees the SWAT team coming. "They got us, Big Al. They got us good. They're lined up about thirty yards from us. If you can get word to the people inside, tell them to get out of there." The speaker then turns to other inmates with him and says wrathfully, "When we needed you guys, you turned your back on us. Now you're going to suffer. Tell them guys [the Hispanic negotiators] never to call me homeboy again, or they're dead." Seconds pass as the radio is mute. Big Al then tries to contact Chopper One. "Attention Chopper One ....Come in Chopper One...." There is no answer. For the first time since Lucero first heard that startling voice from E-2 in the control center Friday night, the convicts' radios fall silent. Santa Fe's revolt has gone off the air.

The National Guard is now deployed close around the building to take into custody the captured cons and to cut off any attempted escape during the assualt. The psychological unit has begun to burn again, and trapped inmates are signaling desperately from the small living area on the second floor. Now Santa Fe County sheriff's deputies try to break into the unit from the outside. They smash a hole, evacuate nine prisoners, and then move north to cell block 6 to round up more than twenty other rioters. But the SWAT teams inside have no warning that the sheriff's men are coming in, and there is another near disaster. Outside 6, the county police meet SWAT troopers, who mistake them in the smoke for cons and almost fire on them.

Now the two SWAT teams move north and into the charnel houses of cell blocks 3 and 4. In 3, which is burning, they find eleven survivors still in their cells, and Long and the pen locksmith free them. They also come upon two bodies;

one is that of "Pancho Villa," the mentally ill Mexican national. His face is obliterated, and his basement cell is jammed shut and cannot be opened to remove his corpse for two days. Meanwhile, another SWAT contingent is liberating the shaky, weak, but grateful Vigil and Martinez from the crawl space beneath 5. After some confusion, the SWAT men also free medical technician Ross Maez and the seven inmate patients he has secreted with him while savagery swirled outside their hospital hiding place for thirty-six hours.

In cell block 4 SWAT officers walk over two mangled bodies at the entrance and begin the gruesome mission of searching the tiers and the blood-smeared basement. Three or four men are still alive in the unit. Four contorted, nearly unrecognizable bodies lie on one side of the basement, four on the other. There are dead on the third and the middle tiers.

At 3:30 P.M. the SWAT teams complete their sweep and leave the pen, but they must go back inside minutes later when inmates are reported reentering the back of the prison from the recreation yard. Outside near the perimeter fence one rioter kicks a guardsman, but the trooper alertly throws his M-16 over his head to other soldiers before the prisoner can take it. In another case, however, cons grab a rifle and toss it to one burly convict standing nearby. He starts to cradle it, but the sound of a dozen guns being instantly cocked and drawn on him compels him to drop the weapon.

The chaos of the assault continues. Right after the SWAT teams comes a train of curious civilians—members of the Corrections Commission, Aragon, prison personnel, onlookers. They wander through the institution during the attack, without identification, causing several near tragedies. And through the smoke and slop and sheer vileness of it all, they and the law enforcement officers scavenge the pen for souvenirs of the butchery, carrying off in grisly fascination knives, fragments of pipe, drug paraphernalia, and other bits of refuse from the massacre.

This is only the beginning of the negligence and official folly in the handling of legal evidence that will stun observers for months to come. The siege command has had unmistakable proof of criminal violence inside the pen for more than twenty-four hours: eyewitness accounts, bodies, tortured guards, and an arsenal of weapons, some of them literally dripping blood. Yet the preservation of crime scenes and physical evidence becomes yet another casualty of the calamity. Spectators paw through the large box of confiscated and surrendered weapons at the base of tower 1. The State Police are supposed to photograph the crime scenes, while the National Guardsmen, under uncoordinated and entirely contradictory orders, are supposed to remove corpses from the pen as soon as possible. As a result, this afternoon guardsmen will take out at least two bodies before they can be photographed, and State Police photographers, fearing more removals, will race through their task, taking four shots—the prescribed number of pictures of a murder victim—of only one of the thirty-three reported bodies. Weapons will trickle into the police lab over the next week, some tagged, some not, and many will never be discovered at all. Only on Thursday, February 7, will the pen's murder chambers be roped off for the hopelessly tardy investigation.

Outside in the yard the last of the rioters are being disarmed. Some are manacled with the plastic handcuffs that seem to be everywhere. The wounded are taken off for treatment, and others are left to shiver in the 40-degree cold in shoes soaked from the muck inside. "No matter what they say," Colby now tells a passing reporter near the front fence, "when this is over and you people leave, they're going to come in and beat us, and beat us bad."

"I think we're back in control, which is a darn good thing," Governor King says to reporters and the crowd by the gate house. He has come back to the siege camp for the retaking of the pen, and now he is here with his wife Alice for the victory. "I congratulate everyone involved," he adds.

Military columns are now moving in and out of the building. After the SWAT teams have secured the institution, some National Guard contingents go in through the front entrance to bring out bodies, treat and evacuate any seriously wounded men, and, in some instances, simply to look around. As the soldiers begin to tramp inside, some of the rioters in the yard taunt them. There is some commotion among cons in the northern part of the front yard just as the governor congratulates everyone. The guard in tower 1 yells down about the disturbance, "Hey, they're burning their cocks off with cigarettes!" Though the crowd at the gate house unmistakably hears this, no one seems to react. There have been rapes and stabbings and self-mutilation among the yard refugees during the night and morning. Sporadic violence continues now in the confusion of the assault.

Moments later a National Guard platoon on special order draws up in front of the prison door in two facing columns, apparently a guard of honor. Bruce and Alice King, she a small woman of kindly mien gripping her husband's hand tightly, then march through the formation toward the prison. They seem to be about to go in. They walk up to the door and stop. There is a wordless pause. They look at each other. And then the governor and his wife turn and walk quickly back to the gate house. One observer, a prison teacher who has come on the grounds without being challenged and who is standing with other spectators at the gate house, thinks it "an incredible symbolic gesture." "I felt they just wanted to establish that the prison had been taken back again," he will write later in a reminiscence. Perhaps. To many, it is indeed King's pen. He and Alice are content to go to the door. The plantation is once more in the hands of the overseers.

It is probably just as well that they do not go in. Those inside already, some of them battle-hardened veterans of the Vietnam War, are shocked and sickened at what they find. "As a helicopter pilot in 'Nam I never saw atrocities that I saw here," a National Guard major will tell a journalist afterward. A flight medic who is a veteran of the savage riverine war in the Mekong Delta will wander into cell block 4 to find "ashes and pelvic bones." She says she will never forget the smell as long as she lives. Guardsmen and others mistake some Anglo bodies for those of black men; the faces are so charred that it is impossible to determine the original skin color. Other corpses are small, waxen, yellow. Some are covered in blood. The liberators will all remember "a tremendous stench" and will recall that the dead men seem unnaturally small, reduced by blowtorch and knife. "I'm not a gory person. I'm not in any way a violent person. In fact, I'm a queasy person," one eyewitness will write of his compulsion. "But no matter how much I saw, I could still see more." The pen is almost quiet now in the slanting Sunday afternoon sun. It is after 3:30. Voices are subdued inside the corridors. There is just the slosh and splat of boots on the flooded floor, the opening of doors, the indecipherable squawk of walkie-talkies. All that and the sound of men coughing and heaving in the corners. They vomit their siege camp breakfasts into the bloody debris.

More dazed inmates are taken to the mental hospital in Las Vegas for treatment. Some National Guard medics will need psychological counseling. Experienced medical examiners will be offered psychiatric therapy after dealing with the bodies. Dozens of men and women who go inside will have nightmares for weeks afterward. "I opened this pen in nineteen-fifty-six," Rodriguez will tell reporters after emerging from a tour. "It was really depressing to see the state it was in—it was really bad."

Amid the horror and revulsion, there is a minor medical miracle. By late Sunday afternoon some ninety wounded inmates, many of them in critical condition, have been evacuated from the prison and treated in Saint Vincent's, in the Indian public health hospital in Santa Fe, and in the field hospital at the prison. Doctors, nurses, and medics have been working around the clock, and they save every life entrusted to them. Convict medics have been the heroes of the takeover, risking their own lives again and again to help hostages and fellow prisoners. Now there is the same sort of humanity at Saint Vincent's and in the field tent on the pen grounds. The heroism in both instances will go largely unrecognized.

Not all the liberation is so laudable. State officials reentering the pen—the attorney general's later report will tactfully call them "non-inmates"—will loot at least 7,500 dollars' worth of state and inmate property from the hobby shop, which, like the law library, has gone untouched during the riot. They steal expensive tools, art supplies, leather goods, and jewelry. Officials pillage as well the prison industries building outside the fence, where the three escapees are discovered on Monday. They steal, too, the master key-cutting machine from the locksmith's shop. A new young prison guard assigned to one of the towers watches in disbelief Sunday afternoon and evening as state troopers make off with penitentiary two-way radios, tools, and other property. Some carry out large television sets and drive them away in pickups. "The State Police took radios, pictures, anything that wasn't ruined," he will recall later. "But what am I going to say when a senior state cop goes over and loads his car?" A convict clerk housed outside the penitentiary in an added unit on the grounds has for some time been documenting chronic official theft from the pen warehouse. Double vouchers are filed for actual shipments and for the recorded receipts after the graft is deducted. He has managed to assemble a collection of the incriminating vouchers in the hope of presenting them to a grand jury. Before the riot he has hidden them, safely he thinks, in a modular office unit on the reservation. But this, too, is sacked by officials during the siege and surrender, and along with furniture and office equipment, the telltale vouchers are gone when he checks his cache on Monday morning. None of the rampant official thefts, offenses that could bring courts martial to an occupying army, will be investigated or prosecuted.

Nor, in a virtual sea of law enforcement officers, will there be any reckoning for the most thoroughly documented official abuses. Two days after the riot, the terrorized and exhausted refugees are still huddled in the yard. Four prisoners refuse to go back inside the pen out of fear of reprisal for having talked with State Police investigators. There is a scuffle as officials try to force them back inside, and Deputy Warden Montoya is hit with a wooden plank in the skirmish. The inmates are finally overpowered, handcuffed, and led away toward cell block 6. But Montoya then stops them, calls them over, hollering that he knows where to put them. According to a subsequent attorney general's inquiry, the deputy approaches the bound men. Screaming profanities, he strikes one, orders the other to take off his shoes, and then stomps the inmate's bare feet. This is "typical" of Montoya's attitude toward the men in his custody, one State Police witness will later testify. "I'll know where to find you," a witness recalls Montoya telling the frightened men. One of the inmates is later mysteriously stabbed while in the prison. His family believes there was an official "contract" on his life. Looking into the incident after numerous complaints, the attorney general's investigators conclude that Montoya has been involved in what could be a felony assault. Even after a formal public report, however, he is not prosecuted.

Elsewhere, with different men, the tension of the siege is handled differently. At four o'clock Sunday afternoon there is a dispute between inmates and guardsmen in the yard when the prisoners are told to move to another area. The refugees hurl verbal abuse and even push the soldiers, injuring one. The National Guard officers order their men to fix bayonets, then reverse the command seconds later. One convict leader comes forward and asks to talk to the officer in charge. A major steps out, and he and the convict leader meet between the two angry groups. After a few minutes, the guardsman promises more blankets, dry socks, food, and water in return for prompt inmate compliance with guardsmen's orders. The inmates then move off peaceably to their new area.

At 5:30 the sun is setting in an orange blaze to the west, sharply silhouetting Sandia, the great watermelon-shaped mountain that hides Albuquerque on its far side. The institution continues to smoke. Firemen will fight its fires for the next two days. A burning American flag, perhaps the one worn by the inmate wandering through the north wing so long before, hangs smoldering from a window above the education unit at the far south end. National Guard bonfires begin to glow again in the twilight. There is the din of the camp and of more than a thousand refugees in the yard. It is almost like the evening before, except that tonight there are no screams. The pen is silent, left to the dead.

On Sunday evening there are the first haphazard efforts to begin accounting for the prisoners. Some men are counted twice, others not at all. Some give false names and numbers. Some are never asked their identity. The number of bodies is "estimated" at thirty-three, and there the official number will stay. Two days later, however, State Policemen interviewing one inmate will tell him they are "still finding" corpses inside, that the number is already at thirty-nine. Some 24,000 calls will flood the governor's service center, and numberless others will go to the lieutenant governor or to members of the Fraternal Order of Police who man emergency lines. But there will be no final count of the living and dead for more than a month, and in the meantime inmate accounting will fall into a sequence of official blundering and prevarication that will make the numbers forever suspect.

This Sunday night, the agony of accounting has already come to the families waiting outside on the highway. Despite repeated requests from the clergy to pen officials, there has been no food or coffee, no sanitation facilities, for those standing vigil. Only on Monday will the Red Cross bring in provisions and portable toilets. At nightfall on Sunday, knowing the pen has been retaken, the families gather to hear a corrections official read a list of names. Although there are many loudspeakers on the grounds, he does not make use of them, and the families do not hear his initial explanation that the names he will read are those of living inmates. As he reads and relatives hear only names, many break down in grief, assuming their men are dead. The list stops with the letter G, and the official retires with no further explanation.

Two families will hear on television of the murder of a son and brother before the state tells them. One mother hears her son listed as dead by a TV announcer and then, hours later, after calling various state agencies, learns that he has actually survived.

On Monday officials will release a list of 979 survivors, but the next day another list of 300 will be read to the families on the highway, repeating some of the 979 names. Once more, there is no public address system; the listeners do not realize that these are the names of men who are alive. Several relatives believe it is a casualty list and weep and grieve at the announcement of their loved ones' names.

National Guardsmen and police dogs will be arrayed Tuesday to hold off the relatives when they threaten to march on the pen to see their men for themselves. "They just hadn't thought about the families," a local minister will remember of his days with stricken parishioners on the highway outside the pen.

Over the following week anthropologists from the University of New Mexico will kneel on the floor of the gutted gymnasium, as the rays of the winter sun knife through the smoke and ash, collecting two cigar boxes full of bone shards. ("It wasn't the usual dig," said one account.) And thirty-five people of the medical examiner's staff will work around the clock trying to identify the murdered men and determine the causes of death. They will find, to their further horror, that some of the worst, most extensive mutilations were performed post mortem.

But for now the relatives must rely on the authorities for news. They surround Archbishop Robert Sanchez of Santa Fe, who has been inside. He tells them they can take comfort that the Catholic chapel was unharmed. He does not mention the corpse in the aisle, its blood stained into the floor, the torso burned so badly that medics mistake the victim's race. After the surrender King makes a brief appearance among the relatives to announce the triumph. He bends over to kiss an elderly Hispanic woman. A reporter later writes that her face turns stony. "But what happened," she asks the governor, "what happened to our men?" King has—and will have—no answer.

"I want it pinpointed why this developed," the governor will later tell the *New York Times*.

"It is clear that the long-standing and desperate conditions at the penitentiary have created desperate men. Desperate men commit desperate acts," says the ACLU in a Sunday statement. "The conditions and practices which led to the events of the last two days must be addressed urgently." Dwight Duran and ACLU lawyers have been at the pen during the siege, and they now prepare to push the suit as never before.

Meanwhile, in the legislature Monday morning, senators and representatives will savor leaked forensic photos of some of the riot's worst atrocities. "We gave them a fair trial and the benefits of our system," a member of the corrections oversight committee has said Sunday night, "but inside the prison they play by their own rules."

In the cold on the highway late Sunday night, a Hispanic ex-con, a survivor of the 1973 riot at Santa Fe, huddles near a camp fire. He has driven from Farmington after hearing of the takeover because he has relatives in the pen. Next Saturday he will bury his cousin, a young inmate bludgeoned in front of the education unit. But tonight he is still waiting to see if his brother is alive. "You don't know what's going to happen to you in there," he tells a reporter. He warms his hands over the fire and silently remembers his own time inside. "Things haven't changed much," he finally says into the flames. "They were bad then and they're bad now."

AFTERMATH

In short, insurrections do not end with
the return of official control but become
a part of the structure, like a flaw left
in a piece of steel which has been subjected
to excessive strain.... A riot is not one
criminal tried in court, unknown, unnoticed,
and then quickly placed behind the wall ...
[but] rather... records the failure of
penal policy.... Riots are of course...
embarrassing to the party in office.

Gresham Sykes,
The Society of Captives

The conclusion is that imprisonment
cannot be fully understood by those who
do not understand freedom. But it can
be understood quite well enough to have
it made a much less horrible, wicked, and
wasteful thing than it is at present.

George Bernard Shaw,
The Crime of Imprisonment

*i*f the riot was a continuation of the prior administration of the New Mexico penitentiary, then the administration of the prison for more than three years after February 2–3, 1980, was in many ways a continuation of the riot.

Most inmates spent the first icy nights after the surrender huddled in the yard. Rape, gang attacks, racial violence, and official brutality all continued in various corners, depending on the authorities in charge. Men jockeyed to be under the jurisdiction of the National Guard rather than that of police or corrections officials.

On Tuesday there began a chaotic expulsion of inmates to other prisons: 90 to an institution in Oklahoma, 148 to Leavenworth, 79 to Atlanta, 30 to Colorado. The pen foisted off 14 of its toughest cons on Arizona, where state prison officials swiftly returned 10 of them after learning about their records. Then, however, New Mexico gave some of the transferees false snitch jackets, hastily manufactured dossiers as informers, to persuade systems like Arizona to take them in. A piece of administrative deception designed to speed up relocation, the invented records were later handled with the usual lax security and thus served to brand innocent men as snitches. For a moment, however, the expelled, betrayed men would have their revenge in a sad little incident. During one of their transfers to Florence, Arizona the New Mexico cons savagely ridiculed before Arizona officials the poor English and frail authority of an accompanying Hispanic guard from Santa Fe. They would be silenced only when a burly

Arizona guard stepped onto their bus and announced that from here on they would speak only when spoken to.

At least Arizona would know roughly the identity of its New Mexican imports. Most departing prisoners were never finger-printed, photographed, or otherwise conclusively identified. Lists were compiled in the smudged longhand of guards who hastily wrote down names as men filed past. Shocked corrections de-partment aides would remember Felix Rodriguez keeping a tally of numbers of transferred men on a soiled matchbook cover. Federal officials expecting to pick up 350 inmates on Tuesday, February 5, arrived to find only 30 men ready to go. One State Police officer pulled men off a transfer bus to interview them about the riot. Colorado, like Arizona, returned some transferees when initial assurances about them from Santa Fe proved false. Maximum-security cons, shipped to Georgia under the wrong classification, promptly escaped. It was another phase in the unfolding though still hidden scandal in inmate accountability.

Back in Santa Fe, some of the remaining men were shunted off to county jails or to other state facilities; others were paroled or discharged outright. Most, however, had returned to the dev-astation and stench of the pen by Thursday night. They were jammed into eight salvageable dormitory floors, and were housed two to a cell in the relatively unravaged blocks 1, 2, and 6. Many were left there to defecate on the floor and to exist without water for more than fifteen hours until guardsmen complained of the cruelty of the situation. Only then did Rodriguez order Koroneos to allow men out to go to the toilet or get a drink. "To hell with you guys," one prison guard told men pleading for water. "You wrecked the place." On Tuesday and Wednesday maddened men in cell block 6 smashed more sewage pipes and set more fires in desperate protest.

Montoya soon organized inmate work details to clear away the worst of the debris and blood. Yet men described the odd, random reminders of the madness left for days and weeks after-ward: the red upholstery of the barber shop burned and slashed, the sinks smashed, but a large, thin mirror untouched; the gutted Protestant chapel and the Catholic priest in his sanctuary next door going about his business wearing a gas mask against the sour smell of death; wooden doors reduced to charcoal and piles of trash that contained neatly folded napkins, a small, blood-stained tennis shoe, a salt shaker; the menu above the mess hall doorway, the bill of fare obliterated and the date frozen at "Feb. 2," and atop it the dismembered sign announcing the prison's chief, " RY GRI IN, W RDEN." To many of the men back inside now, the pen had come to resemble a small-town virgin. They had taken it. It belonged to them, the ordinary prisoners as well as the hardened cons. And no matter who now became its official master, they knew that they could always have it back.

On Wednesday, February 6, a U.S. Air Force medical unit arrived from Cannon Air Force Base in eastern New Mexico to give each inmate a basic physical exam and to provide emergency care. Limited visits with relatives were allowed by February 13, and some outdoor exercise as well as a forty-six-man education program and a prison industries operation with eleven men began over the next two months. But otherwise, official compassion for the survivors soon dissipated. Prosecutors took on the tone of vigilantes. Santa Fe's district attorney, for example, announced on February 5 that he would "ask for the stiffest penalties possible." While the DA's assistants and prison officials began interviewing hundreds of men for prosecution, most convicts were denied the basic constitutional right to see their own lawyers. "We are not recognizing court orders directing prison officials to allow lawyers to see their clients," an assistant attorney general said, explaining the state's extralegal policy during the post-riot "emergency." "Those court orders," he said of decrees by local district judges calling for legal access to inmates, "just aren't worth the paper they're printed on, in my judgment."

Though a previous federal court order by Judge Campos provided for due process in opening inmate mail and especially immunity for legal correspondence, a State Policeman would later testify that during these weeks he saw a prison official "crumple up and throw away" a prisoner's outgoing letter, and at least one lawyer found his properly marked legal correspondence with a client returned to him opened, the client never having seen it. These were the first of many acts, witnessed and recorded by law enforcement officers, in which New Mexico officials flaunted the law contemptuously and with impunity. Before the riot, the New Mexico legislature had stricken from an appropriations bill some $6,800 needed to continue an inmates' legal aid program at the pen. Now, after the calamity, despite appeals from lawyers and despite the millions voted for new bricks and bars, the assembly still refused to restore the money. On February 13 a writer asked a prosecutor who had been combing the prison for informers about the irony of trying riot murders solely on the strength of snitched testimony, of relying on still more informants in a society where treason had brought so much bloodshed. "I suppose it's a philosophical point," the prosecutor replied impatiently. "From my perspective, I hope we get a lot of snitches. I hope we get a whole lot of snitches."

The results of the prosecution's zeal for retribution would not be plain for years. But what the pen gained in the first days after the riot was a vast amount of money. The New Mexico legislature hurriedly authorized nearly $90 million to repair the old pen, design and build a new fortress penitentiary, conduct an inquiry into the riot, and prosecute and defend the riot's criminals. "If the people hired or appointed to run those facilities are not capable of doing it, it reflects very directly on the administration that appointed them," said the house minority leader, a Republican, forgetting that many corrections officials were appointed during the last Republican governor's tenure a decade earlier. But most legislators voted for the new funds and left prison politics, as usual, to the governor and his men. Meanwhile, the riot would become a veritable growth industry for those who received contracts as a result of the muck and blood—architects, builders, contractors, suppliers, plumbers, electricians, and, not least, lawyers. Of the huge post-riot financial outlay, the largest of its kind in the state's history, only $3 million went to hire, train, and pay more equitably new prison guards. There would be something, it seemed, for everyone. All but secreted in the appropriation was over $56,000 for a new portable National Guard field kitchen the legislature had rejected in the past as a needless extravagance, a gleaming facility with a capacity of over eight hundred for a guard contingent numbering less than three hundred.

To all this the first wave of public reaction was shocked but fleeting. Prison experts around the country explained in the pages of the *Santa Fe Reporter* the folly and waste of simply rebuilding the old pen. They were duly ignored by a legislature rushing through its thirty-day session. A few writers of letters to editors in Albuquerque and Santa Fe spoke of citizens' guilt and advocated reform. Others offered proposals for mass executions of "hard-core" cons and suggested that the prison purchase water beds to "eliminate the problem of setting fire to mattresses." By the end of February, however, public agitation had visibly waned.

Once more the prison disappeared behind its shroud of silence. By then, too, all save four hundred inmates had been transferred temporarily to other institutions across the country. And from primitive stone jails in Oklahoma, from new Orwellian electronic isolators in Arizona or Ohio, from harsh work details and rigid discipline and strange, new, hostile convict societies, they soon began to petition desperately *not* to be returned to Santa Fe. It was as if, far away from and only a few blurred weeks after the riot, they had already sensed the sequel.

The new Saenz regime in corrections soon became an ominous flashback. By mid-March the attorney general's investigators for the riot inquiry noticed that the south wing corridor grille, the first threshold of the holocaust, was "open frequently and for extended periods of time." So, too, was the grille next to the control center "ajar repeatedly." At the same time, the official observers noted a guard carelessly walking among a crowd of inmates in cell block 6 with a full ring of prison keys dangling from his belt. What the appalled onlookers did not know, and what no one in authority would discover for another seventeen months, was that the cons already had a complete set of penitentiary keys that they had hidden after the surrender and that was found only by accident long afterward when a guard was murdered. The keep still belonged to its captives.

Early in April Saenz removed Griffin, shifting him to a position in which he would direct the parole system, and brought Rodriguez back as acting warden. Joanne Brown was soon to be acting deputy secretary, and Eugene Long returned to take charge of security when Koroneos, the old security chief, and Lieutenant Gonzales, for whom rioters had been so eager to trade hostages, were elevated to corrections department headquarters as experts on penal standards, positions in which they would continue to draw hazardous-duty pay for months after they left the pen.

Over the ensuing months the prison system was wracked by new turmoil. During twelve days in April, two inmates were stabbed; two were beaten in cell block 6; six men refused to extinguish lights in a dorm and yielded only after negotiations; there was a hunger strike; teargas was used to quell two more disturbances in cell block 6; and cons later staged a food and work strike to protest the continuing regime. By May 1 nearly thirty guards had resigned, including three lieutenants. An escape was foiled in one cell block only when the sawed-through window bars fell off into a guard's hands during a chance check. Saenz responded by closing the penitentiary and the corrections department to the press, by threatening employees with lie detector tests, by branding critical journalists as Marxists, and by dropping a curtain of official secrecy over the system—all this scarcely three months after the most horrible penal revolt in American history. Conducted on periodic tours of the pen to show suitable progress that spring after the riot, Governor King pronounced things "just fine."

But perhaps the most shocking disarray was hidden amid the more transparent examples of misrule. On March 8 King and Saenz announced the final riot tally of thirty-three dead and said that they had accounted for all other inmates. Officials had curtly dismissed numerous reports of more than thirty-three deaths as the result of "emotional distress" among the witnesses. If men were missing, they explained, relatives would still be calling, but the calls had stopped, King explained, ignoring the fact that only half the inmates in the pen kept in contact with anyone on the outside. Now came the final official count, and the corrections department, said Saenz, was "totally satisfied." At the moment he and the governor spoke, according to the department's own alarming documents, twenty men were still unlocated entirely, eight others were not where officials lists had them, five were unaccountably shown to have been paroled months ahead of eligibility, and six were supposed to be in federal prisons that had no record of ever receiving them.

Out of the failure to identify every prisoner through fingerprinting and photographing, there grew a documented trail of confusion, neglect, and dissimulation as a result of which New Mexico officials could never say conclusively how many men survived, fled from, or perished in the riot. What aides remembered as the unprocessed files that Friday night were apparently never entered in the computer, never counted in the census. The total greaseboard count at midnight February 2 was obliterated. Names given at hospitals never appeared on penitentiary rosters, and the discrepancies were never resolved. Post-riot computer printouts of the prison population were repeatedly contradictory—now showing too many men, now too few.

On February 20 departmental records showed as many as 120 men missing in the maelstrom of transfers, releases, re-housing. By February 25, with no thorough systematic identification, the trail had already begun to cool as men left the system. On February 26 department analysts found eighteen men missing with "reasons for concern for the inmates in question." On March 4, this disturbing news having passed from Saenz to Rodriguez to Brown, Joanne Brown responded with a "clarification" memo that only raised new questions. Two men Brown listed as released were supposedly in a county jail and not eligible for parole for months. One ostensibly released *before* the riot was listed as having been transferred to a county jail *after* the riot. Two inmates mentioned in Brown's March 4, 1980, memo were listed as *already* paroled on dates months *later* in 1980. Another prisoner whom she described as paroled never appeared on a subsequent accounting of parolees. And so it went.

Worried about the obvious muddle, Saenz asked Rodriguez and a pen deputy about accountability. All survivors, they assured him, had been properly identified. With that, Saenz made his March 8 public pronouncement that the tally was final. Meanwhile, a March 7 computer roster showed a census that was 19 names short of the 1,157 men who were supposedly in the prison that night of February 1–2, and the nineteen did not include the reportedly unentered men filed from Friday afternoon. When the U.S. Center for Disease Control began a special sociological study of the riot victims (as part of a national survey of victims of disasters), the federal researchers encountered several obstructions by pen officials. They found fourteen men with no recorded names and four more with no previously listed names. They simply described the fourteen and four as "statistical discrepancies."

When the thirty-three dead were "confirmed," with the gruesome distinction of being fewer than the forty-three killed when state troopers stormed New York's Attica prison in 1971, it was by bureaucratic default. Despite myriad reports of corpses far more numerous and elsewhere than those officially found, despite the documented chaos of the surrender and retaking and body-handling, no more corpses had turned up. Yet if the victims had been scientifically identified from their body bags or in anthropologists' cigar boxes of bone fragments, all the survivors had not. In grisly imitation of the pen's unauditable public stores, the actual human toll of the riot was—and would remain—unknown.

By June, Saenz had announced his intention to establish an

"inspections" staff within the system to "uncover criminal violations" among officials. His hold on the job was weakening visibly, however. He had run afoul of Governor King's powerful nephew, a cabinet officer who had urged the closing of a dangerously decrepit women's prison in the southern Rio Grande Valley. With Secretary Saenz under mounting fire from the press and legislature, King and Rodriguez went to a governors' conference at Lake Tahoe. When they returned, Saenz was swiftly removed and replaced by a longtime King aide who was to act as caretaker. Describing himself as "angry...deceived...disappointed," Saenz claimed in a heated interview that he was spied on, perhaps bugged, undermined by the old clique and by King's nephew. He said he was under pressure, "tremendous pressure" from a legislature that opposed change. And after a brief flurry of publicity, the former police adviser was gone from the scene less than five months after his appointment.

Saenz's departure brought no change in the regime. Days before his ouster, a newly appointed federal judge in Albuquerque, local Democrat Juan Burciaga, upheld the pen's gag rule by denying ABC access to the prison to interview inmates for a documentary on the riot. "Neither the First Amendment nor the Fourteenth Amendment provides any right of access to information within government control," ruled Burciaga, a West Point graduate, a former U.S. Air Force officer, and a local Albuquerque lawyer for fifteen years before his appointment to the federal bench amid charges of racial bias by fellow Hispanics. "The prison authorities have the right to establish order and continue that good order," the judge concluded.

"The New Mexico penitentiary has been getting by on the apathy and ignorance of the public," an ABC attorney had remarked. "Because of what happened there is no more apathy so the remedy is to maintain the ignorance."

In a stormy open hearing on corrections policies a few days later, King clashed bitterly with ex-convicts and prison reformers who testified. "You're excused. I've heard enough," he barked at them angrily when they spoke moments beyond the five minutes allotted to them. No clique and no official wrongdoing would be tolerated, he told the hearing. His defense of Rodriguez was emotional and unqualified. Later in the fall the governor would actively promote and present to Rodriguez an award from the North American Wardens and Superintendents Association. The plaque would cite Rodriguez for "his 25 years of commitment and dedication in the field of corrections as exemplified by his courageous acts at the penitentiary of New Mexico, Feb. 2–3, 1980."

Out of the June hearing came a series of attorney general's investigations into some of the most current public and inmate complaints of official abuse in the prison. The evidence tended, as always, to be slim but often graphic and the consequences, or lack of them, telling. Four revolvers and a rifle were still "missing" from a tower armory, Bingaman concluded, but no charges or further inquiries were pursued on what was obviously more official theft. Inmates had been placed in body casts on "possibly seven occasions" as late as January 1980, but no action was recommended against the responsible officials. Montoya had indeed assaulted inmates in the yard just after the riot, an apparent felony witnessed by State Policemen, inmates, and others. But Saenz's successor responded by shifting the deputy warden out of the limelight to a still more powerful position as chief of planning at corrections department headquarters. Like Koroneos and Gonzales, like Rodriguez in 1975, Montoya was to go on to still greater power in spite of such controversy.

As for the charges of brutality, it was the inmates' word against that of officials, and the attorney general concluded that none of the charges could be substantiated. A convict's personal valuables were indeed "missing," yet the evidence was "inconclusive" that officials had stolen them. An officer had indeed "confiscated" an inmate's watch, and the watch was gone, but the evidence of that was "inconclusive," and the guard remained a lieutenant. "I hope to end this office's involvement in investigations of misconduct at the penitentiary," Bingaman concluded the reports, nimbly passing on the future political onus to someone else.

In June and September 1980, Bingaman's two-part inquiry into the course and origins of the riot appeared, to similarly little effect. Commissioned not only to trace the "cause of the events" but also "to recommend any necessary changes in the administration" of the pen, the study was first directed by Michael Francke, the former corrections department lawyer and future King-appointed district judge, before being completed under a Bingaman friend. The resulting two volumes formed a scathing indictment of the old regime and contained a wealth of information. But read loosely, as such inquiries inevitably are, the study seemed to fix more of the blame for the riot on the mid-seventies administration of Governor Jerry Apodaca and his ex–federal wardens, and in any case plainly exonerated Rodriguez. Those who knew the history were astonished when the inquiry essentially ignored the files already at hand on the only previous attorney general's investigation of the penitentiary, failed to take into account Anaya's heavily documented 1975 findings of impropriety during Rodriguez's wardenship, and glossed over the deputy secretary's responsibility for decay and abuses during the period immediately prior to the riot. Nor did the inquiry probe into the long history of brutality, corruption, and scandalous accounting at the institution.

"The record was clear enough in our research," said an investigator who prepared the report and then left. "But Rodriguez's part got watered down to nothing." In the end, the supervisors of the report would be struck with the same old haunting ambivalence convicts felt toward Rodriguez's abilities amid so much incompetence.

"It should be painfully obvious that there are men there [the pen] whose actions contributed directly to the riot.... It's so discouraging, the governor, the corrections secretary, the warden all have done nothing. There are [staff] people inside the penitentiary who should not be involved in corrections," Reese Fullerton, Bingaman's riot report coordinator, told a reporter after publication. But he believed that Rodriguez should not be removed. "Even though he may lack the formal education and training," Fullerton went on, "Felix has the right instincts. He knows how... to get things done, and he understands how inmates think."

With the pen and corrections department shuddering in the fall of 1980 in their post-riot breakdown, the causes of New Mexico's prison disaster seemed to fade away in a search for simple administrative calm. Soon after issuing his history, Attorney General Bingaman announced his candidacy for the U.S. Senate, with Fullerton as his campaign manager.

The politics of the riot aftermath continued through the autumn in spite of occasional rays of exposure let in on the scene by honest officials. One episode in particular conveyed the atmosphere. On November 15, 1980, Dr. James Weston spoke out. He was the state medical examiner who led the effort to identify the charred and mangled remains in the aftermath of the riot. A man of unquestioned integrity, Weston was no ordinary observer. Internationally known, he was a past president of the American Academy of Forensic Sciences, author of a congressional report on the John F. Kennedy assassination, and founder of the State's Office of Medical Investigations. He was "one of the grand masters of forensic pathology," said a colleague.

Addressing the annual meeting of the National Association of Medical Examiners at Hilton Head, South Carolina, Weston revealed that many of the men murdered in the New Mexico riot were not, after all, pen snitches or hated informants, as officials had claimed. Instead, Weston told his fellow medical examiners, several of the victims were inmates who had not been able to pay bribes and kickbacks to prison supervisors and guards. When such "protection" or "shakedown" money was not paid, Weston explained, inmates were falsely labeled by the blackmailing officials as snitches and moved into the pen's infamous informers' unit, cell block 4, where many of them were trapped, murdered, and mutilated by rioting prisoners. According to a tape recording and transcript of his remarks, Weston said specifically:

> *There were some eight or nine dishonest people ... Of this eight or nine, about six of them from time to time accused various members of the prison crew—who had not been in a situation financially to come up with the wherewithal of the bribery that was expected of them—of being snitches. So that the victims, of whom there were thirty-three, actually only seventeen had actually been snitches in the eyes of the eyewitnesses who were called ultimately to give evidence. The rest of them had just been accused of being snitches.*

Weston later told reporters that the bribery and blackmail murders had been confirmed by "someone else involved in the riot investigation." He would not name his source, but he felt "confident the information was accurate." "I am quite certain they were taking bribes," he said. A correspondent for the *Dallas Times-Herald* tape-recorded Weston's address. Three days later the newspaper published an article based on his remarks, and condensed versions appeared in some New Mexico newspapers.

Almost immediately, an obviously alarmed and angry Santa

Fe district attorney, Eloy Martinez, sought to discredit Weston. "I believe both that the remarks by Mr. Weston were taken out of context by the *Herald* reporter and that Mr. Weston showed poor judgment in making the remarks in the first place," Martinez told the press. "I believe that if the allegations were true," the district attorney went on disingenuously, "the attorney general's investigation would have revealed that by this time." He added curtly, "The case is closed." Nor was Martinez the only high New Mexico official who was distressed about the medical examiner's remarks at Hilton Head. Immediately after his return to Albuquerque, Weston received anxious telephone calls and visits from key officials supposedly responsible for getting to the bottom of the riot and its causes. "They told me," the medical examiner later confided to a television journalist, "to keep my mouth shut."

Periodically hounded to say no more about the riot, Weston died suddenly while jogging alone one night around an Albuquerque golf course eighteen months later, his indiscreet Hilton Head revelation never having been pursued by an officialdom from statehouse to courthouse that seemed to know the answer already.

Nine months after their ordeal, the twelve hostages had grudgingly been given 50 to 60 percent disability settlements by the state. Psychologist Orner would be quoted as telling a Denver audience that autumn that three of the men were "vegetables" who were "totally destroyed as human beings" and "will never work again" and that each one was "mutilated in some way." As soon as they were freed from the rioters' reign of terror at the pen, the guards faced a new ordeal. The corrections department largely neglected them and shunted them back and forth through a bureaucratic maze so frustrating that the young woman staff member responsible for liaison with them left her job in tears and disgust. On one side, the former hostages were ensnared by a state government intent on denying its culpability in their torture lest it be forced to admit a liability in millions of dollars in wrongful-death suits being planned by families of inmates murdered in the riot. At the same time, the hostages' apparent physical recovery seemed to jeopardize their chance of receiving compensation. "The state wants them to disappear," said a psychologist who treated some of them. "The theory [of their lawyers] is that to collect, they'll have to be vegetables." By the end of 1980 none of the captured guards had returned to work of any sort.

Over the next two years they would be largely forgotten. Michael Schmitt won late in 1982 an invasion-of-privacy suit against the *Dallas Times-Herald*, whose reporter had listened to Schmitt in a Santa Fe hospital room hours after his release bitterly and graphically describe the agony of his abuse. But the local jury verdict was appealed; even if upheld, the ever-present lawyers would take their fees from the settlement. Meanwhile, Governor King announced that he was donating his $5,000 gubernatorial pay raise to the twelve men. Eventually, the issue of liability was quietly resolved when the guards decided early in 1983 to sue for over $52 million in damages, albeit *not* the state, but the manufacturers of the control center glass.

Whatever the plight of the tortured hostages, the guards who came after them at the post-riot pen faced their own terrors and administrative neglect. By late October 1980 frightened officers and other staff had appealed, in a formal "safety grievance," to the state personnel director, begging that "something be done before it is too late." In more than thirty internal prison memos— reports sent to Rodriguez from June through October but continuously ignored—the corrections officers, many of them new men hired after the riot, had documented numerous incidents of abuse, threats, and physical attacks by inmates. The maximum-security inmates of cell block 3, the most unstable and dangerous in the pen—several of whom were about to be indicted for killings during the riot—had been stripping away a shoddy chain-link fence in the unit to make knives and picks. They had showered guards with urine and bleach, hit them with rocks and with their fists. They had roamed the cell block unhandcuffed, crawled under unanchored fences in the exercise yard, congregated by scores when there should have been no more than five outside at any one time. This had all happened as the senior guard commanders—Rodriguez's men, members of the clique—stood by. And the situation reached a climax at the end of October in a week of stabbings, inmate murders, and mounting terror.

Security was lax throughout the penitentiary, said the protesting guards—no binoculars in watchtowers, patrol and pursuit vehicles with flat tires and dead batteries, riot-control grilles left open, as always, sally port gates that had not worked for a year, new electronic locking mechanisms carelessly placed so as to be vulnerable to hot-wiring by inmates, guards with faulty radios or none at all, and often only two officers assigned to supervise the 350 to 400 inmates of the entire south wing.

To the guards' carefully drafted and documented public protest, however, there was no effective response by corrections or other officials. Though legislative appropriations had raised guards' salaries to a level at or above those of surrounding states, though state propaganda made much of the new guard corps' stability and professionalism, a suppressed corrections department study in the spring of 1981 would record that 32 percent of newly hired guards stayed on the job less than a year. Among the early casualties was an educated young officer who had been valedictorian of his corrections academy training class. "Society doesn't like that place," Gary Weimer said of the pen from his new job as a hospital security guard. "And people in this state willingly went on in ignorance while the politicians didn't want them to know anyway. Men like Felix Rodriguez took care of the prison when no one else wanted to, and now we're shocked at the consequences. We have only ourselves to blame."

Weimer and others were gone, but some new men remained. And the following April it would be "too late" for Louis "Bud" Jewett, young guard who had given up an optical business in Albuquerque and come to Santa Fe with his wife and three small children after the riot to become a corrections officer, "to try," as he told his family, "to make a difference." Left by senior guard officers to supervise the jungle of cell block 3 with only a few months' experience, Jewett quixotically tried to stop a knife fight between convicts who were supposed to have been shaken down and was savagely stabbed in the melee. His heartbeat stopped twice and was twice brought back by a convict medic, as he was evacuated to the hospital only after tortuous confusion and hesitation. At Saint Vincent's he lingered for weeks before dying of his wounds. He would be buried with a guards' honor, though his widow had to beg prison officials to allow her husband his uniform and an American flag. Afterward they asked the grieving wife to pay for the uniform.

Jewett died under still another heralded new regime at the penitentiary. After a purported "national search," King the previous November had hired as Saenz's successor Roger Crist, the forty-six-year-old former warden of the Montana state pen. To obtain his talents, the governor offered the new corrections secretary an extraordinary three-year contract, breaking the next governor's constitutional right to name his own penal director, and a salary of $50,000 yearly, 25 percent more than that of other cabinet officers, as well as free housing at the penitentiary. Crist was said to be thoroughly professional. "When I was eighteen," the appointee told the Santa Fe press, "I knew I wanted to be a warden." Like Saenz, he was swiftly confirmed by a legislature that assumed it had at last a competent administrator for the troubled prison system. Once again, New Mexico had hired a corrections secretary, this one at exceptional cost and with elaborate ceremony, without bothering to scrutinize his past.

Less than two years earlier, the Human Services Committee of the Montana state legislature had compiled a voluminous amount of evidence during an investigation of Crist's 700-man state prison. Documents and testimony included some 350 diverse allegations from guards, federal officials, inmates, and others detailing official wrongdoing and mismanagement and portraying a penitentiary plagued by many of the same problems Crist was now expected to remedy in Santa Fe. The inquiry had revealed, according to one summary, "poor guard training, inept business management, hopeless classification of prisoners, poor food, inadequate rehabilitation programs, lax security, allegations of misappropriation of public funds, and persistent harassment from guards," including "indiscriminate use of Mace," guard "brutality," and "a filthy hole for punishment." The independent Montana Foundation for Medical Care confirmed nine out of ten charges of horrifying dental treatment and atrocious medical care. But New Mexico's talent scout, Bill Giron, a longtime King aide and Rodriguez's friend, was "unaware" of the 350 charges or of the medical findings when he appraised Crist, he told a reporter when the Montana record finally came to light in Santa Fe a year later. "I assured Governor King that this was the man," Giron remembered.

Crist's mentality, perhaps apparent in the eighteen-year-old's ambition, soon became clear. "I won't do your dirty work for you," he reportedly told the Senate Rules Committee when pressed to dismiss Rodriguez, and promptly retained him as his principal deputy. Crist not only retained Montoya as chief policy planner but also placed him in charge of the $50 million building program for new prisons. A former Crist associate from the Wisconsin prison system, Harvey Winans, was named warden although he had no previous experience running a major penitentiary. Winans brought with him his own security chief and ranking guard officer. A new corrections personnel board and a twenty-five-year retirement provision created by the legislature to clear out deadwood were swiftly swept aside, and the entrenched middle-level members of the old guard corps, along with Rodriguez, remained. By the spring of 1981 Crist had reacted angrily to all embarrassing press accounts of prison conditions, shocked federal researchers for the Center for Disease Control study by referring to inmates as "animals," and conscientious officers and department staff who tried to point out continuing problems felt increasingly demoralized. To those who had known Crist in Montana, what now followed seemed predictable. "I'm surprised, with your problems," a Montana legislative investigator later told one New Mexico reporter, "that you chose Crist."

In July 1980, as the new corrections secretary was being recruited, the state had finally concluded with the ACLU a consent order in the *Duran* case. Signed by Judge Campos, the lengthy decree was the product of the negotiations begun so fitfully before the riot and pursued more intensively since between convicts' lawyers, corrections officials, and the attorney general's office. The order fixed a population ceiling and covered living space for prisoners, disciplinary procedures, medical care, recreation, mail, schooling, jobs, and pre-release programs. In the thick, elaborate set of new regulations lay one of the most comprehensive prison reforms ever entered in American law, the culmination of the weary research and handwritten briefs by Duran and his colleagues years before. Presiding over the public unveiling of the consent order in his office, Governor King pronounced it "a landmark kind of agreement."

Less than six months later, violations of this consent order at the New Mexico penitentiary were well documented and widespread. Before the close of 1980 Compliance Consultant Vincent Nathan, a nationally respected federal court master in other prison systems, found illegal classification procedures, derelict psychological and medical care, inadequate food supervision, an absence of educational programs, dangerous understaffing, negligent security, and, not least, a cell block 3 that was "irrational, insecure, explosive."

On May 15, 1981, came a far more complete report on

prison administration by Daniel Cron, an attorney experienced in supervising federal prison orders in Georgia and other states and the formal, full-time New Mexico prison compliance monitor provided by Campos's decree. Cron's findings were the result of several months of daily observation at the penitentiary. He detailed "severe and widespread" violations of the law, including "across the board disobedience of the standards mandated for maximum-security inmates, inconsistent classification procedures, totally unsatisfactory conditions for food preparation [an outside sanitation consultant had called the pen kitchen an "imminent public health hazard"] unsafe and unsanitary living units and an absence of reasonable provisions for the physical safety of inmates." He also reported understaffing, unconstitutional tampering with inmate mail, deficient medical care, poor access to legal help, lethal wiring, defective plumbing, rat feces in food, and more. The unheard, unbelieved convict cries of more than a decade now reverberated yet again in the terse official prose of a young lawyer from Ohio.

A week after Cron's report, ACLU attorneys petitioned Campos to close the penitentiary, name a special master modeled after those employed by several other state and federal courts to oversee compliance with the law, and fine King, Crist, and other officials $1,000 a day if prison conditions did not meet court-ordered standards by August 1, 1981. In response, the state announced that it would not renew Cron's contract when it expired June 30. Then it began a full-scale legal fight to evade the court order officials had signed only months before. Defending the outlaw prison at taxpayers' expense was an Albuquerque lawyer, Robert McCorkle, a member of a large legal firm which often represented the state. For his part, in the spring and summer of 1981 as in the past, Federal Judge Campos looked on.

The prison Campos and others now saw was a place of resurgent crime and savagery. All the old vices flourished. Corruption was said to be rampant yet officially denied. New medical and psychological horrors were added to the already crowded historical chamber. Intimidation of both inmate witnesses and outside critics was violent and blatant. Murder and brutality became commonplace.

Early in 1981 guards as well as convicts began to come forward to describe to reporters the official theft in prison industries and the detailed routes by which narcotics were smuggled into the prison—right down to the color of vehicles and the names of officers. At the Los Lunas honor farm a new food administrator saw guards stealing his meat, which was freshly wrapped in brown paper. He reported it to superiors and was soon fired. His successor was asked to falsify records submitted to the American Correctional Association for accreditation of the institution; he refused and was forced out. A caseworker reported to prison officials on March 3, 1981, that contraband was coming into the institution, but the pen investigative files showed officials telling the caseworker "not to reveal the information . . . case closed." Similar files on the pen intelligence officer, Conrad Keller, revealed case after case of guard wrongdoing—a score of incidents from theft of penitentiary property to drug use to drunkenness on duty to repeated abuse of prisoners and manipulation of records— all duly recorded, and almost entirely undisciplined or unprosecuted. A gang of drunken guards was alleged to have brutally raped a female corrections officer; the story was hushed up.

Outside the walls, things were much the same. A construction supervisor reported the theft of tools worth $2,000 from a prison yard shed to which only the contractor and guards had keys. Convicts claimed to have run a booming solar energy construction ring out of the Los Lunas prison. More than $80,000 was reportedly unaccounted in a 1982 budget when the funds were appropriated for new beds at a juvenile institution, and the money was spent, although the beds never appeared. New prison construction management contracts in the millions of dollars went to the same firm awarded contracts by Crist's prison in Montana, despite comparable bids and under circumstances that moved corrections department staff members to leak the story. Records of prison construction contracts and certificates of completed work for more millions were found missing from the state central files at its Property Control Division, where discrepancies would later trigger an investigation by the Attorney General. Under Montoya, before an angry legislative staff found it, new building plans at one facility called for expensive electric heating and the resulting flush contract, despite the easy availability and much lower cost of natural gas. A construction supervisor was hired to oversee one major multimillion dollar project over the choice of a screening committee. Work was so shoddy at the new Los Lunas medium-security prison that nearly $100,000 was needed to replace doors and locks alone in 1980–81. Meanwhile, legislative studies revealed that prison construction costs in New Mexico were running higher than in most neighboring states, including California, and twice the cost-per-bed in Arizona.

In response to repeated public allegations that as warden he had taken meat from prison stores, Felix Rodriguez indignantly told a local reporter in 1981 that "one thing people probably don't know" was that the law provided that wardens could take food. "You used to have to draw your weekly rations and you got that instead of pay," he admitted. "Shortly after I became warden I went to Dave Cargo [then governor] and asked him for a pay raise," Rodriguez went on. "I told Cargo I'd rather have the pay and the state could keep its groceries." Personnel records would show that the warden apparently received his requested raise. What Rodriguez did not explain to the press was that the old 1889 territorial statute under which a prison superintendent used pen rations had been repealed on July 1, 1969, at least eight months before he became a warden.

Back inside the penitentiary, one inmate died of a heart attack in the summer of 1981 after officials scoffed at his complaint of chest pains and hesitated to evacuate him even after an electrocardiogram showed serious trouble. Another man seemed to die suddenly when his untreated lung cancer had gone so far that he choked while vomiting his own blood. An older con, suffering an acute venal breakdown, was near losing his leg as officials put off necessary surgery until he was paroled and the state would be spared the expense. Though ten prisoners were transferred to the state mental hospital in June 1981, the first of a planned thirty, another inmate was thrown in a punishment cell when he swallowed razor blades. The new corrections medical director admitted publicly that there was still no full-time psychiatrist at the prison and that "mental health remains a real problem."

For those who tried to protest conditions, report abuses, or defend inmates, the price was high. Families of prisoners were photographed and threatened as they peaceably demonstrated in front of the pen. Reformers were nearly run down on Santa Fe streets, terrorized by night calls, harassed as they visited convicts. Their cars were sabotaged, their homes burglarized. One of the inmates whom State Police watched Montoya abuse in the yard after the riot was stabbed in November 1980, and Crist pronounced it "awfully farfetched" that the incident might be linked to testimony against the deputy warden. A Santa Fe probate judge reported that his family was threatened when his son, an attorney, successfully defended a convict against an escape charge by presenting vivid testimony of how two guard captains beat the con and threw him in the hole for three days. The frightened judge quoted one anonymous caller as having said, "You tell that son-of-a-bitch lawyer we're going to kill him and his mother and take their bodies to the penitentiary so the cons can view them."

For the men behind bars, there were the old variations on the theme of intimidation. One riot witness, for example, was offered several inducements, including a free shopping trip to Santa Fe, in return for testimony to prosecutors. In another case, a cell block 3 con sent an April 14, 1981, kite to the warden: "You people have to get me out of here or there will be another killing [and] I'll be dead real soon. I'll help you find out what you want. . . . I'll help you. You get me out of here alive." A pen investigations officer asked district attorneys to move the threatened con, but prison records showed that Warden Winans was incensed and intent on using the con's fear to extract information from him. "We had intended to pump——— on the way to court," Winans rebuked aides. The warden was quoted in official documents as having said he "was not going to approve any move until he received all the information they [the DA] had gotten from———."

By the spring of 1981 a threat to anyone's life in the New Mexico State Penitentiary was hardly idle. From November to March, court-ordered monitor Cron reported twenty incidents of violence. Between March and April 15 there were ten stabbings. On April 17 inmates took over cell block 6 amid seven more stabbings when grilles were left open and guards lost control. By mid-1981 Cron had systematically recorded twenty-four separate incidents of guard brutality including some nearly fatal beatings in the hole and elsewhere, and one alleged official contract on an inmate's life. Many of these incidents involved senior guard officers; most accounts came from prisoners willing to take lie detector tests to support their stories; all were duly reported to prison officials and the U.S. attorney; *none* was pursued or prosecuted. In November 1980 guards savagely beat and kicked handcuffed inmates who were lying on the floor of cell block 3, in the presence of a pen investigation officer who documented the brutality in detail, took color Polaroid photos of the bloody convicts afterward, and was himself hit by an officer with a billy club and was threatened when he tried to stop the beating. Reported to corrections officials, the incident was swiftly covered up and never prosecuted.

As it had been so often in the past, official brutality was only an accompaniment to senseless death. Under the post-riot pressures, men killed each other and themselves as never before, save during the riot itself. In addition to the killing of officer Jewett, there were seven officially acknowledged murders of prisoners in the eighteen months after the riot as well as several other suspected killings and some men who were simply casualties of the system. One inmate slashed himself to death with a razor blade. Another reportedly overdosed on cocaine, although he had a small, unexplained puncture wound in his neck. Still another con was found hanged and cut in his cell but his death was swiftly announced as a suicide. A survivor of the cell block 4 massacre, pressured to testify by prosecutors, hanged himself with a bed sheet in a federal prison in New York days before he was due to return to Santa Fe. In the late summer of 1981 an eighteen-year-old inmate wrote his mother in Gallup, "I want to cry but it doesn't want to come out." He hanged himself the next day with his blanket in cell block 4.

One murder was remarkably foreshadowed, and the negligence well documented in prison and FBI files. On April 5, 1981, a longtime Rodriguez informant told pen investigators about a killing planned for the next day in the yard outside cell block 3. The alarmed officials duly told Crist, Winans, the warden's principal deputies, and an assistant district attorney of the warning. Winans told senior guards to shake down cell block 3 and not to let the intended victim into the yard. According to investigators, the officers openly refused to obey Winans's order, and the warden acquiesced. The next morning, with no shakedown or thorough search of prisoners and with no protection for the target, convict Joe Antunez, a thirty-year-old father of six, a con who had protected hostage guards during the riot and who was soon due for parole, was let into the cell block 3 yard and was still handcuffed when other inmates crushed his head with a barbell and stabbed him some forty times. Yet when the investigating officers who knew of the warnings and negligence later complained to the district attorney, there was no further inquiry. The officers who allegedly flaunted Winans's order went unprosecuted, though they were later cited in an ACLU court document listing violations of the *Duran* order. The guard who failed to conduct an adequate search before the convicts were let into the yard that morning was afterward promoted to lead the new penitentiary search-and-response team, a helmeted, baton-wielding contingent of patroling guards whom inmates soon christened the "super goon squad."

The lawlessness culminated in August 1981, with the slow murder of yet another guard. Thirty-three-year-old Gerald Peter Magee, a former policeman in Newton Falls, Ohio, had joined the guard corps in June 1980 as one more optimistic, conscientious post-riot recruit. At 1:00 A.M. on August 29, as an official log later showed, he was on the graveyard shift when bars were discovered cut in an apparent escape attempt from the dayroom of cell block 6. Despite the evident trouble, Magee and two other unarmed officers were ordered some twenty minutes later to go in and close down the block. There they were immediately seized by gun-wielding cons, as officials variously hesitated, nervously fired at fellow guards from towers, and listened to shots from the cell block. While terrified inmates in cell block 4 expected another takeover, the convicts began to torture Magee. At 3:15 A.M. his screams could be heard far away in tower 4. He screamed in agony for two or three more hours before he died, according to several witnesses, though Crist would later tell the press, "I was in the prison that night. I didn't hear anything." When the cons finally surrendered cell block 6 the next morning, Magee was dead. He had been repeatedly stabbed, and his skull was crushed.

Afterward, the Newton Falls police chief, who was Magee's former boss and confidant, a New Mexico State Police agent who also was Magee's friend, and several of the slain officer's pen colleagues spoke out publicly. Magee had been conducting, they revealed, his own personal investigation into official corruption at the prison. He had evidence on two "supervisory officers," said the police chief. There were notes and even tape recordings on narcotics, contraband guns, and prison industries fraud, said the other officers. Magee, they said, had planned to go to the

—210—

FBI the following week. But many of the sources were never even contacted by police or district attorneys during the subsequent investigation of the murder. And after officials listened to some tapes found in Magee's apartment and turned up at first sweep no incriminating notes or recordings, the case was treated as one more routine pen murder. Three cons were eventually indicted. Then, early in 1983, another prisoner who had been present in cell block 6 that night, a man already facing life in prison for another recent slaying, suddenly came forward to say that he and a partner killed Magee and that prison officials had entered into a "conspiracy" with the two cons to blame the murder on the three who had been indicted. Nonetheless, prosecutors insisted on pursuing the original suspects, who were subsequently either acquitted or quietly cleared of the charges. By the summer of 1983, nearly two years after it happened, the torture and murder of the officer remained one more unsolved, largely uninvestigated execution in the New Mexico prison, the issue of corruption buried with the zealous young officer. On the monument plaque honoring the state's prison guard martyrs at the Santa Fe corrections academy, Gerald Magee's name remains as it was entered after his death—misspelled.

In the wake of the Magee murder, the penitentiary was completely locked down, all provisions of *Duran* suspended in the "state of emergency," as the new search-and-response team prowled the corridors in tardy zeal for security. A district attorney, looking at the scene of the guard's killing, discovered by chance, hidden since the riot, the set of keys to almost every pen unit. But despite repeated reports on prison corruption from his own Organized Crime Commission, despite rising criticism and revelations from local press, television, and radio—and even from *Time*, the *Washington Post*, and the *New York Times*, Governor King continued to deny all serious charges and to reject any independent inquiry.

In October 1981 the state legislature's Criminal Justice Study Committee under a new chairman, a state police officer and senator named Caleb Chandler, began its own probe of the pen and was promptly thwarted by a formal written corrections department gag rule that prohibited employees from talking with committee investigators. When the committee completed its inquiry three months later, it had confirmed many of the charges already exposed in the media, though serious cases of brutality and corruption remained to be pursued, and action even in specific findings would be typically meager.

Hundreds of thousands of dollars remained unaccounted in the corrections budget, and there were seeming improprieties in the awarding of huge contracts, but the legislators could only pass the inquiry on to the attorney general's office, where it rested. Thefts by State Police during the riot were "unconfirmed," so the case was closed. One official had falsified records in the *Duran* case, in contempt of the court order, but he was simply allowed to retire. Much, however, had been learned: pen intelligence files were indeed found to have been destroyed; certain guards had apparently raped a fellow officer; the prison industries operation was mired in malfeasance and employee exploitation; a murder had been committed as a result of drugs brought in by a guard; the contraband reported by the caseworker, and ignored at Winans's insistence, was real. But, in spite of all this, no charges were leveled and no legal penalties exacted. In the end, only four guards alleged to be rapists and nine more officers caught in a confidence game with an inmate were formally dismissed for wrongdoing. Looking out at it all from the dormitories and cell blocks, the men Crist had called "animals" could reflect once more, as they had so often in the past, that some offenders and some offenses were more equal in American justice than others. When the Criminal Justice Study Committee met with King in a closed showdown session in October to urge Rodriguez's removal, the governor again refused the request and publicly called the action blackmail. Thus were the politics deadlocked at the close of 1981, as the penitentiary continued in a state described by Cron report as "explosive."

There would be, however, a coda to the brief flurry of investigations in 1981. While various inquiries into official criminality at the New Mexico prison were referred to state or federal agencies where they would languish or be quietly dismissed for the usual lack of evidence, a special Santa Fe County grand jury was formed in January 1982. Impaneled as a result of an extraordinary citizens' petition to look specifically into corruption and mismanagement at the pen, the jury seemed to promise at last some independent local action. But its brief inquiry was nine weeks old before it was given or even informed of crucial documents. Prosecutors called only thirty-five witnesses among potential hundreds and provided the jury with little more than official reports and media accounts rather than basic investigative files or independent audits of its own. Hostage to a district attorney's office with a long history of obvious distaste for authentic prison investigations, the jury forlornly produced one more set of familiar and toothless recommendations on guard training and management efficiency.

By the second anniversary of the riot, the hope for change at the New Mexico State Penitentiary had been reduced largely to what it had been before the holocaust, to the law itself, and now specifically to enforcement of the *Duran* order. The state would be "money and time ahead" by complying with the order, Crist had said shortly after his appointment late in 1980. The standards, he told legislators, were "minimal." But a few months later the regime seemed to be fighting the decree at every turn. At the last moment, in July 1981, Cron's monitoring contract had been extended for another six months in return for the ACLU setting aside a contempt motion against the state and granting new deadlines for compliance. But over the ensuing months, as Joanne Brown was named by Crist to supervise compliance, conditions steadily worsened, the new deadlines for compliance went unmet, Cron issued a final report as thorough and damning as his others, and the ACLU entered its general contempt motion, along with a specific contempt action against a senior Winans aide who was accused of falsifying disciplinary documents. By every independent account throughout 1981 and into 1982 the pen was still in nearly total violation of the federal court order and once more was dangerously overcrowded. Cell block 3 was now a classification nightmare that left men indefinitely in lockup and in an idle, despairing rage.

At one point, as ACLU attorneys attempted to send letters to their inmate clients, prison officials seized, read, and held the correspondence, in utter defiance of the *Duran* order. They claimed that the lawyers' discussion of prison conditions—something of which the inmates were presumably already all too aware, and which had been exhaustively reported in the press in any case—constituted a threat to pen security. In a remarkable judicial sequence, all of which occurred *in camera* in what the *Albuquerque Journal* would call a "great leap backward," Judge Santiago Campos first allowed the unconstitutional seizure of the legal mail with impunity, slapped a gag order on ACLU attorneys, and sealed the innocuous letter in which prisoners' counsel asked for release of the correspondence. Then, under pressure of publicity, the judge advised the parties privately to negotiate release of the letters, though only with a rebuttal letter from Crist and an explanatory note from Campos himself. Subsequently, Robert McCorkle, the attorney for the state, would move to gag again prisoners' attorneys and press reporting on the penitentiary. By then, however, Campos himself was already under scrutiny for an alleged *ex parte* communication with one of the state parties in the case, and the judge declined the McCorkle motion with strictures from the bench about "misinformation" in the media.

The judge, it seemed, had discussed the case with his dentist, who was also for years a well-paid part-time pen dentist who was opposed to the *Duran* order's abolition of his contract in favor of a full-time dentist. Dwight Duran had discovered the apparent violation of judicial canons only by accident in the compliance monitor's reports. In the ensuing hearing when the ACLU moved for the judge's recusal, a federal appellate court in Denver found against Campos in a lengthy opinion. He was removed from the case by a fellow judge at the end of July 1982, an extraordinary act by the federal bench under the circumstances.

Among the paper avalanche of *Duran* v. *King* the recused judge left behind were telling symbols of his stewardship. The taxpayers of New Mexico, one of the nation's poorest states, would pay hundreds of thousands in lawyers' fees while the state struggled to resist the federal court order both it and Campos had solemnly signed in July 1980, and while a dozen more men died at the pen. In a March 1982 formal request for admissions filed with Campos by ACLU attorneys, which included some 205 statements relating to violations of the *Duran* order, ranging from glass in the food to abuse of solitary confinement, the state of New Mexico had openly *admitted* to 134!

As the politics were played out, those accused of committing the riot murders and other crimes were at last prosecuted, a final apt interment of the event. Weeks after the surrender of the pen to authorities, Santa Fe district attorneys, who were assigned the prosecutions in full, talked of pursuing nearly eighty separate crimes and more than a hundred prisoners. A special riot prosecution staff of forty was assembled, including a chief prosecutor imported from New York and a highly paid local "administrator." Their periodic appearances before the legislature to secure more appropriations and meetings with the press assured the public of progress as the months became years. In June 1981 the administrator told the legislature that the prosecution was "operating perfectly." The following January he pronounced it an "unparalleled success" with a "record number of convictions at a reasonable cost to the taxpayers." New Mexico's justice was said to be far more effective and cheaper than comparable post-riot reckonings after the revolts at the Attica or Pontiac, Illinois, prisons. At the close of most of the cases in 1982, the prosecutors held a seminar in Santa Fe to instruct other attorneys and officials on their achievement. A consultant hired from Chicago used the record, and suitable photographs of District Attorney Eloy Martinez, in a new commercial brochure advertising his firm. The mayor of Santa Fe proclaimed Charlie Baldanado Day in honor of the chief prosecutor, and Bruce King told the seminar audience, "We've come a long, long way."

Less prominently, other voices told a somewhat different story of the two-year prosecution. Defense lawyers, convicts, families, and even prison staff had charged that the district attorneys had repeatedly used pressure as well as the inducement of early parole and other favors to secure testimony. Key witnesses, who first told State Police investigators they either did not see killings or could not identify the killers, came forward later in miraculous recall to relate minute and gruesome details of murders. Unable to finger particular prosecution targets after hearing the first part of a tape recording, some eyewitnesses suddenly remembered faces and names clearly after the tape had been stopped and then turned on again. "Well, for some reason, they [the investigators] mentioned Colby's name a lot, like they wanted people to say he was there," one witness told a jury. Though denying any impropriety, even prosecutors confessed that their witnesses were frequently rewarded with release. "To be honest with you," Baldanado later told a reporter, "not *everyone* I wrote a letter for got paroled" (emphasis added).

"The jury trials," one participating lawyer wrote the *Albuquerque Journal* afterward, "brought public attention to superficial investigations and to ill-advised deals where charges against the guilty were dropped in exchange for testimony against the innocent."

Said another attorney who was involved in the trials, "I just don't think that the truth about the riot came out."

The final accounting on the prosecution would be in its statistics. After nearly fifty indictments, eleven trials, thirty-two pleas, and over $2.2 million spent for prosecution, after seminars, advertisements, and self-congratulations, the state's attempt to bring the riot to justice seemed to many a costly failure. Seventeen of the thirty-three murders were not prosecuted at all. Tom O'Meara, the Ortega brothers, Joe Madrid, Robert Quintela, those murdered in the shadows, and those butchered in the open, had been killed with impunity.

Rioters who tortured the hostage guards also went unpunished; no charges were brought in the savagery perpetrated on the captive officers. The prosecution's "success" could be traced to nineteen plea bargains in thirteen murders. Fourteen of the pleas were for second degree murder and eleven carried concurrent sentences that added nothing to time being served by the same men for other crimes. In the end, prosecutors would sustain before juries only two convictions in *two* of the thirty-three murders. There were two retrials and one hung jury.

It was the public defender's special riot defense team—working with a smaller staff, a much smaller budget, and no civic proclamation awaiting it—that could point to real triumphs. Five convicts were acquitted by juries in four of the murders. Thirteen more men had charges simply dismissed in seven killings. When the sentences had been pronounced, there were few claims of harsh punishment or even deterrence. There were no death sentences. The two jury-trial murder convictions resulted in thirty-year consecutive sentences.

But, of the eight guilty pleas that issued in consecutive rather than concurrent sentences, the longest would be nine years. One con, pleading involuntary manslaughter in a riot killing in cell block 3, had been released by early 1983. Of nine men convicted of conspiracy to take over the pen, most of them from E-2, only one went to trial, and seven of the eight plea arrangements were for concurrent sentences, leaving the men largely where they had been before the guards walked in that February night.

Behind the debacle were several factors: the careless handling of evidence during the siege and after the surrender; the drug-besotted, smoky, fear-crazed atmosphere in which the killings took place; the perversions of the pen snitch system; the

—216—

sheer fact that some murders went unwitnessed. To all this were added the questionable, often self-defeating tactics of the prosecution and an all too obvious disparity of intellect and education between public defenders trained elsewhere and home-grown district attorneys, a contrast that overcame even a prevailing hostility to the defense by the equally local bench.

Three years after the carnage the conclusion seemed inescapable: in stark legal terms of proof and punishment, many if not most of the men who rampaged, raped, tortured, murdered, and mutilated at the Santa Fe riot got away with it.

FORESHADOW

anta Fe, at the close of an unusually bleak, snowy winter, 1983. The town is discreetly alarmed about sub rosa efforts by officials to manipulate a large tract of public land for considerable private profit. The worry appears futile, the gradual desecration of the Holy City relentless. Lineages of bold conquistadores and gentle artists have degenerated into municipal zoning sharks.

The penitentiary out on the Cerrillos Plain is again mostly invisible. Beyond the Sangre de Cristo and the Jemez, in the vast country beneath its soiled skies, prisons are perhaps the greatest single failure in American society. A $4 billion, one-hundred-murder-a-year disgrace, they cage some 400,000 men, women, and children in a crude cycle of inhumanity and degradation that feeds on itself, creating crime and punishment, then more crime and more punishment, with no relief. Exemplar of human rights, leader of the free world, the United States of America sends more people to prison for longer terms than does any other industrialized Western nation, save racist South Africa. There is no shortage of documented evidence of the disaster, and there are no sane answers to the questions about why it goes on. Public fear of criminals and crime is pandemic. In some states there are fewer offenses, yet more arrests and more incarceration than in others. Rehabilitation is out of vogue in the 1980s, leaving the cell blocks once again to the mercy of the turnkeys. In any case, the payback is always there, waiting. Prisons protect no more than they punish and reform. No legislator, no voter, no child of either, is immune to the crimes that will be committed by those recidivists who have had "the benefit of the system," as the New Mexico law-maker put it, those who have been in the custody of this most irrational—in a literal sense, most criminal—of public policies. Penitentiaries remain man furthest from God, an enormity imprisoning society and the outlaw alike, and from which there has been, and is, no escape.

Meanwhile, the men and women who represent the nation's legal conscience struggle with the scandal. Twenty-eight states operate prisons under court orders that have found officials guilty of cruel and unusual punishment. Seventeen more are under challenge. There are policy issues to be debated: alternatives to incarceration; sophisticated diversion of unthreatening offenders who constitute the vast majority of the prison population; restitution and reeducation; the self-defeating logic of determinate sentencing; the insidious chemistry by which the addition of more cells seems to propagate the men to fill those cells; the true role of a prison; and beyond, the social causes of crime itself, rooted deep in the nation's economics, character, and history.

But Santa Fe has not even begun to grasp these issues. New Mexico's legislature is sitting again, as it was that February three years ago. Now the citizens are building a new pen in the southern part of the state, a new isolator at the old institution at Santa Fe—cinder blocks and contracts in lieu of policy. There is a community corrections statute on the floor of the legislature, but that will be only a modest beginning at diversion. There is also a bill permitting conjugal visits; it is unlikely to succeed. Corrections Secretary Crist is against it, he tells legislators, because he doesn't want *his* pen to be a brothel—a least not a heterosexual one. In Santa Fe they are not yet quite ready to face the policy issues because they first have to stop the killings, the escapes, the swallowing of razor blades, the glass and the rat excreta in the food.

In February 1983 two cons armed with wire cutters walked around half the yard in full view of two towers, snipped a hole in the fence, and were out for some forty-eight hours and through twelve head counts at the pen before they were discovered missing by the new security-conscious Winans regime. In the last few months more than fifty men have escaped from the state prison system. Its vaunted security has become a joke. But like that earlier escape in December 1979, this latest flight had an electric effect in the cell blocks, another dramatic sign that the prison belongs, as it always has, to its old owners.

Attorney General Jeff Bingaman is gone, elected to the U.S. Senate after a lethargic campaign in which his strident opponent defeated himself. Bruce King has retired to his large ranch just south of Santa Fe for the time being, having passed the governor's office on to his former aide, Toney Anaya. King is talking coyly these days of a cabinet appointment in the next Democratic administration in Washington, or perhaps an ambassadorship—to a "friendly country," he always adds.

Felix Rodriguez retires during the summer of 1982, at last eased out by legislative arrangement for his pensioned exit. He parts after an embittered press conference, lashing out at "irresponsible journalism," at Anaya, and at Senator Caleb Chandler. He assures the press that he has passed a U.S. attorney's lie detector test on corruption. He obviously deplores the state's ingratitude in pushing him out of office. And he is right, of course, though not for the reasons he admits. It is a tragedy. His Anglo *patrons* should be there with him in the glare of defeat. For all his power, in the end he teaches cons the penultimate lesson of the free world: overseers are always expendable.

The administration has changed—somewhat. Joanne Brown is gone. So are Orner, Long, the former food director, Rodriguez's brother-in-law from prison industries, a few senior officers of the old faction. But Robert Montoya remains a powerful headquarters official. And there are still men of the past everywhere in the system, in administrative services, in jail standards, in the head offices of other prisons, in the corridors of the penitentiary.

Many of the new post-riot generation of guards and many of the more dedicated and educated departmental aides are gone as well. Filling the empty places, forming a thin veneer over the institution's real masters, are Winans's recruits. They are from Wisconsin and elsewhere, and they have Germanic names like Mixdorf and Hassenstab and Hoeft that have an alien resonance in the Spanish cell blocks. "I got to get myself a new clique," Governor King tells a reporter. And so he has. The new men posture with inflated titles and military ranks. They affect Draconian security. But beneath the pretense some of them, too, are accused by the ACLU of subventing the court order and of looking the other way no less than their Hispanic predecessors. They, too, are accused of abdicating authentic control, as Winans is said to do so lethally in the Antunez case, to the old coalition of cons and officials. The inmates and Spanish guards call them the "cheese eaters." It remains largely Rodriguez's pen.

Among the convicts, most of the hard men of cell block 3 and E-2 have been passed off to other state and federal penitentiaries after the anarchy of 1981. The state purchases an interval of calm, briefly, by exporting its problems. But of course new leaders, new respected and reckless cons with even more to prove take their place. One gang implicated in much of the post-riot violence, Los Carnales, is said to have inducted a few members after the riot, and then requires the candidates to kill as a rite of entry. The regime can exile men but not machismo or rage.

Many of the snitches are gone, too, as are the survivors of the carnage in cell block 4 and the new generation of informers spawned by the riot prosecution. Yet new inmates, the new weak and malleable and innocent and ill, have taken their place in protective custody. Predators, prey, precarious regime: they are all there again.

When the new Anaya administration takes over the state in January 1983, it discovers that, in addition to its terminal corruption and despite regular assurances to the contrary, the King government has quietly left the state in dire financial straits. Part of the scavenging of the budget are the lawyers' fees for the *Duran* case, and Anaya instructs his new attorney general to take over from McCorkle and negotiate a settlement out of court with the ACLU. That will probably mean the naming of a federal court master, something Crist has doggedly fought, but if it imposes fresh independence, integrity, and competence on the penal system, it will be the single most encouraging development in the history of the New Mexico prison. The negotiations drag on fitfully through the winter. Some convict clients grow impatient with the ACLU attorneys, distrust the parley, want their day in court. Someone, at least someone, must take responsibility at last.

But even in court, with all the weight of history, the convicts' vindication will be uncertain. The recused Campos has been replaced in the case by Juan Burciaga, the judge who denied ABC's petition for free reporting on the post-riot penitentiary. In New Mexico, the court-eager cons should understand, it is unwise to take history for granted.

And even if the court master is negotiated by Anaya and ratified by Burciaga, he will enter into a long, shadowy struggle with an obdurate prison regime to bring the pen under the Constitution. The smallest change devours time, perhaps too much of it.

Dwight Duran returns to Santa Fe for the negotiations. The naming of a master would be the climax of his heroism that began six years ago when he watched his boyhood friend die, and when he first opened the federal case books to take his laborious notes. He is now a respected figure in his profession, a nationally recognized expert who counsels prison reform from Virginia to Texas. He also moves between two worlds, the convict and the free, suffering the distrust and the fear of those on both sides who are threatened by peace. "Now watch yourself," Crist says to Duran acidly in the fall of 1982 when his parole expires. It is the ex-guard talking to the ex-con whose name will appear in constitutional law texts for the next century.

Duran is tired after the long fight, and he cannot forget. Subpoenaed by yet another grand jury to show them the pen, he will take the jurors on a sunny February day to the basement of cell block 3, to the hole. As he gets up and dresses that morning, he willl vomit at the memories.

Whatever happens with the master—and his supervision will cost the state hundreds of thousands of dollars to do what its officials should legally do to earn their salaries in any event— the riot has truly produced a financial boom. Its cost after three years is well over $200 million, enriching construction and law firms, bureaucrats, consultants, contract beneficiaries of every sort. And the state has not even begun to feel the toll of the wrongful-death suits by families of murdered inmates, the trials for millions of dollars in damages that will strain, against the shared reticence of judges and the state's contract attorneys (some of them ex-prosecutors, some of them McCorkles), to put the penitentiary regime in the dock.

As the relatives seek their retribution in money, the regime will be asked again and again why their men, none sentenced to death, had to die in the hands of the state. There will be no comforting answers. Yet it will be clear in the larger history that their deaths at least secured what change and public attention have come at last to New Mexico's haunted penitentiary. For all the law and politics, all the reformers' devotion and official scandal, the decisive difference has been their blood, their blood smeared on the walls and floors and out onto the tiers. And, in the end, their blood alone.

Then suddenly, at the end of April 1983, Crist too is gone, resigning before the November expiration of his contract to take a lucrative sinecure with the National Institute of Corrections. He has been at odds with Anaya over the appointment of a federal court master and has bridled as well when the feisty newcomer pressures for an investigation into upper level mismanagement in the recent escapes. A political and administrative mismatch with New Mexico, Crist and his once-lustrous Warden-of-the-Year's career is one more casualty of the riot and its chaotic aftermath.

Crist's departure leads to an ironic, almost incredible sequel, and the story now comes full circle. Anaya immediately names as the new secretary Michael Francke, the local King-appointed judge, the former assistant attorney general whose report masked responsibility for the premonitory mass escape weeks before the riot, the erstwhile aide to Anaya and Bingaman while their offices resisted every civil rights suit filed against penitentiary barbarism, the one-time corrections department lawyer at the height of the prison's outrage in the 1970s, a man publicly silent and apparently unseeing in the face of all the evident evil. Francke has no experience running a prison, let alone administering a statewide penal system. But he is said to have fresh ideas and the governor's confidence.

Still, in the long run, what the cons call hard time, Francke and his past will matter less now than ever before. The corrections department that spawned him in the 1970s is gone forever, obliterated by Dwight Duran's handwritten brief. If Francke replaces Crist, another convict leader will take Duran's place as the conscience of the pen. And with Crist's ouster crumbles the last resistance to a federal court master. Early in June 1983 Anaya agrees to name Vince Nathan, a nationally-respected monitor from other states, to begin the long-overdue enforcement of constitutional standards at the pen. The old regime will resist, but its days are now more clearly numbered.

The last lesson of the riot, of the court order, of those haunted cell blocks, is not the endurance of misrule, but rather that the human spirit is indomitable. The devils of the butcher shop will eventually disappear, vanquished by progress and a better understanding of man. And until then, the struggle will go on.

This winter they are still brewing raisin hooch in the dormitories and cell houses. It keeps back the chill of the darkness, when that luminous fat moon rises over the Sangre de Cristo, and the Cerrillos Plain takes on its milky night.

Men still scream in their dreams in cell block 4 and shudder at sudden noises. In the silence after midnight guards and inmates start at the night sounds of the pen. Some swear they can hear them coming again, up the corridor.

EPILOGUE

Winter, 1988. Still another grim anniversary for Santa Fe's now legendary pen.

Outwardly, the scene has changed. Two new prisons have grown like ominous tumors on the face of the Cerrillos Plateau south of the old institution, a maximum-security isolator and another warehouse for the medium classifications, both of them pale brown clumps of ragged wire and blotchy concrete, still oozing corruption of design and policy. In a grotesque sense, they are the state of the art in human cages. New Mexico has been able to buy them as part of its $100 million post-riot construction program, has been able to fill them with sullen, sad-eyed men once the legislature has begrudgingly squeezed out the money to open the doors after a shoddy completion. But the blinking electronic consoles alternately break down or simply baffle the poorly trained guards standing by. And the supposedly high-tech security systems don't work. The state can contract for these penitentiaries and can soon pack them, though it cannot truly build them aright, or run them, or make them safe.

There seems no escaping the history of this plateau, the ghosts of that cold February night in 1980. Nearly a decade after the riot, the new prisons, like the old, are crude, costly cairns of failure.

In the autumn of 1987, the *Albuquerque Journal* published a major investigative series on the penal system. The findings are bleak. "New Mexico's prisons are expensive to operate, crowded, and extremely violent . . . most of the deep-seated problems that led to the 1980 riot . . . are still present at the state's maximum and medium-security prisons," the reporter concludes. "The rapidly growing inmate population in those prisons still lives in a system supervised by underpaid, overworked, and poorly trained corrections officers. Rules governing inmate conduct change frequently and are inconsistently enforced. The system for classifying inmates is flawed. Entrenched gangs wield significant power, and an active snitch system further undermines the authority of wardens and guards." The paper has found what a few close observers of the prisons have long known—that for all the money and anguish and notoriety, the causes of the riot have never been healed, and the riot itself, coursing deep in the underlying currents of prison life, has never really ended.

The conditions of crisis are still visible everywhere. Three guards and thirteen convicts have been murdered since the National Guard units retook the smoldering, blood-drenched pen on February 3, 1980. Month by month, season by season, the stabbings, the work strikes, the escapes go on in relentless cadence. Overcrowding, the catalyst of violence and uprising, is once again routine. The new prisons were to have no dormitories, no stacking of man on man like tinder waiting for a spark. But the musty masonry courtyards of the new cell pods soon fill with beds, and the overflow spills into the dayrooms and other common areas. New Mexico is now fourth nationally in the growth of its convict population. At current rates of incarceration, the state will need a new prison every 2½ years.

Once inside, the inmate of the 1980s and 1990s, like his predecessors of the 1960s or 1970s, will discover the indignity and savagery of overcrowding the least of his torments. If he is one of the scores of mentally ill prisoners, he will still have no adequate treatment. A new million-dollar psychological unit has been erected in the wake of the riot, but like almost all the rest of the new building, it has been mindlessly designed. The truly sick or suicidal cannot be properly monitored by prison staff, and the unit goes largely unused while disturbed convicts, thrown into maximum or even medium cellblocks, now scream in madness, now fall mute in a deadly silence that signals self-mutilation or worse.

For the sane, of course, there are always the diversions of

gang government and warfare, still the real administration of the New Mexico State Penitentiary. The latest dominant faction is called Syndicato de Nuevo México, succeeding the old Nuestra Familia and Los Carnales. The names do not matter. The rule of the gangs with their rackets and intimidation, rape and assassination, symbolizes at once the desperation and barren regression of the caged alongside the incompetence and abdication of the keepers, all of them victims and prisoners.

The quality of the guard corps, its stability and training, was to be one of the learned lessons of the riot, and for a time there has been talk of decent salaries and education. But a New Mexico corrections officer still earns significantly less than most of his peers around the nation, over $6,000 a year less than a guard in neighboring Colorado, and after five years of life-risking work, over $4,000 less than an Albuquerque policeman. In the vacuum the old nepotism thrives, the old clique endures. There are not even written tests for promotion. Much as in those last fateful days before the 1980 catastrophe, the men who manage the prison are there more often by favoritism or friendship than because of ability. Years after it lost its penitentiary in a blatant sequence of folly and negligence, years after its officers were taken hostage and brutalized, New Mexico still seems unable to intelligently recruit, train, pay, promote, or retain the people responsible for watching over its most dangerous felons.

The results are felt from top to bottom. At the Corrections Department headquarters in Santa Fe there is still the same revolving door of senior officialdom, the promising and the educated soon burned out or pushed out. At the bottom, the echoing cellblocks are once more managed by the snitch system, the regime of whispered hate and vengeance that had convicts lining up so patiently to maim and kill that Saturday morning outside cellblock 4. In the new prisons as in the old, there is no real intelligence gathering, no internal affairs operation to monitor staff abuses and corruption.

In many ways, it is true, it all looks and even smells different. The old pen is painted in hopeful pastels; the worst physical brutality and beatings are relatively rare; the kitchen is cleaner and the turkey at Thanksgiving is no longer rancid; the more violent men are locked away in the new isolator or shipped out of the state, or just released to the streets. But the gangs and snitches and root failures persist. As if to make the point, there is even another mass escape from the new maximum-security institution on July 4, 1987, recalling memories of the mass break-out on the eve of the riot. For weeks, the Independence Day escapees terrorize Santa Fe, and some go on a spree of crime in California. In the cynical cellblocks the rest of them watch. They call the fugitives "the Magnificent Seven."

In the early autumn of 1987 the latest warden, George Sullivan, resigns after only two years. Sullivan has succeeded Harvey Winans, and he has been an articulate, enlightened man who planted flowers in the old yard, cleaned and brightened the old central corridor, spoke eloquently to the media and civic clubs about the needs of a modern penal institution. His charges, after all, are also "the children of God," he says in one television interview, words not often heard in New Mexico. Sullivan's genuine impact, however, is slight, his battles with the central bureaucracy and the pen clique eventually lost, and he leaves disingenuously blaming his frustration on court-ordered reforms. "There is a very active element of fear here that you don't find at other prisons around the country," he tells the *Journal* in a parting interview. For those who remember, his words sound a sad, chilling echo of wardens Ralph Aaron and Clyde Malley so long before.

It is not as if other states do not confront, and surmount, many of the same challenges. In its investigative series, the *Journal* reports that the once-violent South Carolina system, with twenty-eight prisons and 13,000 convicts, averages only one inmate killing a year, with only one guard murdered in the history of the system. In Oregon, where Sullivan spent much of his earlier career, one prisoner has been killed in the past seventeen years. Nor is it simply a matter of money. Impoverished, nearly bankrupt New Mexico now spends some $29,000 a year to incarcerate each of its convicts, more than any other state in the nation except Alaska. Then there is the Duran Decree, one of the nation's models of correctional practice and standards that is supposed to be the legal operational manual of the New Mexico penal system.

None of this reckons with the most basic flaw of all. For the disaster of the Santa Fe pen after the riot, like the disasters that led to the event, begins and ends with the tragic absence of political enlightenment, intellect, leadership. There is no authentic answer to the public danger and shame because there is no authentic public policy.

The faltering, short-circuited new prisons have been badly conceived by bureaucrats for bureaucrats. The traditional clique has resorted as it must to the familiar methods of coercion and betrayal. From the lowliest guard to the senior headquarters official, however, the system functions only by the default of the state's elected representatives. Weary of a string of dubious Democrats, the state in 1986 elects a new Republican governor, Garrey Carruthers. And Carruthers promptly supplies more proof—as if more were needed beyond the benighted legislature—that corrections in New Mexico, in America, is a bipartisan scandal.

To replace the incumbent corrections secretary, who has shown a commitment to reform, Carruthers hires O. Lane McCotter, whose main qualifications seem to lie in a checkered background in the military penal system, and who recently left the Texas system after repeated accusations of attempts to evade court-ordered reforms there. With the governor's blessing, McCotter in turn promptly hires as a deputy and as Sullivan's replacement two former Kansas prison officials implicated in a 1987 Justice Department investigation that found Kansas prisoners "subjected to flagrant or egregious conditions which deprive them of certain of their constitutional rights."

In lieu of policy, the governor talks about "privatization," a concept no corrections experts take seriously for the complex, wide-ranging network state prisons have become. In his first legislative session he also vetoes a sentencing guidelines bill, though it is the state's blindly vengeful determinate sentencing laws that feed the relentless overcrowding of the prisons. Behind the facade of conviction and imprisonment is a cruel myth and hoax. Faced with a tide of ghastly crimes, the public clamors to put the criminals behind bars and keep them there. Yet a special study commissioned by the New Mexico Supreme Court has concluded at the same time that in the peculiar perversions of the system, the more violent offenders tend in fact to serve the shorter sentences, while the less violent remain longer—are more thoroughly hardened and embittered—in the universities of crime and hopelessness the prisons have become. Punishment as we conceive and execute it, the study shows too clearly, is not the remedy or deterrent to crime, but rather its accompaniment, its goad. Such paradoxes are difficult to explain, require more than slogans, demand political leadership beyond the pandering veto or vacant convention. This winter, again, Santa Fe is in short supply of those necessities.

Worst of all, the new governor tries ardently and expensively to dilute or even do away with the Duran Decree, which alone has stood between the pen and chaos. Since 1980, the state has already poured more than $1.6 million into various prominent law firms to destroy the court order to which it solemnly agreed in the guilty wake of the riot, before the old arrangements and graft took over again. How that $1.6 million might have been usefully spent beyond the attorneys' voracious meters is another saddening speculation. Now Carruthers moves beyond the usual Albuquerque and Santa Fe partnerships to hire a Washington, D.C., law firm in an effort to have the order declared extra-constitutional. Finding the twentieth century in correctional policy inconvenient or costly or perhaps just incomprehensible, New Mexico is going to pay some more lawyers to try to have it repealed.

And yet, as the Spanish dragoons and the early Anglo artists found, Santa Fe is a place of irrepressible hope. Dwight Duran and the reformers are still at work despite the odds and inertia, trying this winter again to pass a bill for a sentencing guidelines commission that will begin—though only begin—the work of judicial enlightenment that must somehow temper the public's myopic, self-defeating cries for cages and retribution. There are those who still believe that the very shame of the riot and its aftermath will sooner or later instruct us, will sooner or later show that ignorance and distraction, venality and vengeance only spawn more cost and crime. There are still those who believe that the measure of a civilization is how it treats and heals its failures, that the ultimate devils of the butcher shop reside in public indifference and callousness far beyond the walls and wire.

Could it be that, in the end, those feral men of February 1980 were only imitating in some wild, frenzied parody the slow-motion anarchy of public purposelessness they saw on the other side of the bars?

This winter, though, there seems no serious policy planning or philosophical reflection in Santa Fe's government. They are arranging instead a Governor's Ball, a posh, black-tie affair not unlike that gala event some years ago when the ladies in their rustling gowns and the gentlemen in their dark suits came in carriages to celebrate the opening of the new territorial penitentiary down old Pen Road. No one at the dance, of course, will be remembering that old ball inaugurating New Mexico's prison history, or what happened when the dancers went home. It is just as well. Reflecting on history would only spoil the party.

NOTES

Citations of State Police or other investigative interviews are limited to date and transcript page number, enabling scholars or reporters to confirm the quoted accounts from the files of the riot defense or prosecution. Otherwise, the identity of the informants is not noted, a regrettable but necessary concession to the poisoned atmosphere still surrounding the inquiry, and to men who are still incarcerated in New Mexico or elsewhere. Repeated sources are listed initially in full and thereafter simply by author or abbreviated title with appropriate page number or date.

I. FORESHADOW

Page   Citation

9   "So fresh the strike": Paul Horgan, *The Centuries of Santa Fe* (New York: Dutton, 1956), p. 340.

10   "long tradition of sanctuary": Horgan, p. 331.

10   "attracting and holding": Oliver La Farge, *Santa Fe* (Norman: University of Oklahoma Press, 1959), p. 382.

11   "open conspiracy of hedonism": Horgan, p. 331.

11   "the race question": La Farge, p. 343.

13   "lacking this system": *Albuquerque Journal*, February 10, 1980.

14   "no sense of urgency or priority": *Report of the Attorney General on the February 2 and 3, 1980 Riot at the Penitentiary of New Mexico*, Part I (Santa Fe, June 1980), henceforth noted as *AG Report I*, p. 28.

14   "cumbersome": ibid.

14   federal mediation "no longer utilized": *New Mexican* (Santa Fe), February 14, 1980.

15   renovation and transfers from cell block 5: *AG Report I*, pp. 19–20, 27.

15 "smelling, green, rotten": W. G. Stone as told to G. Hirliman, *The Hate Factory* (Agoura, Calif.: Paisano Publications, Dell Books, 1982), p. 18.
15 blackouts: author's interviews.
16 Orner reports, "I get good information . . . ," "a follow-up riot," "they laughed," "keep your mouth shut," et. seq.: transcript of State Police interview, January 7, 1980.
18 Duran letter: author's interview.
18 December 7 meeting: author's interviews.
19 mass escape: *New Mexican* and *Albuquerque Journal*, January 15, 1980. "A lot of dumb luck": *New Mexican*, January 15, 1980. See also *Report of the Attorney General*, January 14, 1980.
20 warning of escape: *New Mexican*, January 18, 1980.
20 "much of the fence line": *AG Report I*, p. 4.
20 broken equipment, without binoculars: *Santa Fe Reporter*, November 13, 1980.
20 "a large click [*sic*]": letter sent to *Santa Fe Reporter*, January 14, 1980.
20 "playing Russian roulette," et. seq.: also quoted *Los Angeles Times*, February 5, 1980.
21 guards fired: *New Mexican*, March 15, 1980.
21 potential conflict of interest in Francke appointment: *New Mexican*, May 7, 1980.
21 drunk in control center: transcript of interview, KGGM-TV, Albuquerque, February 10, 1980.
21 transfers cut off, census climbs: *Report of the Attorney General on the February 2 and 3, 1980 Riot at the Penitentiary of New Mexico*, Part II (Santa Fe, Sept. 1980), henceforth noted as *AG Report II*, p. 31.
22 seizure of "Hot Lix": see Orner interview.
22 "we're going to have a god-damned riot": author's interviews.
22 "one of the primary goals": State Police interview, March 20, 1980, p. 3.
23 warning on tools: *AG Report I*, p. 30.
23 night-lights reported out: *AG Report I*, p. 19.
23 "the biggest party": author's interview with Richard Winterbottom.
23 "plenty of secret meetings": Stone, p. 17.
23 target date January 8 and guns from prison industries: State Police interview, March 18, 1980, p. 9.
23 transfers requested: *AG Report I*, p. 14.
24 "began to wonder": Stone, p. 23.
24 "the first" and shakedown: *AG Report I*, p. 14.
24 Griffin's reorganization: *AG Report I*, p. D-3.
24 control center glass: *AG Report I*, p. 29, E-1.
25 memo and discussion about glass, convict "thanks" officer: *AG Report I*, p. 29.
25 grand jury critical of nepotism: *Los Angeles Times*, February 2, 1980.
25 smuggle raisins and yeast: *AG Report I*, p. 20.
25 Montoya report, Koroneos response: *AG Report I*, p. 14.
26 Griffin asks review of riot-control plan: *AG Report I*, p. 15. "agitators," "reckless, unstable," et. seq., from "Riot Control Procedure, General

Information and Conclusions," Penitentiary of New Mexico memorandum issued September 1977 and reissued March 6, 1980.

26 only two guards: *AG Report I*, p. 15.

26 "you say there's a new riot plan": quoted *Albuquerque Journal*, November 13, 1974.

26 "never to be left": from Deputy Warden Montoya's cover memo dated "3/6/80." "Escape Plan" dated September 5, 1977.

27 "when I come and tell you": *AG Report I*, p. 15.

27 "something's coming down" and report of warning: author's interviews.

27 "Keep on your toes," "locked dorm," and housing records: *AG Report I*, p. 15.

27 Orner memo never given: ibid.

27 "They knew": *Albuquerque Journal*, February 10, 1980.

27 January 31 meeting: author's interviews. See also *AG Report I*, pp. 14–15.

28 no special precautions: *AG Report I*, pp. 15, 27–30.

31 "tripped merrily the jolly waltz," et. seq.: *Santa Fe Daily New Mexican*, August 7, 1885. See also La Farge, pp. 124–125.

31 "If it were properly and wisely handled": quoted La Farge, p. 116.

31 tried to put a penitentiary near courthouse site: *AG Report II*, p. 1.

32 "rushed to and fro": quoted La Farge, p. 125. Three convicts escaped from a work detail during the dedication, establishing from the outset the long tradition of poor security as well. See Harrison citation in following note.

33 For accounts of the penitentiary's history, from which these quotations and episodes are drawn, see *AG Report II*, pp. 1–3 and the *Albuquerque Journal*'s special supplement "Prison Perspective," March 30, 1980. Corruption was venerable among prison officials. One of the first wardens was caught juggling the books, and when one writer traced a history of western pens, he aptly called his chapter on New Mexico "Robbery, Rascality and Sensuality," referring to both sides of the bars: see Fred Harrison, *Hellholes and Hangmen* (Clarendon, Tex.: Clarendon Press, 1968). As late as the 1950s guards designated unruly convicts to collect and empty the buckets of waste from each cell. One ex-con likened the state pen to the "worst" Japanese prison camp of World War II, an ironic comparison for New Mexico, whose National Guard endured the Bataan Death March and subsequent atrocities in Philippine POW camps, a martyrdom commemorated yearly at a Bataan eternal flame across from the capitol.

33 "Monday's riot could not have happened": *New Mexican*, June 16, 1953. The paper's description of the quelling of the riot is worth reading in full as a period piece, with State Police charging the hospital, their machine guns "stuttering."

33 "In the last analysis": quoted *Albuquerque Journal*, March 30, 1980.

34 "Look for the land": author's interviews. Some of the records of the land transactions, including Campos's sanction, are in the penitentiary files of the New Mexico State Archives, Santa Fe.

35 New Mexico's Spanish: Fray Angelico Chavez in *My Penitente Land*

(Albuquerque: University of New Mexico Press, 1974) calls them "a lost tribe within their very own Holy Land," with an apt sense of their martydom, much of it self-inflicted. Chavez, a Franciscan priest and thoughtful writer, also gives a readable account of the rich and scarred history through its Iberian origins and insight into the local scourging Catholicism of the *penitentes*. No region of the United States has a more absorbing heritage, from witchcraft to nuclear weapons.

41   Rodriguez's résumé: *New Mexican*, September 3, 1981. The description of duties and gaps in the record are from a publicly available portion of his personnel file, his own formal "application" for warden, dated October 13, 1970, nearly eight months after his appointment. Available at State Personnel Office, Santa Fe.

41   convict portrayals of Rodriguez: author's interviews.

41   guard turnover: *AG Report II*, p. 6, traces the rate from 44 percent to 80 percent from "available" statistics, though corrections employees claim the full attrition in the guard corps was never accurately reported by the penitentiary or noted on headquarters payroll records.

42   Koroneos, Long, Martinez records: *New Mexican*, September 3, 1981, and available résumés and applications from State Personnel Office, Santa Fe.

42   ties of clan: see *Albuquerque News*, June 4, 1980.

43   Montoya's management: The deputy "had increasing authority in running the prison. This apparently changed nothing," notes *AG Report II*, p. 22, which goes on to deplore "this inability and failure to manage [that] went unabated from 1978 to 1980 . . . inadequate, unclear and inconsistent direction . . . the ineffectiveness and drift of the prison administration."

43   Griffin's background: *Albuquerque Journal*, April 1, 1979.

43   "Lieutenant Forty-one": *Albuquerque Journal*, November 13, 1974.

43   a craven, unstable coalition: see *AG Report II*, pp. 14–32.

43   new captaincies: *AG Report II*, pp. 13–14.

44   recidivism: *Corrections* magazine, March 1976.

44   Lloyd (Miller) McClendon's record: author's interview and McClendon's "Autobiographical Essay," September 9, 1976.

45   "If society had known": author's interview.

45   decay of programs: *AG Report II*, pp. G-2–G-3.

46   "grew up together": author's interview.

46   Duran's background: *Albuquerque Journal*, June 19, 1981, and author's interviews.

47   pen conditions: see *Nation*, February 23, 1980, for a summary of ACLU findings. See also *Los Angeles Times*, February 6, 1980.

47   "a national disgrace," "the filthiest": *New Mexican*, March 2–6, 1980.

47   convict memories and Duran's experience: author's interviews.

48   a place of the poor, et. seq.: *Nation*, March 13, 1982.

48   preparation of *Duran* suit: author's interviews.

50   "unreasonable": quoted *Playboy*, March 1981. The chairman was Senator C. B. Trujillo of Taos.

50   "You know what the political process is," et seq.: Orner interview with State Police.

51   Campos record: from his own "Reply to Questionnaire for Prospective Nomination for U.S. District Judgeship," on file with Federal Court, Santa Fe.

52   "inadequate people": author's interview with Dr. Warren Wilson.

II. TAKEOVER

Page Citation

57   inmate idleness: *AG Report I*, p. F-1.

57   "Man, when I get out of here...": *Santa Fe Reporter*, September 25, 1976.

58   "disturbance," no "specific knowledge," dropout, and large gathering: *AG Report I*, p. 15.

58   "They knew": *Albuquerque Journal*, February 10, 1980.

58   "raw," "my gut-level feeling": State Police interview, March 20, 1980, p. 49. Also the same informant's written statement of March 3, 1980, p. 4.

58   files left: *Santa Fe Reporter*, September 3, 1981.

58   inmate clerk remembers wax board, "116-something": author's interviews.

59   "ghost white": Stone, p. 1.

59   "absolutely reeks," men in E-2 cannot believe: author's interview with Richard Winterbottom, later counsel to many of the convicts involved.

59   "gladiators" have it "together" and "good": author's interviews.

60   scene in E-2, sansculottes: author's interviews, including Winterbottom.

60   "It wasn't over anything great": author's interview.

61   "They didn't secure": transcript of interview, KGGM-TV, Albuquerque, February 10, 1980.

61   shift change: *AG Report I*, pp. 16–18, H-1–H-2.

62   post order, "for a long time": *AG Report I*, p. 29.

62   sneak up on sleeping guards: author's interviews.

63   attack on guards: this account of the initial takeover is based principally on *AG Report I*, pp. 18–21, and author's interviews.

64   wonder whether he would leave alive: *AG Report I*, p. 19.

67   Gallegos "protected": *AG Report I*, p. 21.

68   tapping on tower windows: author's interviews.

68   "We've got the shift commander": *AG Report I*, p. 21.

69   Lucero's calls and Koroneos to Montoya and Griffin: *AG Report I*, pp. 21, 31.

70   Martinez calls Maez in hospital: *AG Report I*, p. A-2.

70   "Everybody out!": State Police interview, March 21, 1980, pp. 6ff.

71   Mendoza and Vigil flee, and fall of control center: author's interviews. See also *AG Report I*, pp. 21–23.

72   "the glass does a fine job": quoted *New Mexican*, February 6, 1980.

73   "If rioting prisoners were ever loose": *New Mexican*, April 21, 1956.

73   "we're doing all we can": *AG Report I*, p. 23.

74   Vigil's call and concealment in basement: author's interviews and ibid.

74   women guards monitor takeover: author's interviews.

75   "when they told me": *AG Report I*, p. 26.

75   "Open up or we'll kill": State Police interview, April 21, 1980, p. 2.

76   dial and handle to hospital door torn off: *Albuquerque Journal*, February 10, 1980.

76   Roybal radios to gate house: *AG Report I*, p. 31.

77   drugs: *Albuquerque Journal*, February 18, 1980.

77   hallway scene: author's interviews.

78   "They wanted the paperwork": State Police interview, March 21, 1980, p. 45.

79   find cash: author's interviews.

79   "*Juras* are coming," "There were people falling down": State Police interview, March 21, 1980, p. 12.

80   "They had to know": State Police interview, March 21, 1980, p. 17.

80   "Everybody into the gym": State Police interview, March 21, 1980, p. 34.

81   Roybal talks to Montoya: *AG Report I*, p. A-4.

81   "We'll at least be sure": State Police interview, April 21, 1980, p. 4.

82   "Are you a guard?" "I used to be": State Police interview, April 21, 1980, p. 8.

82   Hernandez, Gallegos, Curry out: *AG Report I*, pp. 35–36.

82   attempts to reach Rodriguez: *AG Report I*, pp. 31, 34.

83   Montoya takes over negotiations: *Corrections* magazine, April 1980. See also *AG Report I*, p. 33.

85   "throw heads out": *AG Report I*, p. A-4.

85   "I guess the prisoners": *New Mexican*, February 3, 1980.

85   "I guess the biggest contributing factor": *New Mexican*, November 28, 1982.

87   "When two or more": Rodriguez, who reportedly once claimed to have written a research paper on snitches, echoed the phrase coined by Joseph Ragen, the warden of Stateville prison in Illinois. See Michael S. Serril and Peter Katel, "The facts behind New Mexico's bloody ordeal," *Corrections* magazine, April 1980, pp. 17–19.

87   "There isn't much said": *Dallas Times-Herald* team dispatch reprinted in *Albuquerque Journal*, February 11, 1980.

89   "People who have the most knowledge": *Santa Fe Reporter*, February 21, 1980.

90   "The place always had an aura": author's interview.

III. CARNAGE

Page   *Citation*

93   "We got to kill this son of a bitch": State Police interview, April 21, 1980, pp. 5–6.

93   *"No era yo . . ."*: *AG Report I*, p. 41, as well as numerous interview accounts.

93   radio transmissions and searchlight in basement: State Police interview, April 21, 1980, pp. 5ff.
93   "I didn't hurt nobody, man," et. seq.: ibid.
95   "Pancho Villa": memorandum of the attorney general, October 22, 1980, recounts the inquiry into Orner's letter and the issue of transfer. See also Craig Pyes's series on the pen's mentally ill, *Albuquerque Journal,* September 21–24, 1980.
96   convicts meet man with kerchief: State Police interview, February 7, 1980, p. 27.
96   "I didn't do it," et. seq.: State Police interview, March 18, 1980, pp. 15–23. For Madrid's murder see also the *Dallas Times-Herald* team dispatch reprinted in the *Albuquerque Journal,* February 11, 1980.
96   E-1's exodus: *AG Report I,* p. 38.
96   For a complete profile of records of the men in cell block 4, see the forthcoming study by Dr. Sandra Lapham, "Victims of the New Mexico State Penitentiary Riot," Center for Disease Control, Atlanta, part of the CDC's ongoing and larger nationwide study of disasters. A brief official passage on the residents appears in *AG Report I,* p. 25. On the issue of kickbacks to guards, see *Santa Fe Reporter,* September 3, 1981, and references to Dr. James Weston in Part VI, below.
97   "Before the riot started": transcript of State Police interview with Louis Quintana, May 29, 1980.
97   "Hey, they're cutting into . . .": State Police interview, February 5, 1980, p. 18.
97   "I mean all the state troopers": *AG Report I,* p. 26.
98   missing keys: ibid.
99   investigator convinced police could have entered: author's interview with Mark Colvin, principal author of *AG Report II.*
99   "It's their ass": author's interviews. See also Stone, pp. 114–117, who writes that Montoya "knew that a massacre of snitches was imminent."
99   "they came in hollering": State Police interview, February 5, 1980, p. 14.
99   description of onslaught: author's interviews, particularly with Susan Yakutis and members of riot defense and prosecution staffs. See also *AG Report I,* pp. 26, 41–42.
100 "You son of a bitch, you'll never tell": State Police interview, February 7, 1980, pp. 21–22.
101 "I could smell it, man": *Albuquerque Journal,* February 19, 1981, carries detailed testimony on the killing.
102 "kind of like [shut] half-mast": State Police interview, March 21, 1980, p. 57.
102 paddle like golf club: *Albuquerque Journal,* February 19, 1981.
102 "RATA" and whiskers: author's interviews with Sandra Weber, CDC researcher, University of New Mexico. Some national experts pointed out later that "killings of informants are rare" in prisons. See *Corrections* magazine, April 1980.
102 "Anybody here you don't like": State Police interview, February 5, 1980, pp. 8–9.

103   "Those niggers saved my life": *Los Angeles Times, Albuquerque Journal*, April 24, 1980.

103   carries crucifix: *Albuquerque Journal*, February 10, 1980.

103   "You mean, Stars and Stripes?": State Police interview. February 7, 1980, p. 26.

103   Polaroid pictures in riot: Quintana interview, also summary of his statement to the public defender, July 2, 1981.

104   killing beyond 4: the official account, very brief, *AG Report 1*, p. 42. This summary is drawn as well from State Police interrogations and author's interviews.

105   Robert Quintela: *New Mexican*, February 19, 1980.

106   Mario Urioste: *Los Angeles Times*, February 12, 1980.

106   Donald Gossens, "They can't kill me in here": *Los Angeles Times*, April 24, 1980.

106   "I feel like he's gone to a better place": *Albuquerque Journal*, February 7, 1980.

106   James Foley, "He just kept reading": *Albuquerque Journal*, February 10, 1980.

106   Ortega brothers: *Albuquerque Journal*, February 15, 1980. The brothers may well have been victims of long-standing Las Vegas–Carlsbad gang warfare triggered by the riot.

106   Frankie Sedillo: *Denver Post*, February 10, 1980.

107   Paulina Paul: *Dallas Times-Herald* dispatch reprinted *Albuquerque Journal*, February 11, 1980.

107   Tom O'Meara: author's interviews, including Kathleen O'Meara.

108   "There's a lot of people": State Police interview by telephone (DA DISC: SF 80–267), p. 21

108   "If it hadn't been the for drugs"; "If I was an inmate in cell block 4": *Corrections* magazine, April 1980.

108   "To me a human life is the most precious": ibid.

108   "The depth of the violence": quoted *Denver Post*, February 17, 1980.

109   "The fact that nobody was killed": Senator C. B. Trujillo of Taos, quoted *Corrections* magazine, April 1980.

109   "They killed twelve of my people": author's interview.

111   "one of the harshest": *Albuquerque Journal*, September 24, 1980.

111   history of brutality: see *Santa Fe Reporter*, September 3, 1981.

111   the hole: author's interviews.

112   "Being in the hole": Stone, p. 44.

112   "The only reason," et. seq.: *Santa Fe Reporter*, September 3, 1981.

112   finger in eye: author's interviews.

112   1976 gauntlet: See *Santa Fe Reporter*, September 3, 1981. The incident, corroborated by a later legislative committee inquiry, was also the subject of various suits in state and federal courts.

113   "inmate goons": the subject of federal grand jury testimony in 1981, see *Santa Fe Reporter*, September 3, 1981.

113   Thompson case: *Santa Fe Reporter*, September 3 and 24, 1981. See also *Thompson* v. *Montoya et. al.*, Santa Fe District Court.

114   body casts, et. seq.: *Albuquerque Journal*, September 21–24, 1980.

114   "Everybody knew": ibid.

114   medical and dental mistreatment: author's interviews.
114   daily psychological torments: author's interviews. *AG Report II*, p. 21, describes "baiting bears" in which one lieutenant in particular "used to harass inmates ... by calling them degrading names to their face and implicitly challenging them to retaliate." Though the report does not specifically identify the guard, it records that during the riot convicts offered to give three hostages in exchange for him, obviously Benito "Green Eyes" Gonzales. See *AG Report I*, p. A-6.
115   "a convict's code," "Don't let the sensational abuse hide the daily": author's interviews.

IV. SIEGE

Page Citation

119   "The things that I saw": State Police interview, March 18, 1980, p. 12.
120   "how they got it up": author's interviews. See also Robert Mayer's brilliant impressionistic essay, "Thirty-Six Hours at Santa Fe," *Rocky Mountain Magazine*, June 1980.
120   brothel in basement of 3: author's interviews and State Police interview, April 21, 1980, p. 4.
120   blaring television and radio: author's interviews.
121   "E-2 was kind of like a command post": State Police interview, March 20, 1980, p. 49.
121   "I'm over here checking this Lieutenant Anaya": *AG Report I*, p. 42.
121   brutalization of guards: author's interviews. Anaya "pretty bad": *AG Report I*, p. A-5.
122   Montoya "rejected the plan": *AG Report I*, p. 39.
122   Montoya refuses doctor: *AG Report I*, p. 40.
122   "you better come in, sucker": State Police interview, February 5, 1980, p. 25.
122   "well-being ... utmost," "At this moment": *AG Report I*, p. 36.
123   Chopper One and field telephone: *AG Report I*, pp. 37, A-5.
123   King's telephone conversation: *AG Report I*, p. 37, and *Albuquerque Journal*, February 3, 1980.
124   "I talked to Bruce," "You've got fucking uncles": *AG Report I*, p. 37.
124   escape from cell block 5: *AG Report I*, p. 38.
125   Stout negotiations and first list of demands: *AG Report I*, pp. 37, A-5.
125   chaos at tower: author's interviews; *New Mexican* and *Albuquerque Journal*, February 3, 1980, *AG Report I*, p. 39.
126   ominous transmissions: *AG Report I*, pp. 40, A-6.
126   "a couple of groups," "knowledge of inmates being killed": *AG Report I*, p. 41.
126   reports guards tortured, Anaya critical, trade for Gonzales, "chop heads off": *AG Report I*, pp. A-6–A-7.
127   "stack" in gym: State Police interviews, February 5, 1980, p. 33; April 21, 1980, p. 16.
127   survivors to mental hospital: *Albuquerque Journal*, February 8, 1980.

128 briefings for relatives, "He came in last night": *Albuquerque Journal*, February 3, 1980.

128 "like a general": State Police interview, March 20, 1980, p. 34.

128 Mighty reseals grilles: State Police interviews, March 18, 1980, p. 25; March 21, 1980, p. 53.

129 written demands and responses: *AG Report I*, pp. 43–44.

131 order to assault: *AG Report I*, p. 51.

131 "you better bet," "I'm not going to do anything to threaten": *New Mexican*, February 3, 1980.

131 "There's no point": *Denver Post*, February 4, 1980.

132 assault proposals and confusion: *AG Report I*, pp. 52–53.

133 "knowing the mentality," "Fifty percent would have quit": quoted *Corrections* magazine, April 1980.

133 threats and Montoya makes media concession: *AG Report I*, p. A-8.

134 "why wouldn't you look down?" et. seq.: State Police interviews, March 21, 1980, p. 63.

135 "Everybody was just trying": State Police interview, February 5, 1980, p. 31.

135 threat to hostages, "If they rush us," et. seq.: State Police interview, April 21, 1980.

136 Mills, Andrews talk with convicts: *AG Report I*, p. 45.

136 Saturday night atmosphere: see the excellent dispatch by Bruce Campbell and Marc Sani, *Albuquerque Journal*, February 4, 1980.

136 "I've had it": *AG Report I*, p. A-9.

137 orders tower lights off, escape to prison industries building: *AG Report I*, pp. 46, A-9.

137 "doing fine" amid new torture: author's interviews.

137 offer Roybal for media, no "retaliation": *AG Report I*, p. A-10.

138 "infuriated": the attorney general's word, in *AG Report I*, p. 46.

138 assistant district attorneys in negotiations: ibid.

138 "They're stoned": *Denver Post*, February 4, 1980.

139 Shugrue incident: *AG Report I*, p. 47; *Corrections* magazine, April 1980. The author viewed the videotape in the spring of 1981, courtesy of fellow author Charles Raish.

140 "Be careful": *AG Report I*, p. 47.

140 "attention all units": *New Mexican*, February 3, 1980.

140 "not a bit": *Albuquerque Journal*, February 4, 1980.

141 "The situation": *AG Report I*, p. A-10.

143 "That prison": quoted *Santa Fe Reporter* and *New Mexican*, September 3, 1981.

142 plump commissary, "we raised," "seven-fourteen," "I never made money so easily": see the intermedia investigative report, ibid.

145 "you could get a bet": *Playboy*, March 1981.

145 narcotics traffic and Hill case: *Santa Fe Reporter*, September 3, 1981, and State Police memorandum to the district attorney, September 8, 1978.

146 Aspen House scandal: *Albuquerque Journal*, February 24, 1980; *New Mexican*, February 21–22, 1980. See also memorandum of Jane Foraker-Thompson to Corrections Secretary Charles Becknell dated November

9, 1979, resignation letter of November 19, 1979, from Program Director David Hendry, and related documents on file in author's archives, New Mexico State Library, Santa Fe. Foraker-Thompson detailed official cover-up of drug tests and the story of one Aspen House resident who raped his wife with a curling iron. Hendry reported "unregenerate lying, cover-up . . . conflicted interests and general incompetence on a monumental scale" by officials. The Organized Crime Commission inquiry is dated September 1979.

147   pen annual audits, "qualified reports," et. seq.: audits on file in state auditor's office, Santa Fe. See also *New Mexican*, September 3, 1981.

147   shunned federal grants: author's interviews with former Corrections Secretary John Salazar, corrections department program and budget officers, and former clerical workers and lay teachers at the institution.

149   Harry Summers's highway incident, murder of informants, and other incidents: author's interviews with Reverend Summers and Kingsley Hammett's remarkable six-part series in *New Mexican*, March 2–7, 1980.

150   press conference, McClendon quotation, "we didn't get a public response": *Corrections* magazine, March 1976.

151   "Confidential Information": the memorandum is addressed to Howard Leach, secretary of corrections, its cover dated originally "6-8-73," but with entries beginning August 14, 1971. The archive is interspersed with memoranda from parole officials Luther Stephans, Frank Garcia, and Jerry Griffin as well as letters from Quintana to King, and contains handwritten marginalia. It is on file in full in the author's State Library archive, Santa Fe. Subsequent citations are simply to "Quintana" with the appropriate date and page number of the archive.

152   "serious parole violations": Quintana, January 22, 1974, p. 53.

152   Indian jewelry: the allegations run throughout the archive but one typical case is summarized, January 30, 1974, p. 61.

152   "not on merits": Quintana, p. 2. (The case is listed simply as "August 1971.")

152   "pressure," "no real consideration": Quintana, p. 4, case described as "December 1971."

152   "poor psychiatric report": Quintana, p. 5.

152   "using their job": Quintana, June 26, 1973, p. 38.

152   "problems encountered with . . . Anaya": Quintana, August 9, 1973, p. 43.

153   "Anaya tried to pass a whole batch": Quintana, January 30, 1974, p. 63A.

153   "Governor wants this man out": Quintana, March 5, 1973, p. 14.

153   "no reason": Quintana, March 2, 1973, p. 19.

153   "only 18 days": Quintana, ibid., and p. 36 for similar circumstances.

153   "thrown a fit": Quintana, June 14, 1973, p. 26.

153   "let him go": Quintana, June 20, 1973, pp. 28–29.

153   "parole board doings," "I would give one to the grand jury": Quintana, June 15, 1973, p. 37.

154   "personal political gain": ibid.

154   "little Watergate": Quintana, June 25, 1973, p. 39.

154   call from King, "our leader," "not to pay attention": Quintana, June 25, 1973, p. 40.

154   "he wanted all copies": Quintana, June 26, 1973, p. 41.

154   "he would be destroying them": ibid.

154   "shit or get off the pot": Quintana, January 22, 1974, p. 55.

154   "Governor was very concerned . . . if this kind of thing went to the grand jury," "necessary for indictments": Quintana, February 10, 1974, pp. 76–78.

154   "Then after I leave": Quintana, February 12, 1974, p 81.

155   "revealed evidence," "many prominent members," "outside Statute of Limitations": the FBI documents are available in the State Library archive.

155   Anaya's investigation: Organized Crime Commission Report to Governor Apodaca, May 12, 1975. See also *Albuquerque Journal*, May 16, 1975.

156   "he couldn't understand why he would ever write": Quintana was never named in the attorney general's report but the context, added to the FBI file, makes his identity apparent. He was later promoted to deputy warden of the new Los Lunas medium-security prison. His material is a rich source of information on New Mexico politics and personalities well beyond the parole issue.

156   Stockham affair: traced in *Albuquerque Journal*, September 21–27, 1975. For Rodriguez's similar survival when a corrections secretary fired him in 1970 and the secretary ended up being dismissed, see *Santa Fe Reporter*, September 3, 1981.

159   "It is not maintained": *Albuquerque Journal*, September 27, 1975.

159   "by how they smelled," et. seq.: quoted *New Mexican*, March 2–7, 1980.

159   consent order: No. 50874, June 3, 1976, Santa Fe District Court.

160   fight civil rights, cut public defenders: *Albuquerque Journal*, March 12, 1980.

160   grand jury reports: detailed by Hammett in *New Mexican*, March 6, 1980.

160   Becknell episode: author's interviews; *Playboy*, March, 1980; "My wife's": *Albuquerque Journal*, February 7, 1979. See also *New Mexican*, February, 1979.

160   Anglo legislators veto Rodriguez: author's interviews.

V. SURRENDER

Page Citation

165   "Don't get any ideas": author's interviews.

166   "bodies everywhere": State Police interview, April 21, 1980, p. 16.

166   Sunday morning: author's interviews. The *AG Report* largely passes over this period.

166   Lonnie Duran: *Albuquerque Journal*, February 4, 1980. The paper's profiles of the convict negotiators, including Kedrick Duran, twenty-

six; Vincent Candelaria, twenty-seven; and Donald Lee Stout, twenty-seven; as well as William Stephens, thirty; and Michael Colby, twenty-two, described below, ran under the headline "History of Inmate Representatives Violence Filled," emphasizing previous convictions and the participation of Colby and Stephens in the December 1979 escape.

166   "What the hell": author's interviews; also *AG Report I*, p. 48.
166   Victor Gallegos, captivity and escape: *Los Angeles Times*, February 6, 1980; *Denver Post*, February 4, 1980.
168   "hanging on": *Albuquerque Journal*, February 12, 1980.
168   "They killed him": quoted ibid.
168   "sense of endless casualties," "John Doe," "heavy casualties": *Santa Fe Reporter*, February 7, 1980.
168   "Montoya, you chickenshit," "Hey, Felix": quoted and described by Stone, p. 174.
169   Mills's experiences: related by his close friend and colleague Bob Barth in *Santa Fe Reporter*, February 14, 1980.
169   Martinez and Ortega free: *AG Report I*, pp. 48–49.
169   "Kill the blacks": the encounter is officially described in *AG Report I*, pp. 49–50. Also author's interviews.
170   "least, least, least": quoted *New Mexican*, February 8, 1980.
170   "We had to escape": Associated Press dispatch, "Black Inmates Stuck Together during Riot," February 6, 1980.
170   tape recording of reasons for riot: State Police interview by telephone (cited above), p. 10.
171   "Hey, shoot me!": State Police interview, March 21, 1980, p. 56.
171   "Right now," "there's been enough": *Albuquerque Journal*, February 4, 1980.
171   press conference and subsequent negotiations: videotape file of KNME-TV, Albuquerque's public television station. See also the summary account in Stone, p. 175ff.
174   Rodriguez pulls up, orders: *Corrections* magazine, April 1980.
174   "You lied . . ." "blow your heads off": quoted Stone, pp. 185–86.
174   alleged treason: *Corrections* magazine, April 1980, a theme largely picked up by Stone in *Hate Factory*.
174   "at no time," "It was the administration": author's interview with Ernie Mills, June 1, 1981.
175   chaotic retaking: see *AG Report I*, pp. 53–58.
177   "The stupid asses": quoted *Corrections* magazine, April 1980.
178   cons grab a rifle: author's interviews. The *AG Report* relates, p. 55, only the guardsman throwing his M-16 out of reach.
178   scavenging and souvenirs, negligence at crime scenes: *AG Report I*, pp. 59–60.
179   "No matter what": *Albuquerque Journal*, February 4, 1980.
179   "I think we're back": ibid.
179   "Hey, they're burning": from the extraordinary eyewitness account by Steve Elsen (pseudonym for a prison employee), *Santa Fe Reporter*, February 7, 1980.
180   governor and wife approach pen: ibid.
180   "As a helicopter pilot": *New Mexican*, February 4, 1980.

180 "tremendous stench," "I'm not a gory person": *Santa Fe Reporter*, February 7, 1980.
181 "I opened this pen": *Corrections* magazine, April 1980.
181 "non-inmates" loot: *AG Report I*, p. 65.
182 "The State Police took": author's interviews.
182 incriminating vouchers taken: author's interviews.
182 Montoya incident in yard: *AG Report I*, pp. 61–62 and also the subsequent attorney general's formal report on the incident, July 1980
183 clash between cons and guardsmen: *AG Report I*, p. 61.
183 "still finding," "thirty-nine": State Police interview, February 5, 1980, p. 33.
184 plight of families: *AG Report I*, p. 60; *New Mexican*, February 4, 1980; *Time*, February 18, 1980.
184 "It wasn't the usual": *Albuquerque Journal*, February 8, 1980.
185 "But what happened": *Time*, February 18, 1980.
185 "I want it pinpointed": *New York Times*, February 5, 1980.
185 "The conditions and practices": ACLU statement, February 3, 1980.
185 "We gave them": *New Mexican*, February 5, 1980.
185 "You don't know": *Albuquerque Tribune*, February 7, 1980.

VI. AFTERMATH

Page Citation

189 chaotic expulsion: *Albuquerque Journal*, February 6–7, 1980; *AG Report I*, pp. 62, A-13–A-14.
189 false snitch jackets: author's interviews with officials who saw them.
189 ridicule of Santa Fe guard: author's interviews with Arizona officials.
190 numbers on matchbook: *Santa Fe Reporter*, September 3, 1981.
190 defecate on floors, "to hell with you guys": *AG Report I*, p. 63.
190 random scenes: see the graphic dispatch by Jack Cox in *Denver Post*, February 8, 1980.
191 "stiffest penalties": quoted *Denver Post*, February 5, 1980.
191 "we are not recognizing," "the paper they're printed on": *Albuquerque Journal*, February 10, 1980.
191 "crumple up," mail returned opened: *AG Report I*, p. 65.
192 "I suppose it's a philosophical point": quoted *Rocky Mountain Magazine*, June 1980.
192 "If the people hired": quoted in the *Albuquerque Journal*, February 10, 1980.
192 National Guard kitchen: author's interviews with Legislative Finance Committee staff.
192 experts oppose building: *Santa Fe Reporter*, February 7, 1980.
192 letters to editor: *Albuquerque Journal*, February 10, 1980.
193 resist return to Santa Fe: some refugees call a Texas federal prison "heaven on earth" by comparison with the New Mexico pen, see *Albuquerque Tribune*, February 19, 1980.
193 "open frequently," "ajar repeatedly," keys: *AG Report I*, p. 67.

193 continued to draw hazardous-duty pay: *AG Report II*, p. 42. "No one knows what they're doing here," the report quoted a corrections department official. The special pay, reserved for the pen, went on until August 30, 1980.

193 new turmoil: chronology traced in *AG Report I*, pp. A-15–A-16.

194 "just fine": *Santa Fe Reporter*, June 12, 1980. One of Saenz's main duties, King had said on February 1, the day before the riot erupted, was "to keep them [the prisoners] inside the contained operation": *Albuquerque Journal*, February 1, 1980.

194 post-riot accounting of survivors: the sequence is traced in full with its official documentation in *Santa Fe Reporter*, September 3, 1981.

196 "angry," "deceived . . . disappointed": quoted *Albuquerque Journal*, June 21, 1980. See also *New Mexican*, June 22, 1980.

196 upheld gag rule: *Albuquerque Journal*, May 30, 1980, and June 7, 1980, the latter carrying Burciaga's opinion.

196 charges of Burciaga's racial bias: the controversy is traced in *Albuquerque Journal*, September 21, October 5, 6, 7, and 29, 1970. "Burciaga acknowledged he prefers to be called a Mexican-American, saying the word Chicano 'has sort of a political connotation which troubles me at times,' the *Journal* reported. The paper's Washington analyst thought Burciaga's attitude had "obvious implications," but was hardly a matter the Senate could rule on in his confirmation. Local Hispanic opposition to the judge was withdrawn in a pre-confirmation deal in which he agreed to accept minority recommendations for clerkships and to recuse himself from any case involving a lawyer who had opposed him.

196 "you're excused": *Playboy*, March 1981.

197 "his 25 years": *Albuquerque Journal*, October 2, 1980.

197 attorney general's inquiries: see *Albuquerque Journal*, November 15, 1980; *New Mexican*, August 27 and November 14, 1980.

198 ignored Anaya investigation: the sole reference is *AG Report II*, p. 17.

198 "The record was clear enough": *Santa Fe Reporter*, September 3, 1981.

198 "It should be painfully obvious," et seq.: quoted *New Mexican*, September 26, 1980.

198 Weston affair: described in *Santa Fe Reporter*, September 3, 1981; for the sequence of reactions, see *New Mexican*, November 27 and December 5, 1980. *Dallas Times-Herald* transcript is in the author's archives at the State Library, Santa Fe. Weston's biography and obituary: *Albuquerque Journal*, May 11, 1982. "They told me": Weston interview with KOAT-TV, Albuquerque. Hounded: author's interviews.

200 "vegetables," et seq.: quoted *Albuquerque Journal*, Associated Press dispatch, September 22, 1980.

200 "the theory to collect": author's interviews.

201 Schmitt suit: *Albuquerque Journal*, September 17, 1982.

201 "safety grievance": *Playboy*, March 1981; see also *Santa Fe Reporter*, November 1980.

202 32 percent stay less than a year, "society doesn't like": author's interviews.

202 Jewett murder and aftermath: author's interviews with Sylvia Jewett.

203 "When I was eighteen": quoted *New Mexican*, November 15, 1980.

203   "poor guard training," et seq., regarding Crist's background: see King-
        sley Hammett's thoroughly documented "Crist in Montana," *Santa Fe
        Reporter*, October 7, 1981.
203   "I won't do your dirty work": quoted *Santa Fe Reporter*, September 3,
        1981.
203   Crist regime: author's interviews; "I'm surprised": *Santa Fe Reporter*,
        October 7, 1981.
204   "a landmark kind": *Albuquerque Journal*, July 22, 1980. A summary
        of the order is in the *Journal*, July 16, 1980.
204   Nathan report: *Albuquerque Journal*, March 20, 1980.
205   "severe and widespread," Cron report: *Albuquerque Journal*, May 16,
        1981; see also *Dallas Times-Herald*, July 27, 1981.
205   ask to close pen: *Albuquerque Journal*, May 23, 1981. On May 19 the
        Journal had referred to the pen as "that 'Tiger Cage' outside Santa Fe,"
        in reference to the notorious South Vietnamese.
205   McCorkle background: *Albuquerque Journal*, May 25, 1980.
205   corruption and suppression of investigations: *Santa Fe Reporter*, Sep-
        tember 3, 1981; author's interviews. The Keller investigative reports are
        in the State Library archive. University of New Mexico journalism stu-
        dents confirmed in their own investigative report the continuing "sloppy
        accounting" and "potential waste or pilferage of thousands of dollars in
        food." See "Prison Food Delivery: A Tortuous System," *New Mexico
        Business Journal*, June 1983.
206   awarded contracts: *Albuquerque Journal*, July 18, 1981; and David
        Steinberg's probing article, "Politics in Construction," *Journal*, July 19,
        1981.
206   records missing: *Santa Fe Reporter*, September 3, 1981.
206   electric heat: report of Legislative Finance Committee staff, July 13,
        1982.
206   supervisor: author's interviews.
207     $100,000 for faulty locks and doors: "Report to Corrections Department
        Budget Bureau," October 21, 1981, contained in Rodriguez letter to
        Legislative Finance Committee staff, October 26, 1981.
207   construction costs; "Corrections Department Progress Report," Legis-
        lative Finance Committee staff, June 1, 1982.
207   "one thing people don't know": quoted *New Mexican*, September 3,
        1981; repeal of statute: see New Mexico *Laws of 1969*, Chapter 226,
        p. 885. For original provision, see *New Mexico Statutes* (annotated)
        42–1–29, p. 564.
207   "mental health remains problem": quoted *Albuquerque Journal*, March
        28, 1981.
207   families harassed: *Albuquerque Journal*, May 25, 1980.
208   "awfully farfetched": quoted *New Mexican*, November 15, 1980.
208   "You tell that son of a bitch," judge's family threatened: *Albuquerque
        Journal*, April 14, 1981.
208   "You people have to get me out," et. seq.: *Santa Fe Reporter*, September
        3, 1981.
208   twenty-four incidents: copies of the reports, given the author anony-
        mously, are in the State Library archive.

208	November 1980 beatings: see *Santa Fe Reporter*, September 3, 1980, and Keller documents in State Library archive.
209	"want to cry": *Albuquerque Journal*, September 1, 1981.
209	Antunez murder: *Santa Fe Reporter*, September 3, 1981. The FBI file, again supplied anonymously, is in the State Library archive. See also *Albuquerque Journal*, January 10, 1982. As this book was written, the murder was the subject of a wrongful-death suit by Antunez's widow.
210	"super goon squad": "The men that you see walking around, in black coveralls, riot helmets, batons [*sic*] and gas masks..." announced a penitentiary memo of October 23, 1981.
210	Magee murder: Penitentiary of New Mexico memorandum, "Order of Events, 30 August 1981," dated September 2, 1981; see also *Santa Fe Reporter*, September 10, 1981.
211	reforms suspended: *Albuquerque Journal*, September 14, 1981.
211	national notoriety: *Time*, October 26, 1981; *Washington Post*, October 11, 1981.
211	gag order: corrections department memo from Warden Harvey Winans, dated November 5, 1981.
212	Criminal Justice Study Committee Report: dated January 9, 1982.
212	"explosive": *Albuquerque Journal*, October 4, 1981.
212	Santa Fe County special grand jury: report dated June 10, 1982.
213	"money and time ahead": *New Mexican*, December 25, 1980.
213	letters seized, et. seq.: *Albuquerque Journal*, June 17, 19 and 21, 1981.
214	subsequent attempt to gag: *Albuquerque Journal*, October 31 and November 3, 1981.
214	admitted to 134: see "Defendant's Response to Plaintiff's First Request for Admissions," *Duran* v. *King*, No. 77–721 C, March 26, 1982, U.S. District Court, Santa Fe.
215	"operating perfectly": *Albuquerque Journal*, June 13, 1981. "unparalleled success": *Journal*, January 15, 1982.
215	seminar, "We've come a long way": *Albuquerque Journal*, November 19, 1982.
215	pressured cooperation: *Albuquerque Journal*, April 24, 1980.
215	gruesome details: *Albuquerque Journal*, February 27, 1981.
215	"Well, for some reason," "not everyone": *Albuquerque Journal*, January 30, 1983.
215	"The jury trials brought forward": *Albuquerque Journal*, December 20, 1982.
216	"don't think the truth came out": *Albuquerque Journal*, January 30, 1983.
216	accounting on prosecution: ibid. See also the district attorney's report for the crisis management seminar workshop, dated November, 1982, Santa Fe County district attorney's office.

VII. FORESHADOW

Page   Citation

| 221 | $4 billion, 100 murders: see *Time* Essay, May 5, 1980. |
| 221 | some 400,000: *Corrections* magazine, June 1982. |

221   fewer offenses, more arrests: ibid.

222   court orders and challenges: *Washington Post*, May 24, 1982.

223   "I got to get myself a new clique": *Santa Fe Reporter*, March 13, 1980.

225   an obdurate prison regime: three years after the riot with its millions in appropriations and the all too evident need for more guard training, a legislative committee concluded of Crist's corrections department: "*it appears from the obvious lack of coordination and over-all accountability that top management is not truly committed to training as a means of improving morale, or productivity*" (emphasis in original). Memorandum of House Appropriations and Finance Committee, February 11, 1983.

225     $200 million: "Riot-Associated Costs," Legislative Finance Committee memorandum dated August 26, 1982.

INDEX

Mentally ill prisoners, 70, 90, 95, 97, 101–102, 107, 141, 207; mistreatment of, 114, 207
Mexican citizen inmate, 95, 178
"Mexicans," 36
Mexican War, 10
"Mighty" (inmate welder), 128–129
Miller, Lloyd. *See* McClendon, Lloyd
Mills, Ernie, 84, 135–136, 137, 138, 167, 169, 171–172, 174–175
Mixdorf, Lloyd, 223
Montana, 202–203, 204
Montoya, Joseph, 34
Montoya, Robert, 17, 22; background of, 43; before escape of 1979, 17; between escape and riot of 1980, 22, 25, 28; at corrections dept., 197, 203, 206, 223; at inception of riot, 70, 73, 77, 81; in negotiation face-to-face meetings, 125, 129, 136, 138, 167, 168–169; negotiations led by, 83, 84, 93, 122–123, 126, 139, 165–166, 172; in negotiations on hostage exchange, 122, 127, 133–134, 136, 137–139; post-riot promotion of, 197, 203; post-riot retaliation by, 182, 197, 207–208; promises of no retaliation given by, 138, 172; retaliation threat by, 168; after riot, 182, 190, 197; rioter demand for meeting with, 124; rioter demand for resignation of, 83, 85
Murders, in penitentiary: history before 1980, 33, 48, 113; post-riot, 89, 201, 202, 205, 209–211, 212; in riot of 1980, *see* Executions
Muxlow, Ralph, 19

Narcotics. *See* Drugs
Nathan, Vincent, 204, 226
National Association of Medical Examiners, 199
National Council on Crime and Delinquency, 158

National Guard, 83, 84, 122–123, 125, 131, 133, 165, 168, 180, 181, 184, 189; field kitchen, 192; handling of incidents with prisoners by, 169–170, 183; in prison storming, 132, 175–176, 177; removal of bodies by, 179
"Natives," 36
NBC (TV), 138, 139
Negotiations with rioters, 83, 85, 118, 122–127, 129–131, 165–166, 171–174; face-to-face meetings, 125, 129, 136, 138, 167–169, 171–173; meetings with press, 135–136, 137–140, 167, 169, 171–173; unaffected by knowledge of massacre, 126–128, 133–134, 139. *See also* Demands of rioters
Nepotism, 25, 36, 38, 39, 42–43, 124
New-admission inmates, 69, 76
New Mexican (newspaper), 31, 32, 33, 34, 159
New Mexico: American seizure of (1848), 10, 36, 38; defendant in *Duran* v. *King*, 14–15, 18–19, 50–51, 204, 213–214; finances, 224, 225; judicial system, 49; police, 49 (*see also* State Police); state government, 11, 36, 49 (*see also* N.M. state legislature); statehood, 32; state motto, 147
New Mexico Corrections Commission, 150, 152, 153, 158, 178
New Mexico Department of Corrections, 19, 21, 148, 150, 159–161, 193, 198, 201; under Becknell, 160; under Crist, 202–204, 212, 213, 222, 224; Franke appointed, 226; gag rule, post-riot, 194, 196; under Hanrahan, 158, 160; under Leach, 152, 153, 154, 157; Montoya at, 197, 203, 206, 223; Rodriguez at, 13, 14, 25, 41, 158, 159, 160–161, 203; under Saenz, 140–141, 161, 193, 194–196; treatment of guard hostages after riot, 200

Restitution philosophy, 222
Retaliation, 129, 168; assurances
  made to rioters, 138, 168, 173;
  after riot, 129, 168, 175, 197
Reverse racism, 36, 38–39, 46
Riot-control grilles, 14, 34, 62, 74;
  open on night of riot, 62–63, 65,
  66, 71; post-riot laxness, 193,
  201, 208
Riot-control plan, 26–27, 98
Riot guns, 73
Riot of 1980, 65–109; beginning of,
  65–66; prior warnings of, 13,
  16–17, 22, 23–24, 25, 27, 28;
  surrender, 173–180, 189. *See
  also* Demands of rioters;
  Executions and killings; Hostages;
  Investigations, post-riot;
  Negotiations; Siege of penitentiary
Riots, prison, 188; before 1956, 33;
  of 1971, 47, 51, 111, 149, 151;
  of 1973, 47; of 1976, 47, 112–
  113, 159, 172; as political act and
  orgy of retribution, 22–23;
  reprisals for, by ax handle
  gauntlet, 111, 113, 159, 172
Riot squad, in blackout incidents,
  16
Rodriguez, Felix, 28, 40–42, 44,
  51, 89, 159, 170; background and
  career of, 40–41, 149, 158, 159,
  160–161; before escape episode
  of 1979, 13, 17, 19; between
  escape and riot of 1980, 25, 28;
  defended and praised after riot,
  196–197; at Department of
  Corrections, 13, 14, 19, 21, 25,
  41, 158, 159, 160–161, 203–
  204; in *Duran* v. *King*, 14–15,
  19; *el jefe* and *patrón* power of,
  28, 41, 126, 160; exonerated,
  198; at inception of riot, 81, 82–
  83, 84; and negotiations, 124,
  125, 126, 129–131, 139;
  negotiation meetings with rioters,
  125, 136, 138, 167, 168–169,
  171–174; and prison storming,
  132, 133, 175, 176; promises of
  no retaliation given by, 173, 174;

quoted, on riot and killings, 108,
  181; removal urged by Criminal
  Justice Study Committee, 212;
  retirement of, 223; after riot, 190,
  193, 201; rioter demands for
  meeting with, 68–69, 83, 124;
  and theft of meats, 207; as
  Warden, 13, 40, 43, 158, 171,
  193, 195, 198, 201–202, 207;
  Wardenship and prison scandals,
  51, 149, 153, 154, 156–158;
  mentioned, 24, 50, 209, 224
Roybal, Captain Greg, 61, 62, 63,
  65–66, 69, 70, 75, 76–77, 122,
  136, 137; release of, 167; torture
  of, 75, 80–81
Runyon, Bob, 13

Saenz, Adolph, 140–141, 161, 167,
  175, 193, 194–196, 202–203
Saint Vincent's Hospital, Santa Fe,
  124, 138, 167, 168, 181, 202
Salazar, Ymelda, 152
Sanchez, Archbishop Robert, 185
Sangre de Cristo, 10, 23, 34, 221
Sanitation problems, prison, 47,
  205; court order for change, 159
Santa Fe, 9–11, 31–32, 192, 221;
  bicultural society and racism, 10–
  11, 35–38
Santa Fe Downs, 47, 145, 156
Santa Fe *New Mexican*, 31, 32, 33,
  34, 159
Santa Fe Reporter, 89, 111, 192
"Santa Fe stretchers," 47
Scandals, 147, 148, 149–159;
  parole scandal (1973–74), 51, 84,
  148, 149, 151–156, 158;
  Stockham affair, 156–159
Scapegoats, in escape, 21
Schmitt, Michael, 63, 65–66, 136;
  release of, 139; suit against *Dallas
  Times-Herald*, 201
School release, 45
School system, New Mexico, 11,
  36–37
Search-and-response team of guards,
  210, 211
Security: Koroneos in charge, 17,

42, 62, 193; negligence of
administration, 15, 17–18, 20,
23–28, 43, 62, 79–80;
negligence of guards, 61, 62–65,
209–210; negligence continued
after riot, 193, 201, 204, 208,
222; night shift procedures and
post orders, 62, 63, 64–65;
prison design for, 14, 24–25,
34, 73. *See also* Riot-control
grilles
Security glass, control center, 24–
25, 72, 79–80, 85; manufacturer
sued, 201
Sedillo, Frankie, 106
Self-mutilations, inmate, 114, 180
Sentences, in riot trial, 216
Sentencing, determinate, 222
Services, prison, theft by employees,
143
Sexual abuse, 47, 70, 77, 95, 102,
114. *See also* Rape; Sodomy
Shakedowns, 159; before 1980 riot,
24, 25
Shakespeare, William, quoted, 86
Shanks (prison knives), 25, 66, 169
Shaw, George Bernard, quoted, 188
Shugrue, Michael, 139–140
Siege-command team, 82–85, 122–
126, 131, 133–141 *passim*, 165–
169; aware of continuing carnage,
124–125, 126–127, 139; divided
and confused, 131, 132, 139,
175, 178–179; *el jefe*, 126; leaves
guard families in dark, 128; leaves
inmate families in dark, 184–185;
planning of assault on pen, 131–
133, 175
Siege of penitentiary, 83, 122–123,
125, 131, 133–141, 165–175;
assault, 175–178. *See also*
Negotiations
Simms, John, 34
"Snitch jackets," 88, 107, 189
Snitch system, 16, 87–90, 115,
192, 199, 208, 216. *See also*
Informers
Society of Captives, The (Sykes),
188

Sodomy, 47, 120; of dead men, 105;
of guard hostages, 80, 121–122,
127, 137
Solitary confinement, 47–48, 88,
111–112, 171, 173, 214. *See also*
Hole
South Africa, 221
South wing, 34, 78, 202; start of
riot in, 65–69; home brew odor
on night of riot disregarded, 59,
61; riot-control grilles, 14, 62–
63, 65, 66, 71, 193; violent
prisoners housed in E-2, 15, 16,
59
Sosa, Dan, 161
State government, 11, 36, 49. *See
also* New Mexico state legislature
"State of emergency" declaration of
1981, 211
State of Prisons, The (Howard), 30,
142
State Police, 49 and *n*.; looting of
prison by, 181–182, 212;
photographing of crime scenes and
bodies by, 179; post-escape
investigation by, 16–17, 50; post-
riot investigation by, 23, 80, 215;
presence during riot, 73–74, 79,
82–83, 84, 97, 123, 125, 129,
165; and prison storming, 131,
132, 175–178
Stephens, Jack "Two-Pack," 173,
174
Stockham, Frank, 156–157, 158,
159
Storming of penitentiary, 174,
175–178; plan for, 131–133, 141,
175
Stout, Don, 125
Suicides, inmate, 113, 209;
murder faked as, by guards,
112, 209
Summers, Harry, 149–150
"Super goon squad," 210
Supplies, prison: lack of inventory
audit, 146; official theft of, 143–
144, 146–147, 182, 197, 205–
207
Survivor list, 184